Suffering and Evil

Emile Durkheim's death certificate of 1917

Suffering and Evil
The Durkheimian Legacy

Essays in Commemoration of the 90th
Anniversary of Durkheim's Death

Edited by
W.S.F. Pickering and Massimo Rosati

Durkheim Press / Berghahn Books
New York • Oxford

First published in 2008 by
Berghahn Books
www.berghahnbooks.com

©2008, 2012 Durkheim Press

First paperback edition published in 2012.

All rights reserved. Except for the quotation of short passages for the purposes of criticism and review, no part of this book may be reproduced in any form or by any means, electronic or mechanical, including photocopying, recording, or any information storage and retrieval system now known or to be invented, without written permission of the publisher.

Library of Congress Cataloging-in-Publication Data

Suffering and evil : the Durkheimian legacy : essays in commemoration of the 90th anniversary of Durkheim's death / edited by W.S.F. Pickering and Massimo Rosati.
   p. cm.
  Includes bibliographical references and index.
  ISBN 978-1-84545-519-4 (hbk.) -- ISBN 978-0-85745-645-8 (pbk.)
  1. Durkheim, Émile, 1858-1917--Influence. 2. Suffering--Social aspects. 3. Good and evil--Social aspects. I. Pickering, W. S. F. II. Rosati, Massimo, 1969-

HM479.D87S85 2008
301.092--dc22

2008031378

British Library Cataloguing in Publication Data

A catalogue record for this book is available from the British Library

Printed on acid-free paper

ISBN 978-0-85745-645-8 (paperback)   ISBN 978-0-85745-646-5 (ebook)

Contents

Acknowledgements   vii

Prolegomena   1

Introduction: *Suffering, Evil and Durkheimian Sociology: Filling a Gap*
   W.S.F. Pickering and Massimo Rosati   3

Reflections on the Death of Emile Durkheim
   W.S.F. Pickering   11

I. Suffering and Evil in Durkheim   29

1. Le Suicide *and Psychological Suffering*
   Sophie Jankélévitch   31

2. *Suffering and Evil in the* Elementary Forms
   Massimo Rosati   49

3. *Some Concepts of 'Evil' in Durkheim's Thought*
   Giovanni Paoletti   63

4. *Suffering to Become Human: A Durkheimian Perspective*
   Mark S. Cladis   81

II. The Durkheimian Legacy   101

5. *Robert Hertz on Suffering and Evil: The Negative Processes of Social Life and Their Resolution*
   Robert Parkin   103

6. Le Malin Génie: *Durkheim, Bataille and the Prospect of a Sociology of Evil*
   William Ramp   118

7. *Evil and Collective Responsibility: The Durkheimian Legacy and Contemporary Debates*
   Massimo Rosati   136

8. *The Hague Tribunal: Critical Reflections Prompted by Durkheim's Remarks on Suffering*
   John B. Allcock   148

9. *Looking Backwards and to the Future*
   W.S.F. Pickering   163

Notes on Contributors   179

References   181

Index   191

Acknowledgements

The editors wish to thank most profoundly those who have written chapters for this book. We much appreciate the hard work and time they have devoted to their tasks and also their willing acceptance of suggestions by the editors. Their contributions have greatly increased the scope of the book.

There have been others, however, who have helped to make this book – others who, as it were, have worked behind the scenes: in reading chapters, checking references, suggesting reading material, translating words and quotations from the French and, in one case, offering medical expertise. To all of them we give our assurance that they have made a very important contribution to the book. More specifically we would extend our sincere appreciation to Pierre Jacquelin, Jacqueline Sheldon, Carol Pickering, Gale Maclaine, Jonathan Fish, Andrew Fairbairn and Peter Collison.

It has been of great value to be able to quote freely from two recent English translations of *Les formes élémentaires de la vie religieuse*, those of Karen Fields and Carol Cosman. For this we much appreciate their kindness.

Production editors whose responsibility it is to put books through the press do not receive the thanks they should: so on this occasion we extend our sincere gratitude to Mark Stanton of Berghahn Books. He has done sterling work not only for this book but for several others initiated by the Durkheim Press.

W.S.F. Pickering
Massimo Rosati

In Memoriam

This book is dedicated to the late Philippe Besnard (1942–2003), who achieved so much by promoting the study of Emile Durkheim and brought to light what was heretofore unknown about his life and work.

Note

In all the references to Durkheim, the dating enumeration is that of Steven Lukes in his book, *Emile Durkheim. His Life and Work: A Historical and Critical Study* (London: Allen Lane, 1973). The dating enumeration was extended in the 1992 edition, published by Penguin, and further, by the British Centre for Durkheimian Studies, Oxford.

Unless otherwise stated, all the translations into English from French and German have been made by the authors of the chapters in question.

Prolegomena

Introduction

Suffering, Evil and Durkheimian Sociology: Filling a Gap

W.S.F. Pickering and Massimo Rosati

I. The Presence of Suffering

Suffering in many forms has always been an integral part of the human condition. The issue, however, has become a far more demanding topic today in the light of the recent series of national and international disasters on a monumental scale. They have been brought to the attention of the public via the mass media: genocides, earthquakes, floods, hurricanes, famines, acts of terrorism, civil wars, international wars, the ever-increasing scourge of AIDS. The list has no end. No sooner has some cessation or healing of suffering been achieved in one area than new wounds appear in the body of humanity. The suffering of the world today stands above the kind of suffering one expects within 'normal', 'everyday', institutional, 'domestic' life.

There is no need here to elaborate upon obvious and well-documented facts coming from many parts of today's world. The existence of large numbers of relief agencies since the end of the Second World War is incontrovertible evidence of such worldwide suffering and the concerned response of individuals, societies and nations to combat it at many levels.

The more sceptically minded would point to wars and natural disasters that have been interwoven with the history of civilization from its inception. Modern mass suffering is therefore not a new phenomenon. Logically this may be the case but in terms of crude numbers, it is clearly not so. One has only to take into account the population of the world today compared with that of a few centuries ago. It has been estimated that since 1945 170 million people have been murdered by governments and there have been forty-eight genocides and mass murders (see Wilkinson 2005: 79). Such statistics are impossible to gather with any great accuracy but from those just given the enormity of mass suffering in the last half of the twentieth century may be deduced. And what of the first half of that century, with millions killed in the First World War, followed by the millions who died from the deadly flu epidemic that followed in the early 1920s?

Surely there has never been so much worldwide suffering as that which took place in the twentieth century. And it still continues.

II. Studies Past and Present

Until very recent times it was only with the greatest difficulty that one could find sociologists who had written anything at all on the subject of suffering. It might be argued that the one great exception was Max Weber writing in the first quarter of the twentieth century. As is well known, he adapted and then applied the concept of theodicy by examining the way the major religions of the world deal with suffering (see ch. 10). But suffering as a subject in itself has not been considered by sociologists: if it was to be found anywhere, it was in religion and philosophy. One German sociologist, who followed Weber, did consider it briefly, namely, Leopold von Wiese (1876–1969) of Cologne University. He was what might be called a formal sociologist, a systems builder, addicted to classification, and in some ways not unlike Durkheim. He called himself an integralist. In 1934 he wrote an article of a dozen or so pages that bore the title 'Sociology and Suffering'. It was intended as a response to what Müller-Lyer had written in 1924 when he said that 'suffering [was] the fundamental problem of sociology'. Von Wiese adopted a contrary position in stating that sociology was not to be focused solely on suffering – in fact, it had to stand aloof from either condemning or ameliorating suffering. Such a concern stood within the realms of social philosophy and medicine, he argued. Sociology was a science and therefore was value-free – a point he strongly emphasized, and that was doomed to become a favourite sociological refrain. Knowledge and action must be kept separate. Today, according to much mainstream sociology, 'is' and 'ought' questions still have to be kept apart, and sociology must engage itself only in factual (is) and not normative (ought) questions. Von Wiese raised other matters, but to the best of our knowledge this article of his, which examines suffering from first principles, was the first to be written by a well-established sociologist. In it he raised fundamental issues, such as: 'Is suffering indeed a valid subject for sociology to study?' and 'How should suffering be classified?' One may not agree with his answers but at least he is to be credited with raising the questions.

At this point another sociologist should be mentioned, namely Pitrim A. Sorokin (1889–1968). He was a Russian refugee who created the department of sociology at Harvard in 1930, but today his many books tend to remain on the shelf. Although he was a sociologist of deep and wide learning who entered unexplored and unexpected areas of social life, his conclusions did not turn out to be as fruitful as might have been hoped

(Timasheff 1963: 242). Having already attempted to produce a sociology of revolutions, there appeared from his pen in 1942, *Man and Society in Calamity*. There is no mention of the word suffering *per se* in the text: he disregarded it as an operative concept. But calamities assume suffering – suffering on an immense scale. The long subtitle explains the contents of the book: *The Effects of War, Revolution, Famine, Pestilence upon the Human Mind, Social Organization and Cultural Life.* Sorokin was a sociologist of stature who was prepared to deal with subjects of great proportions, as in the case of mass suffering. He concentrated on a form of suffering that might be called calamitous. His brand of sociology fell out of fashion in the 1960s and he either desired none, or was unable to create any disciples. However, from him has come an interest in the sociology of war.

So we turn to Durkheim, the central figure of the pages that lie ahead. He was no pioneer in using suffering as a key concept. Thus, we might well ask: Who today would turn to this great *fin de siècle* leader of French sociology to gain insight into the phenomenon of suffering? He wrote no book, no article, that had in its title the word 'suffering' or any of its cognates. Suffering would appear to stand well outside his range of interests. Morals and religion, however, were very much his *métier* and certainly in many ways and in various degrees they are associated with suffering. The only person amongst Durkheim's followers to whom one can point who might have been interested in suffering is Robert Hertz, who, while he did not consider suffering *per se* at least wrote on such allied concepts as sin, salvation and death (see Chapter 5 and also Chapter 6 for the work of Bataille).

Nonetheless, one should be aware of the fact that the only other person at the time who did consider suffering did so in connection with theodicy. He was Gaston Richard (1860–1945), a contemporary of Durkheim, a former disciple and, in the end, an antagonist. A book written in his last years had the surprising title, *Sociologie et théodicée*. It will be treated in detail in a later chapter (see Richard 1943; Pickering 1975b: 343–9; ch. 10 here).

So it is that, without further documentation, the subject of suffering seen through the eyes of the sociologist has remained virtually dormant. Recently, however, an attempt has been made by Iain Wilkinson to work in the field with his book, *Suffering: A Sociological Introduction*, published in 2005. One of his aims was to demonstrate, against popular opinion, that classical sociologists were much more concerned with suffering than has been generally realized. In another direction, we are made fully aware of the vast amount of literature that has emerged since the end of the Second World War, and particularly in the last decade, which examine the Holocaust, and now books on the subject have become a virtual industry. But the world since then has also suffered other disasters, more genocides, massacres, violence, torture, famine, earthquake, and so forth. These, too, have given rise to a plenitude of books, though the number written by sociologists appears to be abysmally small. This book is not concerned specifically with any of these dramatic events, but with suffering in general, as it can be seen through a Durkheimian lens.

III. More on the Sluggishness of Sociologists

We have been convinced for a long time of the sluggishness of sociologists in considering suffering, and recently our ideas have been confirmed by other scholars who have come to the same conclusion. We will not labour the point much further than to draw the reader's attention to the 1996 issue of *Daedalus*. It was asserted that 'the social sciences have consistently failed to explore the existential meaning of suffering in social life' (in Morgan and Wilkinson 2001: 200). It is not without point that, so far as we know, no journal exists, certainly no sociological journal, that deals solely with the subject of suffering *per se*. One has only to compare this fact with the many journals that focus on various other aspects of sociology. 'We need a new kind of discourse to disturb our collective consciousness and stir it into practical application that moves beyond mere pity' (Langer in *Daedalus* 1996: 47). In this matter one might mention an exception found in France, namely, the publication of a book in 1993 by Pierre Bourdieu and others and translated into English in 1999, with the title *The Weight of the World. Social Suffering in Contemporary Society*. It consisted of over fifty-four interviews with people who had suffered in one way or another.

In anthropology there has been a substantial growth in the realm of medical anthropology. In fact, the growth in the whole area of suffering and health has been quite remarkable. It covers notions of health, primitive medicines, the way in which suffering is rationalized and so forth. Perhaps these advancements should be looked at in order to discover if they have relevance for the sociologist.

Some more recent books include Barrington Moore's *Reflections on the Causes of Human Misery and upon Certain Proposals to Eliminate Them* (1972); also, the well-known book by Z. Bauman on *Modernity and the Holocaust* (1989). Again, on the Holocaust from a sociological or socio-philosophical point of view is R. Fine and C. Turner (eds), *Social Theory after the Holocaust* (2000). Another book to be mentioned is that of Luc Boltanski on *Distant Suffering, Morality, Media and Politics* (1999). However, in the effort to be sociologically systematic, it was not until 1993 that a book appeared in America by Helen Fein, that bore the title *Genocide. A Sociological Perspective*. It fully acknowledged the lack of interest by sociologists in the Holocaust.

In the matter of evil, one might mention K. Wolff's article 'For a Sociology of Evil' (1969), in which he maintains that contemporary social sciences are characterized by their inability to raise the question of evil because of a neo-positivistic notion of science.

More recently, one sociologist who has dared to employ the notion of evil from a culturalist and Durkheimian point of view is Jeffrey Alexander (see Alexander 2001). From his standpoint, as with that of many of our contributors, there are social representations of suffering and, we suppose, evil. The consequence is that suffering and evil can be approached sociologically.

IV. Why the Sluggishness?

It is always interesting to know why some writers – why some academics, philosophers, theologians, scientists – study the subjects they do. The reasons, both personal and social, are numerous. The other side of the coin is to ask why certain subjects, obvious to the commentator, are *not* studied, when to the commentator they ought to have been dealt with. Once again personal and social reasons are multifarious. Attempted answers have to be focused on specific cases and so we consider briefly the work of sociologists.

Why is it then that sociologists as a whole have been so slow in coming to grips with the subject of suffering? The answer is by no means simple and only the briefest of outlines is possible here.

The first and foremost is that the concept of suffering is difficult to handle since it covers such a wide area. For example, the same word applies to someone who is suffering from a tooth ache, and to another person who is undergoing torture by the police, or one experiencing a mild depression and another writhing in pain with cancer. Some kind of classification is required before anything meaningful may be said about suffering in general, as von Wiese suggested. It is only with difficulty that one can make suffering a key concept subject to a number of social variables.

Secondly, suffering and evil speak of the dark and unpleasant side of individual and social life. Not every researcher wants to look around a torture chamber or read accounts of massacres and persecutions. There are more amenable aspects of social life than these sordid and distressing subjects. Perhaps not surprisingly, certain researchers find details of suffering, especially man-made suffering, such as torture and brutality, so disturbing that they cannot undertake studies that involve such degradation and pain.

Thirdly, it is interesting to know why researchers in sociology choose the subjects they do, or why they travel along certain professional paths and not others. Grants indeed dictate the direction a researcher may take. Nor are governments inclined to give money to sociologists to delve into the seamier sides of their political actions. One area where sociology has developed – and with government funding – is in the sociology of medicine. We are of the opinion that such research relates to the administration of medical services, hospitals and the welfare of patients. It is not concerned with suffering as it is seen in this book. For obvious reasons government money has been available for some time for those working in the field of crime.

It has just been said that empirical studies in suffering may involve political or religious issues. In so much suffering as in the case of genocides, war and persecution, those who suffer tend to blame others for their suffering, which may mean blaming individuals or nations – Hitler, the Slavs, Muslims. When studies are made of mass suffering, the historian or the sociologist, comes face to face with blame that is deeply held against the alleged oppressor. One thinks, for example, of the Turkish and Armenian accusations and counter-accusations over the so-called Armenian massacres – 'so-called' because the Turks deny the validity of the word 'massacre' to what happened in 1915. For the sociologist to analyse what he or she is convinced actually went on may very well mean taking sides with one party or another. Disputes over the Rwandan massacres presents the same problem for the investigator.

In this light the researcher – and it equally applies to the anthropologist – does not want his or her professional 'neutrality' or objectivity questioned or tarnished by enquiries into, say, a massacre, where he or she may inevitably feel driven to take sides. Hence, politically and professionally, the best advice is to keep away from such matters.

These are but a few, scantily sketched, reasons for sociologists finding suffering either a difficult or an unpopular topic to investigate.

V. The Sociologist's Starting-point in the Present Context

What has just been said raises the question in a wider context. As suffering is such a complex phenomenon, covering physical and mental components, can the sociologist deal with it meaningfully?

Psychologists would appear to be in a better position to undertake the task of studying suffering 'scientifically', as the emotions of the individual are within their province and suffering is inevitably intertwined with the emotions. Nonetheless, for the sociologist there is ample scope for study. Pain and suffering may contain social components: for example, social facts relating to the way suffering is administered, as in punishment and persecution, or suffering within the process of socialization.

Religion and philosophy have often viewed suffering as an evil, or as the result of evil. The connection between suffering and evil, however, is not an intrinsic one. Evil is an interpretation of suffering, where suffering is viewed as an empirical phenomenon. God, traditionally defined as some force at work in the world, is not accepted by the sociologist. However, the way people regard God is a legitimate field of sociological enquiry. Similarly, with evil. That there may be a real force called evil which operates in the world is outside the concern of the sociologist. A consideration of evil can easily lead to the notion of personification, for example, Satan. Nevertheless, how and why people believe in evil and its alleged effects on society is indeed part of the sociologist's remit.

A particular problem confronts those who have contributed to this book. It rests on the fact that, not surprisingly, a great deal of the basic data comes from French authors in which a key word is *mal*. The difficulty is that *mal* is an ambiguous word. It can mean, on the one hand, evil and, on the other, illness, sickness, disease, pain, harm, suffering, misfortune, ill. In the word *mal* the French do not differentiate the two ideas of evil and suffering. Evil is essentially a theological or metaphysical concept, sometimes associated with sin. It is of the same genre as God or spirit. Suffering, by contrast, is associated with pain, physical and mental. Where *mal* appears in a French text, its English equivalent has to be determined by the context. The outcome may not always be clear. For this reason this book includes in its title the two words 'suffering' and 'evil'. *Souffrance* is a common French word for suffering but it is not much employed in the texts relevant to this book.

In translating *mal*, there would seem to be a shift away from the word evil to one relating to illness. Such a change is seen in comparing early and very recent translations of Durkheim's *Le suicide*. The first English translation made in 1951 by Spaulding and Simpson consistently translated *mal* as 'evil' (1951a: 378 – 89). In the translation of 2006 by Buss of the same instances, the words he uses are 'sickness' or 'ill' (2006a: 422 – 35). In the change, there would appear to be a reluctance to use a word that might suggest metaphysical or high emotional overtones.

VI. The Way Forward

As we have hinted, a glance at the publications in the sociological world that deal with suffering in the way we envisage it shows the landscape to be particularly barren. And certainly this is so within the sociological legacy of the Durkheimian tradition. As with Wilkinson, of whose work we were ignorant when we began our project, this book attempts to show, amongst other things, that whereas Durkheim and his followers did not tackle the issue of mass suffering head on, there is in their writings, and especially in those of Durkheim himself, a considerable interest in *mal* and *souffrance* (especially the former). To reverse current thinking about Durkheim, the subject of suffering, it will be shown, was far from absent in his writings. Nevertheless, not all the contributors to this book will subscribe uncritically to what he wrote or did not write on the subject. It should be pointed out that it is not the aim of this book to present a unified approach to the topic on hand. As suffering in Durkheim is not an issue that has been tackled to any extent before, one can hardly expect that the contributors will all be of the same mind.

We are deeply aware, however, of the complexity of theoretical questions and problems that must be raised in any systematic sociological study of suffering and evil. They are beyond the scope of this book. However, in examining the work of Durkheim and his disciples several theoretical problems will be raised concerning the study of suffering.

Our modest claim here is simply to show that within the boundaries of the Durkheimian tradition, sociologists can find concepts and a rich vocabulary to raise further questions and ways to approach the complex problem of suffering and evil. To be more precise, this book aims to fill gaps. First, we want to fill a gap within the area of Durkheimian studies. Although Durkheim's thought has been analysed from so many different points of view, it has not, until the present time, been systematically considered in this light. We also want to show, in the plurality of our voices, that Durkheim's personality was much more complex than is usually understood. He was not insensitive to the 'dark side' of human existence and, in consequence, his thought was capable of grasping those dimensions of social life related to suffering and evil. It is certain that further research in this direction deserves to be undertaken. Secondly, we intend to show that Durkheimian categories can be useful today for the analysis of contemporary forms of evil and suffering, thus filling a gap in current social theory.

Since our starting-point is the conviction that until recent times the subject of suffering and evil has been much neglected in the sociological world, and is also almost absent in Durkheimian studies as well, this book aims to fill the gap, with particular reference to the Durkheimian tradition. We begin by exploring the different meanings that the concepts of evil and suffering have in Durkheim's works, together with the general role they play in his sociology (Part I). Our interest then turns to the meanings and roles of these concepts in relation to suffering and evil in other authors within the Durkheimian tradition, up until the beginning of the Second World War. We further explore the Durkheimian legacy in its wider aspects, with particular reference to the importance of the Durkheimian categories in understanding and in conceptualizing contemporary forms of evil and suffering (Part II).

As has just been hinted, what more apposite way of beginning to come to grips with the subject at hand than to reflect on Durkheim's death and what led up to it? To this we now turn.

Reflections on the Death of Emile Durkheim

W.S.F. Pickering

I. The Cause of Death?

In the new or Second Series of the *Année sociologique*, Marcel Mauss, as the editor and nephew of Emile Durkheim, wrote:

> Durkheim died on 15 November, 1917, at the peak of his life at fifty-nine and a half years of age, after a long illness that started at the beginning of December 1916. (*L'Année sociologique*, n.s., 1923–24, I: 9)

He went on to say that Durkheim had been aware that the end was nigh and that he had had time to arrange his manuscripts and leave instructions about their disposition. Elsewhere it is recorded that he died at 2 p.m. on that day without any suffering (see death certificate and Durkheim1998a: 586).[1]

Durkheim was buried in the Jewish section of the Cimetière de Montparnasse in Paris. The cemetery contains the bodies of many famous French men and women – intellectuals and artists of the nineteenth and twentieth centuries. The funeral was strictly private at the wish of the family (*Le Temps*, 17 November 1917).

What was the immediate cause of death? This has never been definitively ascertained. At that time there was no entry on French death certificates that demanded such information and indeed they were not signed by a doctor. However, even if such information were available, it might have been unreliable, as the cause of death is best ascertained after a post-mortem examination: in the case of Durkheim no such action was taken.[2] At one time there was a rumour in Epinal, Durkheim's birth place, that he had died of cancer.[3] To this possibility we shall return later.

More details about Durkheim's last days come from the obituary notice in the *Revue de métaphysique et de morale*. Although it does not specifically say so, it was in all probability written by Xavier Léon, who was its editor (Léon 1917). He had helped Durkheim create the *Année sociologique* in the late 1890s and later became a close friend of the family. Like the

Durkheims, he was of Jewish descent. In the obituary, Léon wrote that late in 1916 Durkheim made a passionate speech at one of the many committee meetings he attended (ibid.: 750). Afterwards he suffered his first attack of an illness which, Léon said, was to prove fatal (ibid.) Lukes states that it was a stroke (Lukes 1973: 558). The date of late 1916 appears to coincide with that given by Mauss. It might be noted that earlier, in January of that year, Durkheim reported that on one occasion, at a meeting, with his papers in his hand, everything became eclipsed and around him everything went out of sight. For two hours he did not think what he was saying (1998a: 497). Could this have been a warning of the illness that was to come later? According to a close friend of the family, Georges Davy, and in connection with the alleged stroke at the end of December 1916, Durkheim recovered somewhat and did a little lecturing extemporaneously for an hour at a time (Davy 1960: 20ff.).[4] He weakened, however, and in the early summer of 1917 went to Fontainebleau to recuperate in peace and fresh air (ibid.). There he wrote to Davy: 'I feel that I am speaking to you about men and things with the detachment of someone who has already left the world' (ibid.). He returned to Paris to his home at 4, Avenue d'Orléans and, according to Davy, he wrote his last letter in his own hand on 30 September. On 4 November he dictated another, with his wife as amanuensis (ibid.). (According to letters published in Durkheim 1998a, Davy may have been wrong in the matter of the 'last letter'.) All too sadly, Durkheim wrote to his nephew in November, just before he died, 'I do not see myself writing another book, however short. What torture!' (1998a: 585).

It is certain that we shall never know what the medical verdict might have been on the cause of Durkheim's death. One can only speculate. So, what was the long illness, beginning in December 1916? Did it really begin with a stroke as Lukes stated? Léon, in speaking about it, had used the phrase *la première atteinte du mal*. But these words tell of nothing specific. An illness, to be sure, but relating to what? Of course it could well refer to a stroke as Lukes assumes. One needs to be reminded of the fact that in those days people tended to refrain from talking about the precise nature of illnesses, especially if they were serious. If it was indeed a stroke, it is best described as a cerebral haemorrhage. In present-day French the words are *coup de sang*. It is common knowledge that a stroke may or may not give rise to death. For our purposes we assume that Durkheim did have a stroke, or something akin to it.

When a stroke is diagnosed, it is tempting to ask what brought it about. It is precisely here, however, that it is very difficult to postulate a scientific answer. Doctors, even today, often refer to *possible* contributory factors but cannot prove that any one factor directly gives rise to a stroke, or even whether several factors together bring it about. They speak of risk factors that *may* produce a clot in the brain. Such factors relate to blood pressure or to psychological stress. The latter might come from the lifestyle the sufferer has led. One thus enters into the world of speculation, for not all people who work under stress, who drink a great deal, who have high blood pressure, suffer from a stroke.

Further, it must not be assumed that someone who has had a stroke and then recovers, dies later from the effects of the stroke. Some mortal illness or accident may intervene. Nonetheless it is profitable to look at the kind of life Durkheim led and the events that occurred towards its end to see if they might have contributed to a stroke.

II. Lifestyle

Although the word 'stroke' was never specifically mentioned in connection with Durkheim's death, there have been several commentators who have pointed to Durkheim's psychological make-up and events in his life that might have been factors leading to a stroke.

There is a well-known precedent that encourages sociologists to turn to psychological factors in recalling the lives of the founding fathers. The case in point is that of the mental breakdown of Max Weber in 1900, when he was forced to resign his professorship. There is, however, one significant difference between Weber's breakdown and any that Durkheim might have had. Weber's was obviously very serious as he did not take up a senior academic post again until 1918. With one exception, Durkheim's so-called neurasthenia, as was the expression of the day, was never serious enough to cause him to withdraw from teaching and other academic duties.[5] That exception was in January 1917 as the result of the alleged stroke (Davy 1960: 18).

In the light of extensive speculation about Durkheim's socio-psychological problems, some attention must be given to the facts of the case. As has been noted, doctors today consider carefully the lifestyle of those who have had a stroke and see it as a possible, but not the certain 'cause' of an attack.

Rather than beginning with Durkheim's early life, for example, his adolescence and his relations with his father and mother, we propose to work backwards from events and from his correspondence in the period that immediately preceded his death.

III. 1914–17

Thus, we start with the war years. There is scarcely a commentator who does not mention the devastating effect on Durkheim of the death of his son, André. It has been held by many that Durkheim died from a broken heart. Claudette Kennedy, Durkheim's great-niece who, as a child, knew him in his last years, was always convinced that this was the case (personal communication). It is also the conviction of Etienne Halphen, one of Durkheim's grandsons. It seems to have been accepted by all the family that this was the case. Others outside the family were also of the opinion that Durkheim died of a broken heart. The writer of the obituary in the *Revue de métaphysique et de morale* (as we have noted, most probably Léon, editor and friend of the family), wrote precisely in that vein. 'He [Durkheim] died as a result of his son's death' (Léon 1917: 750). Davy stated, 'The death of the son vanquished the life of the father' (Davy 1960: 20).

From the time André joined the army he began to suffer from ill health. In early 1915, having been slightly wounded on the Western Front, he was given twenty-one days' leave for convalescence under the care of his mother. In late 1915 he was sent to Salonica on the Bulgarian front – a posting about which Durkheim was apprehensive. On 10 January 1916 André was declared missing, but it was not until 25 February that his death was officially confirmed. The delay, it is said, was because it was difficult to find his body. He had been shot and died from bullet wounds on 5 December 1915.[6] The effect of André's death overwhelmed Durkheim, although he said he was prepared for it (Davy 1960: 19). He was nervously exhausted by the long wait he had to endure until his son's death was officially declared. 'I do not have to tell you of the anguish I am living through', he wrote to Davy (ibid.). The distress caused by André's death is evident in what Mauss wrote in an obituary of Durkheim's wife, Louise, after her death in Paris in 1925: 'To lessen the tragic suffering of Durkheim she rose above the terrible agony which she experienced when André was killed by the enemy' (*L'Année sociologique*, n.s. 1924–45, II: 9). As a thoroughly devoted wife she did everything she could to encourage her husband to carry on with his work. Durkheim's attachment to his son, as is well known, was very strong indeed. Not only was he an only son, but academically he was said to be extremely able. He was taught by his father and he wished to develop his father's thought. Surely every father would have been proud of such a son! Moreover, Durkheim realized that with the death of André his cherished hopes in many directions were over: the family would never be the same again. As Davy expressed it, the death of André 'tore the tender heart' of Durkheim (Davy 1960: 19). Here we have a parallel with King David's grief on the death of his son Absolam described in the Hebrew scriptures (2 Samuel 1). With obvious reference to his son, Durkheim was reported to have said, 'Do not think I have never cried'(Davy 1919: 181). And on another occasion, 'Regarding my son, … today I think I can speak to you [Davy] about him' (ibid.). Davy noted that Durkheim faced the situation with an impeccable stoicism. 'His ascetic thinness was further accentuated, his eyes more hollow, his gesture more feverish, and his posture less assured' (ibid.). The father was brave enough to write the obituary of his son. He stated that the intellectual bond between them was as close as it was possible to be (1917a). He lost not only a son but also an intellectual colleague.

Durkheim's death was frequently expressed in terms of dying for one's country – the sentiment attached to fallen soldiers. Davy wrote, 'though far from the Front [Durkheim] was a victim of the war'(Davy 1919: 181).

Thus we may hold that he sacrificed himself as much as those who died in the trenches. Sacrifice was a word much on people's lips at the time. Durkheim himself had written much about it in *Les formes élémentaires* shortly before the war (1912a: 465ff.). He never realized how apposite the word was to describe those who died for their country.

There can be no doubt that Durkheim's family was an extremely close one.[7] In his many letters to Mauss there are a number of affectionate references at this time to his grandson Claude, born in 1914, who, with his mother, was living with the Durkheim family (e.g. see 1998a: 524). Durkheim thinks the young child *charmant* and worries about him when he becomes ill. Perhaps he begins to see in Claude something of his beloved André? As it turned out, however, Claude was to show no interest whatsoever in matters academic. He did, nevertheless, come to Oxford for a short time to study.

During the terrible First World War thousands of families sustained such losses, and worse, compared with those Durkheim experienced. Yet how many fathers 'died' away from the Front as a consequence of the loss of sons? Grief they would have had, certainly deep grief, but would they have died as a result? It might be said in defence of those who hold that Durkheim died of a broken heart that there are cases of people who die, and yet, where an autopsy is carried out, no cause of death can be found. The consequence is an open verdict. In Durkheim's case, however, this would hardly have been so, in the light of the illness he suffered (see below). In passing one should note the ambivalence of Léon in his somewhat emotional obituary of Durkheim. On the one hand, as we have seen, he referred to André's death as the cause of Durkheim's own death and, on the other, spoke of the sudden 1916 illness as its cause (Léon 1917: 750).

One must put André's death in context. That context was the war itself and the enormous suffering it engendered. Humanity was seen to be carving itself up. It completely shattered Durkheim's optimism and humanistic thinking that he had acquired during adolescence. These were the basic values on which he built hopes for the future of mankind. They were expressed in the cult of the individual. If it was to be the religion of the future, as he hoped it would be, it could do nothing to prevent or ameliorate the slaughter then raging. Such miseries doubtless deeply saddened idealists, and may have caused them to be depressed.

But how did Durkheim deal with his grief and other miseries? The answer he found, as many others also have found in facing grief, was to embrace work. On hearing the details of André's death his response was, 'Happily, I am very occupied. I dread leisure' (1998a: 501).

Against such an obsessive attitude to work, the fact should not be overlooked that Durkheim and his family were assiduous in the taking of holidays. When he was in Bordeaux he frequently visited his home town of Epinal. He also often went to Biarritz, Saint-Valéry-en-Caux, Sèvres, Versailles, and Cabourg, as well as other places. It seems most likely that he always took work with him. Towards the end of his life, as we have noted, he spent considerable time at Fontainebleau. There is one famous photograph of the family on the beach, where he is reading the newspaper, oblivious to the photo being taken. One wonders who pressed for the holidays, Emile or his wife?

The burden of work

Durkheim was obviously too old for the army and in any case he was too important a person to be given a post in the services. He found himself in great demand and was soon weighed down by academic work and other duties. One has to consider seriously the vast amount of work Durkheim undertook during the war years. He had always been a dedicated, hard-working university teacher but the war made even greater demands on him (for a description of his general workload see 1998a: 477). Early in the war he wrote to Mauss: 'I work as I have not worked for 30 years. It is extremely rare for me to leave my study before 10.30 to 11 each evening' (letter dated 11 December 1914). It was not, however, so much a matter of hard work in itself, but of working under great pressure that can be so telling on a person's psyche. The extra load that Durkheim had to carry, and its attendant demands, can be viewed in two dimensions.

The first focal point is to be found in his professional base, the Sorbonne, to which he went in 1902 as *chargé de cours* and where he rose to be a prominent professor. As the teaching staff left the university to enrol in the army, so, inevitably, those who were left had to take on more responsibilities. Durkheim soon became a leading figure as teacher and administrator. In 1916 he found his duties in connection with the baccalaureate very heavy. There were 1,900 candidates in philosophy and, on account of mobilization, there were only five professors to cope with the papers: Lévy-Bruhl had left for work in munitions and Delbos had died. What exhausted Durkheim was the mental fatigue of assessing so many papers. He said, 'the effort that one has to make to carry out this impossible task gives rise to an inability to dispel these harsh demands' (ibid.: 530; see also 553). It made him ill (ibid.: 542). As the years went by he continued to complain about the heavy work in assessing the baccalaureate papers. On one occasion, a day's marking was followed by a council meeting, followed by a reception by the council for visiting Spaniards. This gave him no leisure at all (ibid.: 556). In addition, he had theses to direct, notably that of a disciple, Paul Fauconnet, on the subject of responsibility (ibid.: 456).[8] But there was also public lecturing. In 1916 he gave two courses. Durkheim appeared to want to leave the university to do more important work. He wrote, 'If only I had someone to replace me at the Sorbonne. At the moment there is only Bouglé, but that is not enough to solve the problem' (ibid.: 504). There was no escape: in fact, he never left the Sorbonne.

The second component of his increased duties brought on by the war lay in working for the government. He was either recruited for, or volunteered to be, a propagandist. Certainly he seems to have readily and willingly written tracts to aid the French cause. But it took a great deal out of him. He wrote, 'Our propaganda industry goes on all the time.' As he said, he is 'always working up to his neck' (ibid.: 453).

The primary task was to arouse French enthusiasm to resist the enemy. It was also to castigate the Germans for their immoral action in attacking France. He passionately set out to revitalize the 'moral[e] de la nation' (Davy 1960:18). To this end he wrote a tract with E. Denis, *Qui a voulu la guerre?* (1915b). Another followed shortly on the German *mentalité*, *L'Allemagne au-dessus de tout* (1915c). And then in 1916 appeared *Lettres à tous les Francais* (1916a). The first two of these were seen to be of such value for the war effort that they were translated straight away into English. All three were published with the support of Ernest Denis, Raymond Poincaré and Marcel Semblat (Davy 1960: 19). For one tract Durkheim travelled to Brest, to the naval base there, where, incidentally, he met André. He was without his wife and the journey back was a sleepless one occasioned by nervous tension (1998a: 461). He was often despondent about the moral situation in France and wrote to Davy that the country lacked a firm hand and a tireless will (Davy 1960: 20). It was a tireless will that typified Durkheim's own character.

On 26 December 1915 a commission on the presence of Russian Jews in France raised the question as to whether or not they should be conscripted (see Pickering and Martins 1994: 179–201). Needless to say, Durkheim was at the helm of the commission and a report was completed in February the following year – a short space of time indeed. The commission gave rise to very heavy work and caused him great emotional weariness, coupled with a loss of sleep (1998a: 497; see Pickering and Martins 1994). In April 1916 he went to Biarritz to study the Jewish question in Russia (see *Durkheimian Studies*, vol. 6 n.s., 2000, pp. 1–4). It was about this time that the death of André was confirmed. It will be recalled that Durkheim suffered the alleged stroke at the end of that year.

At one time things were so bad that he was tempted to retire altogether. Worried about the demands made on him, he wrote to Mauss in March 1916 saying that he wondered whether he would not say goodbye to his very active life and pass the rest of his days working quietly. He seemed to have much energy but at the same time he appeared to long for the chance to work in an atmosphere of tranquillity and seriousness. He could have the children live with him for he did not want to move. He concluded, 'I am going to see about it, try it out, and will allow myself to be guided by experience' (1998a: 504).

His life during this period was made even more difficult by the political attacks that were, surprisingly, made against him. The charge of being a Jew and therefore being disloyal to his country was raised in *La parole* in

January 1916 (see Lukes 1973: 557). Then, two months later, he was again attacked in the Senate on similar grounds. Such vitriolic statements hardly made life pleasant for him: they were just one more burden he had to carry.

Domestic life

One must not overlook the domestic situation that was both a joy and a source of worry for Durkheim. As we have already noted, he became very agitated if his grandson Claude became ill (see, for example, 1998a: 574). But as much, if not more, concern to him was his anxiety about his nephew. Many indeed are the references to Mauss and his money troubles, to his failure to complete his doctorate and his many omissions to reply to his letters (see various letters in ibid.:). Anxiety is shown both by Durkheim and by his sister Rosine, Mauss's mother. Rosine was worried about the ill-regulated life her son was leading. These concerns went back a long way, to the time when Mauss first went to Bordeaux to study under the watchful eye of his uncle. Further, from the time that his father, Moïse, died, Emile had the responsibility of being the head of the Durkheim family.

What were the effects on him of this very hard work and his worries? There can be no doubt that during the war years Durkheim suffered from sleeplessness. At times this disability seems to have been quite severe. He wrote to Mauss:

> I have been able to sleep again. But three weeks ago I suffered from severe insomnia. Moreover a simple conversation easily brings on very great tiredness. I believe but am not sure that this tiredness is diminishing. But I ought to be still very careful. At the moment there is a very slight tendency for the troubles that I had in November last year to reappear (ibid.: 575).

This letter written in 1917 would appear to contain a reference to the alleged stroke of a year before that has been mentioned above. Earlier he had written, 'All goes well. I continue to sleep well and each day I cut back on the dosage of valerian' (ibid.: 563). In March 1916 he commented, 'With the help of the medicine, about which I have spoken to you, we can sleep. Boulloche authorises a large dose of it' (ibid.: 503). Here is another reference to Durkheim's use of valerian as prescribed by the doctor. Valerian was commonly employed at the time for the treatment of hysteria, other nervous complaints and for insomnia. It was not a painkiller. It was used as a tranquillizer that 'calmed the nerves', as people used to say. It would seem in Durkheim's case that it was used to induce sleep. However, toxicity can arise from a continual use of valerian, but this does not seem likely in his case. In another letter he states that a very little veronal is added to the valerian (ibid.: 504). This is a sedative or barbiturate. Durkheim made every effort to reduce the dosage of valerian, which he admitted was quite strong. Did Durkheim suffer from migraine?

Certainly the combination of valerian and veronal is not to be recommended because of their combined side effects. It might be noted that whenever Durkheim had a headache he relaxed and used it as a sign to ease off work (ibid.: 575). As with headaches and migraines, symptoms come and go with their ups and downs (ibid.).

Depression

All the evidence would suggest that during the war, and indeed before (see below), he suffered from some form of depression. Its nature and intensity are difficult to assess. Certainly, as we have already noted, it never caused him to stop work, save at the very end of his life.

Whether it was real depression or not, serious or otherwise, it showed that Durkheim had some kind of nervous trouble. On 5 February 1916 he wrote to Mauss, 'You see my depression [*dépression*] continues but I am not overwhelmed by it. What impedes me is the fact that these are harsh times, especially when whatever one is doing, there is always in one's mind something more to be done' (ibid.: 499). Somewhat later, on 4 November 1917, just before he died, in a letter he dictated to Louise, he said: 'The illnesses from which I suffer, and which have not totally disappeared, seem assuredly to be of a nervous origin. It is true that one does not know entirely from where this nervous illness came, and why it descended on me as soon as we returned [from Fontainebleau?]' (ibid.: 584). Someone called Dupré, perhaps a doctor, advised him to live in the Midi. Durkheim thought Pau would be desirable and said he would look into it (ibid.). Notice that he spoke of illnesses, not just one illness.

The following is quite unlike the Durkheim we imagine. Writing on March 1916, he said to Mauss: 'It is in the evening after a day's work is done that I am overtaken by these sad thoughts, especially on the days when I feel depressed, as on the days when I am teaching. I come back exhausted. There is no other word to express the state I am in at the moment. In addition I do nothing in the evening. Soon after dinner I lie down' (ibid.: 503).

Religion

Here and elsewhere it is evident that Durkheim's worries were counteracted by hard work, which is a common enough remedial experience. In similar circumstances others have received consolation and help from religion. That religion helped people in various ways Durkheim often enough attested. Indeed, a study of religion seems to have largely dominated his academic interests (see Pickering 1984: 20ff.). Although an agnostic or mild atheist, he exhibited personal characteristics that might be called, in a loose way, religious. He fervently believed in a humanistic religion – the cult of the individual. When it came to the crunch and he was facing death, he wrote a sad letter to Léon. Here are two well-known sentences of the letter that are worth repeating:

> Of course I know the religions are there, and that their practices are rich in experience that is unconscious and full of accumulated wisdom. But their wisdom is crude and empirical; nothing resembling ritual practices has been of use to me or seems effective to me. (in Lukes 1973: 556)

The newly emerging religion which he supported was brushed aside, as were other religions: they did not speak to his condition. Interesting also is the fact that he focused on ritual rather than belief (see Pickering 1984: ch. 20).

IV. 1902–14

In going one stage further back, we look briefly at the period from 1902, when Durkheim started lecturing in the Sorbonne, until the outbreak of the 1914 war. Although he may have been keen to leave Bordeaux for Paris in order to be at the centre of French academic life, he had some misgivings about going there (1975b, 2: 434). His early days in the French capital were far from joyful. He carried out his work in fear and trepidation and evidence for this is revealed in his correspondence with Octave Hamelin (see below).

As Durkheim came face to face with the realities of living in Paris (when he first went there he lived in Boutroux's apartment) and in being on the staff at the Sorbonne, he felt in some way intellectually and emotionally inadequate. He wrote to Hamelin, 'I was overtaken almost immediately by a bad state of mind that was responsible for melancholic moments and it is reflected in everyone around me' (1975b, 2: 455). He went on to say that he wanted to write to Hamelin 'in this bad period' – 'in the midst of my lamentable exhaustion', but he did not want to give Hamelin valueless suffering. However, he appears to have got over his troubles fairly quickly and he reported that he was now sufficiently recovered to talk about it objectively. The cause of his mental illness was at the same time, he said, both physical and mental. He went on to say that it was not impossible that the sea (as in Bordeaux?), and the absence of sleep had stimulated him and that was the reason for his nerves being at breaking point. He had a feeling of intellectual feebleness. He argued that this had come about by renouncing the 'strict life' – one might deduce, the rule of life – that he had led in Bordeaux along with Hamelin. If the regimen had been rather dull, it had been in some way his life. 'I held to it: it held me together'. Now that he had come to Paris he had made himself a rule of life intended to last four years and the result was that he was now much calmer.

What is one to make of this revealing letter?

The *mauvais état moral* – the lamentable *affaisement* – could not have been extremely serious since he so quickly finds his equilibrium restored by simply adopting some rule of life or plan for the future. His mental health goes up and down: restoration to normality always seems on hand.

Further, there is reference to physical illness and one wonders what this was.

V. 1887–1902

So we come to the beginning of Durkheim's university career which, in the fashion of the day, was preceded by appointments in various lycées. He was in Bordeaux from 1887 to 1902. During these fifteen years he undertook a great amount of lecturing and writing and produced his two theses for the doctorat – the Latin thesis *Quid Secundatus* (1892a) and the major thesis *De la division du travail social* (1893b). The latter was to become a very important contribution for the development of sociology. Further, in 1897, he started to produce and edit the *Année sociologique* which became a national journal of the highest order. But there were other achievements and they took their toll on him by way of great tiredness and mental strain.

Perhaps the most vivid description of how matters stood comes in a letter, dated 22 March 1898, to Celestin Bouglé (1870–1940). In it Durkheim spoke of his mental rather than physical fatigue that resulted in his finishing *Le suicide* (1897a) and then going on to prepare volume II of the *Année sociologique*. He had also worked on an important article for the *Revue de métaphysique et de morale*, which was entitled 'Représentations individuelles et représentations collectives' (1898b). He said he had endured a very doleful winter. He spoke of the lamentable events surrounding him that were so morally enervating. Here, surely, is a direct reference to the Dreyfus Affair and its impact on the university, where most teachers were anti-Dreyfusards. It isolated him and his colleague Octave Hamelin, along with the Rector, from the teaching staff; however he gained much consolation from those two.

When Durkheim went to teach in Bordeaux he found a colleague in the up-and-coming young philosopher, Octave Hamelin (1856–1907). Indeed they were more than colleagues – they became very close friends (see Nemedi and Pickering 1995). They were an isolated couple and, apart from any emotional rapport that might have drawn them together, they were both philosophers of one kind or another. The one was a Jew and the other a Protestant. They were both in various ways outsiders. Durkheim looked up to Hamelin as having a superior mind and when Hamelin died tragically through drowning in 1906, Durkheim wrote his obituary (ibid.).

In referring to his own mental state, Durkheim wrote to Hamelin during the Dreyfus Affair: '… deep down I am an optimist. All I need is to get back to normal. From the moment when I no longer have this insupportable feeling of solitude, I shall indeed find time and energy necessary to write the article' (1975b, 2: 423). This, of course, referred to the famous article, the apologia for liberal individualism, 'L'Individualisme et les intellectuals' (1898c). In it individualism is firmly advocated and contrasted with egoism, which is rejected. Interestingly, he found difficulty in choosing the right publisher. Further, in March 1899, he started preparing volume III of the *Année sociologique*, while correcting the proofs of the second volume consisting of 600 pages.

At the end of his time in Bordeaux and on the point of going to Paris, his mother died. It has already been noted that she is said to have suffered from cancer of the liver. There is, to date, no evidence for this from the pen of Durkheim, but he does mention graphically Mélanie's last days in a letter to Hamelin (1975b, 2: 542).

VI. Interpreting Depression

We go no further back in the life of Durkheim for the simple reason that evidence from the man himself regarding his mental state is extremely difficult to discover. One event might be mentioned, however. Durkheim failed his baccalaureate at his first attempt, it is said, through illness. That illness seems very likely to have been some form of psychological stress.

Our intention is not to produce a psychological or psycho-analytical case study of the man. Rather, the reason for enquiring into his mental state is to try to unearth information about his lifestyle which might account for the possible stroke he suffered in 1916. His own words reveal the stress he was under during his academic endeavours. They involved very concentrated work that brought on some form of depression. There is no evidence, however, to show the precise nature of that depression or nervous illness, or to unearth its causes. He suffered badly from insomnia and it is now well established that such a complaint may be associated with depression. If one might venture an opinion, Durkheim's depression was not very severe for, as we have said, he was able to carry on with his work despite suffering from psychological disorders. Nevertheless he was prescribed palliative medicine. His neurasthenia rose and fell like the tides of the sea.

Steven Lukes, in his classical study of Emile Durkheim, gives little attention to the mental problems of the man who is the subject of his biography. In a short footnote he simply attributes them to overwork (Lukes 1973: 100, n.7). There have been others, however, who have taken the opposite direction and tried to explain Durkheim's mental troubles in terms of Freudian analysis, and more particularly by referring to the Oedipus complex (see Lacroix 1981). In a less sophisticated way, Mucchielli has pointed to the 'nevrose créatrice' (creative neurosis) employed by Durkheim as a way of overcoming his depression (Mucchielli 1998). This is seen in the enormous amount of work he undertook, coupled with the creativity of his ideas. *Nevrose créatrice*, Mucchielli holds, is a kind of sublimation of nervous energy, although it does not necessarily have sexual connotations, as Freud maintained (ibid.: 92). He also suggests that Durkheim concentrated on particular sociological subjects, such as religion and communal life, for instance, that were derived from basic personal characteristics going back to his childhood. There is no doubt, as we have already noted, that work was part and parcel of his life. To his nephew Durkheim wrote, 'But I ought to be more prudent. What would affect me would be to have no power to undertake work, however moderate. How could I fill my life? Such an existence would be no existence' (1998a: 575).

Theories about Durkheim's mental troubles have their place in Durkheimian studies but cannot be examined in detail here. They are certainly not the remit of this essay. While focusing on suffering and evil within the Durkheimian context, this chapter is specifically concerned with Durkheim's death and what might be related to it in the matter of his mental condition.

VII. Another Possible Cause?

With the presentation of such evidence as can be mustered, a position has been reached where one should try to form a conclusion on the cause of Durkheim's death. As has been asserted above, no final scientific answer can be given, but one should at least try to point to the likelihood of the cause of death.

The issue of mental illness has been prominent in what has been written and it is necessary to evaluate it. There can be no doubt that Durkheim suffered from some form of depression while he was working as a university teacher but it seems almost certain that it had nothing at all to do with his death.

Further, his lifestyle in general, which does not seem excessively indulgent, would hardly have contributed to a stroke. One fact has been constantly emphasized – namely, that if it was a stroke it was not a severe one. To the end of his days he seemed perfectly rational and had full use of all his mental and physical faculties. Not long before he died he was able to give lectures, although he admitted to feeling not very strong on such occasions. He wrote letters to the very end.

But all this begs the question as to whether or not he did in fact have a stroke. There seems to have been a rumour that he did suffer one, though there is no concrete evidence for it. It is clear that whatever occurred there was no damage to the brain. Instead, he may have had a mild heart attack which could have caused only a transient disturbance of cerebral functions. Further, strokes are of varying degree and duration and the alleged one, in November 1916, might not have lasted long. Strokes bring about a sudden and often a persisting disturbance of cerebral functions; this was not evident in Durkheim after November 1916. Migraines can cause transient effects similar to those of a mild stroke. In one case an observer noted that Durkheim's eyes seemed sunken, which is not a characteristic of a normal stroke.

In brief, the question is debatable. It is not likely, from the available evidence, that a stroke was the cause of his eventual death.

And so we are left to consider a physical ailment, not connected with the brain, that brought about Durkheim's death. It has already been noted that, despite the longish periods of medical treatment Durkheim had experienced, a toxic cause of death appears improbable.

There is, however, another possibility: cancer. This has already been alluded to in rumours circulated in Epinal. A clue to the fact that Durkheim may indeed have had cancer lies in an extraordinary few lines written to Mauss in 1916. Durkheim had gone with his family to Biarritz in April of that year to have a rest following the work he had been undertaking. The Commission on Russian Refugees had been completed in a very short time but, needless to say, he was tired. Nevertheless, he wanted to study the place Jews held in Russian life. On 4 May, after returning to Paris, he wrote to his nephew saying that he had profited from the rest and that Claude was in good health. He then continued:

> As far as I am concerned I am physically refreshed. I am looking much better. Mentally I have made more progress. Things are as follows. The body – I mean the mental [*moral*] body is healthy. It has not been invaded by destructive forces [*mal*]. I refer to something hidden – a wound and one that bleeds. But the wound is local; it is clean and is carefully watched over. Fresh blood is constantly flowing from it. Ten, twenty times a day – I can't tell you really how often – it opens suddenly and lets out a few drops of blood. This is exactly the situation. I cannot describe the situation any better. (1998a: 520)

This quite extraordinary piece of writing by Durkheim is difficult to interpret. He is physically refreshed; he says he is fine mentally and then within the same breath refers to a wound and blood. Nowhere in his letters or anywhere else does he write like this. It is hardly a symbolic communication that might refer to his depression; in any case this side of his life, it seems, was quite satisfactory. The details are too precise for it to be some kind of mental fantasy or cryptic communication – such imagining is not for Durkheim. The words must refer to reality: to what was actually happening to him physically. The inference is that it was a cancer of some kind, probably a skin malignancy, a melanoma perhaps, which can be accompanied by bleeding. There is no hint of where in his body the melanoma might have been.

Why has this illness never been mentioned by Durkheim before? Why was it that close friends and relatives appear not to have known about it? One answer lies in the fact that if indeed it was cancer, this dreaded disease was at the time shrouded in secrecy. The discreet way of referring to cancer then and now is to use the phrase, 'une maladie qui ne pardonne pas' (an unforgiving disease). This is how Bossu, the historian of Epinal, refers to the cause of Durkheim's death (Bossu 1982, 2: 149). More than likely the immediate family – and obviously Mauss himself – knew about it but hardly anyone else. In general it was only the doctor and certain members of the family who would speak about it. Even the patient himself might have been ignorant of the real nature of the malady.

A worthwhile task is to ascertain whether any of Durkheim's relatives had had cancer. Once again, accurate medical records are not obtainable. However, Durkheim's mother, Mélanie, who died in 1901, is said to have suffered from the disease. In her case it was alleged to be cancer of the liver (see note 3). Durkheim described her closing days in a letter from Epinal in which he said she scarcely opened her eyes and that she had no life in her, save that her heart and lungs functioned (1975b, 2: 452–53). Here is some genetic linkage in the matter of cancer between Durkheim and his mother. With no such linkage we turn to Durkheim's wife, Louise, who died in 1925. Of her, Bossu wrote, 'Mme Durkheim died of the same disease (*mal*)', that is, the same as that of Durkheim (Bossu 1982, 2: 149). And Mauss, when he wrote his Aunt Louise's obituary, said, 'She was not sixty years old when a horrible illness took her away from us' (*L'Année sociologique*, n.s. 2: 9). Surely the 'horrible' illness was cancer?

We can conclude that the strongest evidence for the cause of Durkheim's death was cancer, although the true cause of death will never be known. The other possibilities that have been considered carry far less weight.

Those who would reject any indication of cancer in Durkheim's crucial quotation have to offer an interpretation of its peculiarity. If it is a symbolic way of describing depression, then, as we have said, one has to face the fact that it is totally out of line with his general use of language.

Nevertheless, there is a problem with the cancer hypopthesis. It is this. The letter Durkheim wrote in which we have assumed there is a reference to cancer was dated 9 May 1916 but he died on 17 November a year and a half later. Throughout that time no reference can be found that he was suffering from such an affliction.

VIII. Final Assessment

In looking beyond medical evidence for a cause of death, certain aspects of Durkheim's personal life, not generally known, at least in the English-speaking world, have been brought to light. Although he enjoyed an apparently happy family life and achieved a great deal in the academic world, we see that he suffered considerably. One thing is certain: he was a much more complex personality than has generally been assumed. Behind the rational, ascetic man, totally dedicated to matters academic, stood someone whose life was emotionally intricate. At the same time he appears to have been able to control those intricacies and keep them from public view. He was a worried if not a tormented soul.

Finally, a point that focuses directly on the theme of this book is that Durkheim saw the First World War as an evil giving rise to a terrifying amount of suffering and slaughter. It is not surprising that although he often called himself an optimist, there are threads throughout his work – threads that never become prominent – that show his concern for suffering and evil as part of the lot of humankind.[9]

Notes

1. References to Durkheim's works and letters are in accordance with those of Lukes (Lukes 1973 and following editions). Where the dating-enumeration in the brackets of this text has no name preceding it, that of Durkheim is implied. All the translations from the French into English have been made by the author under the watchful eye of Mrs Jacqueline Sheldon, whose help is much appreciated.
2. I am very grateful to Dr Gale Maclaine for his contribution to this chapter by examining, in the light of modern pathology, such medical evidence as we possess about Durkheim's death. In many ways his contributions have helped to shape the chapter.
3. This information is to be found in a book by the local historian, Jean Bossu (Bossu 1982, Vol. II: 149). It is impossible to check with Bossu how he came by this information as he is now dead and his papers have disappeared. Durkheim's mother, Mélanie, also died of cancer of the liver. This has been confirmed by Durkheim's grandson, Etienne Halphen, in a personal communication.
4. Georges Davy (1883–1976) once wanted to marry Durkheim's daughter but it proved impossible as Davy was a Gentile (personal communication from Etienne Halphen). This was confirmed by Claudette Kennedy, great-niece of Durkheim. Durkheim once called Davy 'le pauvre garçon' when Davy was about to embark on a dubious marriage. He also referred to Davy's dramatic stories of an amorous kind (1998a: 584).
5. The term 'neuresthenia' came into use in the medical profession in France and Britain in the middle of the nineteenth century and means a weakness of the nervous system – a nervous disability. With the advancement of medicine, psychology and psychiatry, this term is no longer used, owing to its vagueness.
6. After the war, André's body was reinterred in the family grave in Montparnasse. He was originally buried in a little village, Davidovo, in Serbia (1998a: 501). For more on the death of André, see Durkheim's letter to Léon dated 15 September 1915 (1975b 2: 469–70). For Durkheim's reflections on the war, see other letters to Léon in 1975b. Interestingly, he held that the war had put an end to pacifism (1975b 2: 472).
7. Durkheim gives the impression of being a very happily married man. This is seen in his many references to his own family and to his deep affection for his children and grandson Claude. Louise, his wife, was an enormous help to him, not only in normal wifely duties, but in helping him to proofread and copy his manuscripts (*Année sociologique*, n.s.1924–5, II: 9). There is one aspect, however, that should be mentioned and that might raise the eyebrows. Louise was a very able pianist before she was married. After the marriage, however, at Emile's request, she gave up playing so that he could concentrate on his work undisturbed. When he died she took up playing the piano once more.

    It is obvious that he saw family life in strongly patriarchal terms. This can at least be deduced from photographs of the family. But at that time, there was nothing exceptional in it, as can be seen when one examines the family patterns of the middle classes in France at the time. Within marriage itself he was highly moral and, it seems, never had an extramarital affair. The fact is corroborated by what others have noted in Durkheim – that in many ways, he was an ascetic Puritan.

Intellectually, too, he was a great supporter of the family as a social institution, and indeed lectured and wrote about it. He was strongly opposed to divorce and to sexual freedom because they undermined not only marriage but society itself. It is little wonder that Durkheim seems to have condemned the lifestyle of artists of his day (see Durkheim 1925a).

8. For some of the other duties Durkheim had to undertake in the Sorbonne and elsewhere, see (1998a: 521,559). Fauconnet later succeeded Durkheim in his chair in the Sorbonne.
9. Some time before he died, in his late fifties and also before the sudden illness that occurred in late 1916, Durkheim was aware of the imminence of his death. One wonders if cancer had been diagnosed? In a revealing letter dated 19 March 1916 he wrote:

> I feel indeed detached from all temporal interest. But this also brings joy. The joy of the ascetic feeling is above everything ... Since the evening of 2 January I said to those around me: there are two principles ... which if they are true (and I believe them to be true), will apply to me.
>
> The first is that life triumphs over death, that is to say, that beings in whom there is life react with one another: life takes hold of them again and supports them. They cannot stop life from unfolding and manifesting itself. I was remembering grandmother eight days after her son died, unable to refrain from taking an interest in street life. Saturday evening, 26 February (two days after having received the final news), coming back from Bourg-la-Reine, I found the proofs of a 'Letter' by Admiral Degouy that needed reworking completely as I knew they would, and I was wondering how I could go back to this task which meant nothing to me and seemed dull. The next morning I resumed work on it and half an hour later I was saying to your aunt: 'I work; I am saved'. I had caught a glimpse of the means by which to do the work for what needed redoing and I was absorbed by it. Undoubtedly, in the circumstances I am going through, this faculty of mine to ponder over and over again for fifty years on the same thing day and night militates against me. But I can also use this faculty to escape the obsessive idea if I can find some other matter to occupy my mind. And I will always have something to think about. The result is that when I work I forget, and as soon as I stop I think – you can guess what. But I can escape from this thought if I am grabbed enough by some other thought.
>
> The second principle is that life is flexible, even at the age of fifty-eight, and it can take many different forms. All the egoistic side of my life has vanished. ... I feel in fact detached from every worldly interest. But that also gives me joy. It is the joy of the ascetic who feels himself to be above everything. It is a severe and melancholic joy. And certainly in so far as one can foretell the future, melancholy will be my mode of my life. However, I am naturally well inclined towards it. It does not frighten me. I would prefer an active sort of joy perhaps, yet I believe that one can have a different sort of life as well.
>
> I trust I have presented you with a highly accurate analysis of my state of mind in as much as I can ascertain it. I don't know if I will ever laugh much, but I can do without laughing. And my life seems to be heading in that direction. You have no idea of the sensation of joy that comes from the feeling of detachment, because I do not have any temporal interest any more. (1998a: 507–08).

His ambivalence towards the future emerges from this letter. Despite his bouts of depression, he is optimistic for the future. At the same time he is somewhat pessimistic in that asceticism coupled with hard work are really what he strives for. And we have seen the pessimism become stronger as he approaches death.

I. Suffering and Evil in Durkheim

Chapter 1

Le Suicide and Psychological Suffering

Sophie Jankélévitch

In the *Règles de la méthode sociologique*, Durkheim compares the roles of statesman and doctor: like the latter, the statesman 'prevents the birth of diseases by good hygiene, and seeks to cure them when they occur' (Durkheim 1895a: 93). *Mutatis mutandis*, the sociologist occupies a position as eminent as Plato's philosopher king. Just as the latter's science of moderation is placed at the service of the constitution of a just political order, so the sociologist's knowledge of the normal and the pathological is placed at the service of the health of the social body. In itself this knowledge is disinterested: science is distinguished from art by the fact that it approaches its object with the sole aim of knowing it (see Durkheim 1900b). But the choice of the object of study is not a matter of indifference; it expresses concern regarding the health of the social body. In the final analysis, sociology is commanded by a practical aim which justifies it and without which it would be no more than idle speculation.

Durkheim was clear about the means to be used to cure the evils from which his society suffered: a social reorganization based on corporative institutions, an education able to provide federative ideals appropriate to the new moral tendencies. But the occasional, somewhat edifying optimism of a few pages should not mislead us about his confidence in the effectiveness of these remedies; it may be that, for him, the 'universal and chronic state of malaise' he spoke about in 1914 is basically incurable.

I. The Diagnosis

In fact, the sociologist claims to be a doctor. Certainly, he is a special doctor, since he does not address his practice to an individual, or even to individuals, but to a whole, resulting from their association and endowed with a reality *sui generis*, irreducible to the sum of its constituent elements. The suffering of the social body is therefore irreducible to that of its individual components, and inaccessible through what these individuals may feel or express about their subjective situation. In *Le suicide*, the 'doctor' has to deal with a silent patient (how could he not?); he relies solely on the regularities of statistical data which express the tendency of every society to 'furnish a determinate contingent of voluntary deaths' (Durkheim 1897a: 15). Further, suicide can be viewed as a phenomenon of normal sociology – but which also reveals a rapid and significant increase in the numbers of these voluntary deaths throughout the century. This gives suicide the appearance of a pathological phenomenon calling for a suitable therapy.

For Durkheim, the 'rising tide' of voluntary deaths is the most evident symptom of the sickness affecting the social body. Individual suffering always appears as the effect of this sickness, and individual forms of suicide can all be connected to general social causes which determine the phenomenon, even if each suicide considered in itself is marked by the singular temperament and history of the individual who has performed it. In fact, society cannot be sick without individuals being affected at the same time: 'its suffering necessarily becomes their suffering, Because it is the whole, the ill it suffers is communicated to its component parts' (ibid.: 229).

Durkheim thus views individual sorrows as the product of collective sorrows, and the model of equilibrium between opposing forces clearly dismisses the study of subjective reasons for suicide from the field of analysis. Indeed, how in this perspective can autonomous meaning be attributed to the representations individuals may have of their actions? Human deliberations, Durkheim reminds us, are only ever later justifications of resolutions taken for reasons inaccessible to consciousness; these reasons refer to suicide-generating trends in society in which individuals are passively and irresistibly caught up without being aware of it. Altruism, egoism and anomie generate an 'active renunciation', a 'languid melancholy' and an 'exacerbated lassitude', collective tendencies which, 'penetrating individuals, cause them to kill themselves'. (ibid.: 336). Only these trends are truly determining. The clear-cut distinction Durkheim makes between (individual) motives and (social) causes of suicide, concerning himself only with the latter, reflects the founding caesura of Durkheimian sociology between the social and the individual. In fact, by virtue of the principles formulated in the *Règles*, the definition Durkheim puts forward in the introduction to his book – *'we call suicide every case of death which results directly or indirectly from a positive or negative action carried out by the victim and which the victim knew must produce this result'* (ibid.: 5, Durkheim's italics) – excludes any consideration of the subject's purpose or intention. 'Scientific faith', as Bourdieu points out (Bourdieu 1997) leads Durkheim to exclude from his study the raison d'être of an act which common sense regards as fundamentally individual, and which in his eyes is first of all a social fact with all the characteristics stated two years earlier in the *Règles*.

In the chapter of that book devoted to the distinction between the normal and the pathological, Durkheim claims adherence to a strictly descriptive and statistical conception of the normal. This should mean seeing the increasing number of suicides as normal since, however disquieting, it is a matter of a general fact. However, the diagnosis given in the final chapter of *Suicide* is unambiguous: it is a pathological phenomenon. More precisely, it is the speed of increase that is pathological, a speed which should not be imputed to progress in itself according to Durkheim, but to the 'unhealthy agitation' in which it is being realized at the end of the century. In his eyes, this feverish condition would be the specific pathology of modern societies; it is what is designated by the concept of anomie.

The term 'anomie' was introduced into the French language by Jean-Marie Guyau, who in his *Esquisse d'une morale sans obligation ni sanction* (1885) employs it with a positive connotation to designate the absence of fixed law, the disappearance of the categorical imperative and absolutes in future morality.[1] For Guyau, anomie registers the individual's originality and emancipation from group conformity. Durkheim, on the other hand, uses the term in a clearly pejorative sense to designate a state of anarchy, demoralization and deregulation. Durkheimian anomie is the disorder which results from rules no longer exerting any moderating action on collective life, especially in the economic sphere. A sort of permanent war is generated by the passion for gain and the pursuit of individual interest which encounter no limits, as if in the absence of a moral force capable of curbing rivalries and appetites, men were returning to something like the Hobbesian state of nature, governed solely by the law of the strongest.

The study of suicide published by Maurice Halbwachs thirty years later brings out an important aspect of Durkheim's use of the concept of anomie (Halbwachs 1930). Halbwachs notes that the life of increasingly urban and industrialized modern societies is marked by an increasing complexity of human relations. This intensification of inter-individual contacts multiplies occasions for suffering, rivalry and frustration, all the more by virtue of the weakening of collective, federative feelings. If men seek death less during war or revolution, it is because social life is simplified in these periods: men are carried away by passions and common interests that mobilize them around a single cause and divert them from themselves, but also from each other and their inter-individual conflicts. But for Halbwachs, 'the complication of modern societies should not be confused with what Durkheim called anomie'. If human relations are very often the source of all kinds of discontent, disappointment and anguish, it would be reductive to attribute the malaise thus created to the collapse of social discipline, as Durkheim does. To account for a phenomenon whose disturbing nature he recognizes, Halbwachs resorts to the purely descriptive notion of 'complication', whereas Durkheim, through the diagnosis of anomie, directs a normative gaze on the organization and functioning of society. The distinction between complication and anomie thus calls for a consideration of the presuppositions of the Durkheimian concept: a certain way of judging the present in comparison with the past; a particular conception of the relations between order and disorder.

Durkheim's point of view is dominated by the idea that nothing has been constructed on the ruins of the past. The revolutionary shock demolished the traditional frameworks of social life, dissolved the bonds joining men together, shattered the familial and religious constraints to which men were subject and which structured their daily life and representations, and left a void which has still not been filled. Is, then, the Durkheimian analysis of modern societies inspired by nostalgia for the past? To read the pages Durkheim devoted to the malaise of his contemporaries in such a unilateral way would be to ignore his attachment to Enlightenment ideals and the revolutionary values asserted by Kant and Rousseau. They were the dignity of the human person, the spirit of free inquiry and the emancipation of the individual, despite the risk that these values might strain the social bond. But Halbwachs raises the different problem of the conditions under which comparison of past and present is pertinent. On the one hand, the evaluation of the amount of suffering in a society, in whatever period, must be related to the satisfactions men also find in that society. On the other hand, by making anomie the typical evil of modern societies, Durkheim gives the impression that

> in ancient societies economic and social life was conducted without clashes, did not experience critical periods, and individual appetites, rivalries and passions did not produce, relatively, the same quantity of discouragement and sorrows. We say relatively, that is to say taking into account the sum of activity expended and the needs which could be satisfied. (ibid.: 373)

The diagnosis of anomie thus expresses a form of nostalgia through which the past is viewed as an idyllic age, or at least more peaceful than the modern era, and the whole of social evolution is read as decadence, as degradation from an initial condition taken as the norm.

Halbwachs notes that ancient societies also had their illnesses and challenges the idea that the social and economic activity of modern societies is, as Durkheim reckons, 'entirely disordered'. Once again, the problem is that of the surreptitious introduction of implicit value judgements into sociological analysis. We have to understand that capitalist societies also have their own specific order; things do not take place in just any way. With Bourdieu, we can speak of a game, 'in order to express the participation of a set of people in an ordered activity' (Bourdieu 1987: 81); the social world is not a chaos and possesses regularities – an order – which sociology has to explain. Bourdieu's distinctions between the different meanings of the word 'rule' may enable us to get a better grasp of the difficulties raised by Durkheim's analysis and at the same time explain the meaning of Halbwachs's objections. The word 'rule' is ambiguous. Bourdieu says that it designates 'a juridical or quasi-juridical type of principle more or less consciously produced and controlled by the agents'; 'a set of objective regularities imposed on all those who enter the game'; and the 'principle constructed by scientists to account for the game' (ibid.: 81). Bourdieu warns against confusing the second and third senses of the word, which 'in Marx's old phrase', amounts to presenting 'things of logic as the logic of things'. The task Durkheim takes on in *Le suicide* is indeed to give a rational account of the collective phenomenon of the tendency of every society to produce a certain number of voluntary deaths. In other words, the scientific project is to isolate the rules – in the second sense – of suicide, that is to say, the objective regularities at work in the phenomenon in question. In order to do this he constructs a model – this is the third sense of the word – in which the concept of anomie plays a central role. But anomie, which for him signifies disorder – that is, the absence of order – is not only an explanatory concept; it really seems to be inherent in modern societies themselves. Is there not a slippage here from the things of logic to the logic of things? Furthermore, the meaning of the notion of anomie in Durkheim is ambiguous. With regard to the scientific project it involves connecting different rates of suicide to different social structures, anomie then becoming one structure among others. But at the same time this structure is paradoxically qualified as chaos, as disorder. Bergson has shown that the opposition of order and disorder is engendered by the intellectual habits of a way of thinking, intended first of all for getting one's bearings in practice, for directing conduct. Similarly, Canguilhem refuses to see the concept of the 'pathological' as the logical contrary of the concept of the 'normal', 'for life in the pathological state is not the absence of norms, but the presence of other norms' (Canguilhem 1975: 166). The concepts of order and disorder only designate two different types of order. The idea of disorder is evaluative, expressing the presence of 'the order we are not looking for' (Bergson 1959: 1,338), which does not interest us, or, as Bergson says, our disappointment in the absence of the order we desire. Anomie, the disorder peculiar to capitalist societies, would thus be the bad order characterized by poorly or insufficiently regulated behaviour. It is an order Durkheim rejected and condemned in the name of another order deemed to be a more harmonious, natural, normal state which, according to him, it is the task of sociology to restore. Does not likening 'bad order' to disorder involve a second slippage in which the normative concept of a well-regulated order, of a system of disciplined conduct, is superimposed on the descriptive concept of social order?

In the light of Halbwachs's conclusions we can see how Durkheim sees the increase in the suicide rate from the perspective of an evaluation which modifies how the relation between the normal and the pathological is thought. It also determines the nature of the therapy to be prescribed. But the concept of the 'ought' underlying this deliberately quantitative and statistical analysis of suicide, this rigorous application of the rules of method, is also what gives it the weight of an ethical reflection. This brings back to the forefront a questioning which the positivist approach seemed forced to eliminate.

II. 'True' Suicide and Melancholy

Durkheim is contemplating the society of his time and in this respect the different kinds of voluntary death distinguished in the typology of *Le suicide* could not have the same significance. Altruistic suicide is on the decline because the moral constitution to which it is linked, characterized by the individual's total subordination to the community, is only observed in an ancient or traditional type of society. It is a society itself in decline, or in narrowly circumscribed spheres of contemporary society, like the army. It is only the increase in egoistic and anomic suicides which has a pathological character. It is these we should try to check and which are indicative of a sickness of modern times whose measure is given by their growth. But from the point of view of the collective malaise which this phenomenon expresses, are not attempted suicides, that is to say, suicides which do not succeed, just as significant? Moreover, is not profound discontentment on its own, which does not necessarily result in suicide, or even attempted suicide, and so is not quantifiable, already in itself a morbid sign? In this respect, egoistic and anomic suicides are alarming phenomena for Durkheim, much more so than altruistic suicide, then, beyond the figures provided by statistics. Perhaps this is due to the question with which these acts directly confront us – that of the reasons for living in modern societies.

The book's introduction reminds us that the sociologist must distance himself from everyday language and its ambiguities and start by constituting the order of facts he proposes to study. Thus, Durkheim constructs the concept of suicide by abstracting from the subjective determinations which lead to voluntary death, but also from the feelings it arouses in collective opinion. The definition put forward in the introduction allows inclusion, under the category of suicide, of acts which common sense would hesitate to consider as such. In fact, at first sight it may seem difficult to give the same name to the act of someone who kills himself in a spirit of renunciation, or out of devotion to the community, and that of someone who is depressed or desperate. But does not Durkheim, surreptitiously and, with regard to the rules of method he prescribes, paradoxically, return to the common sense with which he claims to break? He examines a possible explanation of altruistic suicide by man's melancholic representation of life. According to him, this explanation has the weakness of being valid for all types of suicide and of therefore concealing the specificity of each. There is sorrow and sorrow: the egoist's sorrow is not the altruist's. The first 'is sad because he sees nothing real in the world but the individual', the second because 'to him the individual seems stripped of all reality' (Durkheim 1897a: 243). With this distinction Durkheim makes a shift which brings out the fundamental difference between egoistic and altruistic suicides: in the former, the man, prey to his feelings of pointlessness, kills himself because life no longer has any meaning for him; in the latter, he kills himself because life has too much meaning, so to speak, and his action is dictated by the hope of better perspectives. If the 'intemperate' altruist attaches no value or even reality to his own existence, it is because all his energy and interest are invested in something which exceeds or transcends him. The person who puts an end to his life in order to win the esteem of the community, who sacrifices himself for a group, an ideal or for God, has resolved the nagging question that torments the egoist: 'What's the point?' He has resolved it – inasmuch as he ever poses it – in the sense that his degree of integration in society and his mode of existence already demonstrate the dissolution of the problem.

But is not this precisely the reason why common sense resists describing as suicide the action by which the altruist takes his own life? Isn't 'true' suicide the act of despair? Moreover, Durkheim asserted this in the *Division du travail social*: the suicides we observe in 'lower' societies, those that two years later he will describe as altruistic, are not acts 'of despair, but of abnegation', expressing their authors' total attachment to an ideal. They 'are not therefore suicides, in the common sense of the word, any more than the death of a soldier or doctor who knowingly exposes himself in order to do his duty' (Durkheim 1893b: 226). For Durkheim, the true suicide is the unhappy suicide, the person we see in 'civilized' societies which are marked by an upsurge of individualism, exposing them to egoism, and by a loosening of the normative system that potentially generates anomie.

What happened between the 1893 thesis and the work of 1897? As we have just seen, according to *Le suicide* the scientific approach involves leaving the terrain of everyday opinion and common language. However, it is as if in rendering the phenomena intelligible it proved impossible to abandon the agent's point of view completely. This point of view being by definition inaccessible to analysis, since the agent's condition is henceforth one of eternal silence, all we can do is reconstruct it. What then becomes determinant in defining the real suicide and distinguishing it from other forms of voluntary death is not the real motives – inaccessible in themselves – but the supposed motives, that is to say, the representations of self, place in society, relationships with others and existence that the sociologist attributes to the potential suicide.[2]

Only egoistic and anomic suicides therefore really pose the question of reasons for living. Why are men unhappy in so-called civilized societies?

Because there is something profoundly perverted in the structure and functioning of these societies which forces men to live unnaturally, if we accept that nature is, in a double sense, the limit. First of all, the limit is that which the group represents in relation to the individual inserted within it (integration), which therefore constitutes the individual as part of a whole which extends beyond him. And then it is that which checks individual ambitions and desires (regulation). The absence of limit in the first sense generates egoistic suicide due to the disintegration of social bonds, the weakening of collective life and the correlative hypertrophy of the feeling of individual personality. The absence of limit in the second sense is cause of the *mal de l'infini* which gives rise to anomic suicide. If the different kinds of suicides can, in the main, be connected to the major types distinguished in terms of an aetiological classification, Durkheim notes that in experience they are rarely encountered in isolation. He also notes the affinities between egoism and anomie (see e.g. Durkheim 1897a: 226) and the possibility of seeing the latter as a consequence of the former: 'we know, in fact, that generally they are only two aspects of a single social condition, so it is not surprising to find them in a single individual. It is even almost inevitable that the egoist has some aptitude for deregulation, because being detached from society, society does not have a sufficient hold over him to regulate him' (ibid.). In both cases what is pathogenic is the absence of society to the individual: in egoistic suicide society is absent from collective activity and in anomic suicide it is absent from individual passions. In fact, although they generate different types of suicide, egoism and anomie are two faces of a single sickness affecting members of modern societies. And although the expression *mal de l'infini* is more often employed to designate the suffering of the anomic, Durkheim also uses it to designate that of the egoist, for if the latter is lost in boundless desire, the former is lost in the boundlessness of the dream. In both cases the pathological element is found in the hypertrophy of reflective intelligence as a function of inner life in the egoist and of sensibility in the anomic.

This idea of hypertrophy refers to a conception of disease as a breach of harmony, in which there may be a distant echo or transposition of the humorism developed by Hippocrates and the authors of the *Corpus Hippocraticum*, and then later by Galen. The soul's health, like the body's, is based on the equilibrium of four humours – blood, phlegm, yellow bile and black bile – and physical qualities – hot, cold, dry and humid – which accompany them. The Renaissance too will see the interplay of the humours, combined with other factors, as the key to the explanation of psychical affections and of melancholy in particular, a disorder characterized by fear and sadness and caused by a black and silty humour occupying the brain and altering its temperature. The same theoretical framework is still maintained in the seventeenth century. At the end of the eighteenth century it has still not been completely abandoned by Pinel and Cabanis.

In Durkheim's time, the break with a theory that exercised hegemony over medical thought for a long while was largely accomplished, notably by Broussais. But is it not still melancholy that we see in the sickness of the egoist and the anomic, the modern face of ancient *acedia*, varying only in its nuances – more languorous in the egoist, more violent in the anomic? The Middle Ages identified it as a physical disorder, and the Church, seeing it as a variant of sloth, condemned it. The rehabilitation of Aristotle's point of view, emphasizing the affinities of the melancholic temperament with genius and creativity, had to wait until the Renaissance.[3] In Durkheim melancholy is reduced to its depressive aspect, identified with *malaise d'être*, and his description of its symptoms especially seems to reveal the romantic sources of his thought. Reference to literary works are rather rare in Durkheim; in *Le suicide* they are only found at the end of the second book, in the chapter devoted to the study of the individual forms of different types of suicide. However, his kinship with some nineteenth-century writers goes well beyond the literary examples that punctuate the reflections in these twenty or so pages.[4] To Lamartine's Raphaël, Chateaubriand's René and Goethe's Werther, each referred to in the chapter in question, could be added Vigny's Chatterton, Tolstoy's Anna Karenina, and George Eliot's Silas Marner, cited by Halbwachs, but also Flaubert's Emma Bovary, about whom Durkheim is strangely silent, Lermontov's Pechorin (Lermontov 1854), or even Octave, the hero of Alfred Musset's *Confession d'un enfant du siècle*. Amongst all these characters, the last is one who does not go so far as to take his own life, but all are affected by what Musset calls the 'sickness of the century', that seems to us to be the essential object of Durkheim's reflection in *Le suicide*. Each in their own way illustrates the two major forms of suffering revealed by egoistic and anomic suicide.

Egoism is a mixture of sadness and unproductive idleness, tinted with a feeling of abandonment. The egoist suffers from depression, disenchantment, moral helplessness and melancholic languor. The collective asthenia reverberates in him in the form of incurable lassitude, gloomy dejection and weakening activity. Life, Durkheim notes, is not so much painful to him as meaningless and empty, and this feeling of emptiness gives rise to suicidal thoughts. 'I no longer wished to die when I was really unhappy', says René (Chateaubriand, 2003 [1802]), when pain fills the abyss of his existence previously shaped by ennui. As Musset says, in his description of the spirit of the century at the beginning of the *Confession*, 'it is sweet to think you are unhappy when you are only empty and bored' (Musset 2003 [1836]: 175).

The sickness of the anomic is also a form of melancholy, but in which irritation and discontent are dominant. Durkheim describes it as an exacerbated lassitude, a painful disquiet, a feverish impatience, a state of constant agitation in which desire, lacking any external power capable of containing it, intensifies and becomes its own end. It is a pathology which affects the relationship to time inasmuch as it manifests itself in an inability to be satisfied with the present, an irrepressible tendency to project itself constantly into the future and pursue inaccessible goals. Whether he experiences a sudden loss, or his desire suddenly encounters an insurmountable obstacle, or he wearies of an endless quest, the anomic passes from illusion to disappointment: he is a malcontent who blames himself, others or life in general. Such is Faust, the very incarnation of immoderation, for whom the 'vulture' of melancholy gnaws away at life, and who 'is always pursuing some distant vapour'.

For Durkheim, however, the individual histories of potential suicides are only the occasional causes of the act by which they put an end to their lives. Their sickness only reflects what is eating away at the social body as a whole. In 1836 Musset had already drawn a striking picture which foreshadowed the sociologist's diagnosis some sixty years later. The beginning of the *Confession* is set against one of the major oppositions of nineteenth-century thought – that of a dying old order and a still uncertain new order – in which Robert Nisbet sees the matrix of the 'sociological tradition'. Meditation on this conflict and the resultant helpless confusion is implicit throughout Durkheim's work (Nisbet 1993).

> Three elements therefore divided the life then offered to young people: behind them a past destroyed for ever, still bustling about on its ruins, with all the fossils of absolutism; before them the dawning of an immense horizon, the first lights of the future; and between these two worlds ... something like the Ocean separating the old continent from young America, indistinct and irresolute, a stormy sea full of shipwrecks, crossed from time to time by some distant sail or by a ship exhaling dense steam; the present century, in a word, which separates the past from the future, which is neither one nor the other while resembling both at the same time, and in which with each step we take we do not know whether we are treading on a seed or a ruin. From that moment two camps were formed: on the one hand, the excited, suffering spirits, the expansive souls who need the infinite, bowed their heads in tears; they were wrapped up in unhealthy dreams, and all we see now are frail reeds on an ocean of bitterness. On the other hand, the men of flesh remained upright, inflexible in the midst of positive pleasures and concerned only with counting the money they had. (Musset 2003: 24–25, 31)

Musset evokes the 'bleak and silent disgust', the 'disenchantment' and 'dreadful despair', the universal doubt, nihilism, 'principle of death' and 'insensibility' which in his eyes characterize the time. In this life recounted in the *Confession*, he says, we should read the story of the sickness affecting an entire generation.

This sickness is solitude, for Halbwachs the sole cause of suicide. The feeling of not being understood and of leading an empty, pointless life actually goes back to this solitude. 'There is nothing a thought formed by society is less capable of looking in the face than the social void', Halbwachs comments (Halbwachs 1930: 321), in a striking phrase which places the void at the level of the sun and death on which, La Rochefoucauld tells us, we 'cannot fix our gaze' (La Rochefoucauld 1974: 13). Halbwachs here takes up Durkheim's reflections on the causes of suffering in the latter's analysis of egoistic suicide. Man leads a double existence: to his physical being is added a social being made up of feelings, ideas, desires and practices detached from organic needs and shaped by the action of society. These higher forms of human activity are both derived from society and directed towards it. If collective life breaks up, if the threads which bind us to others and the whole of society are severed, the reasons for living disappear.'What is social in us is without objective foundation. It is no more than an artificial combination of illusory images … nothing, therefore, which can serve as an end for our actions' (Durkheim 1897a: 228).[5] The moral constitution of man himself, therefore, makes a life without meaning intolerable. This is in fact the situation lived by the literary characters evoked above: without mooring in an external reality and sick from objectless daydreams, their social being becomes empty. Sometimes solitude is seen as an isolation connected to urban life. Musset compares the town to a 'cesspool in which only bodies are in society, leaving souls solitary' (Musset 2003: 75). At other times it is viewed as what Durkheim will see as the very condition of the egoist. This is what P. Souël expresses harshly to René at the end of the latter's account:

> I see a young man intoxicated with chimeras, who dislikes everything, and who has shirked his social responsibilities in order to devote himself to idle reveries … What do you do deep in the forests where you pass your solitary days neglecting your duties? … Presumptuous young man who thought that man can be self-sufficient! Solitude is bad for someone who does not share it with God; it redoubles the soul's powers while depriving them of any subject on which they can be exercised. (Chateaubriand 2003: 181)

René is a part who takes himself for the whole; he deserves no pity.

III. Holes in the Fabric (*tissu*)[6]

The feeling of solitude is a product of the condition of the social fabric, the loosening of which produces these 'vacuums which separate consciousnesses and makes them strangers to each other' (Durkheim 1897a: 317). From what 'type of imagination', to adopt George Canguilhem's expression (1975: 56), does this diagnosis arise? At this level too there is an echo of romantic thought in Durkheim.

Durkheim's use of the metaphor of *tissu*, however hackneyed its current usage may appear, is worth considering for a moment. First of all, let us recall, with Canguilhem, the biological meaning of this term. Bichat sees *tissu* as the constitutive material of the living being. Tissue evokes continuity, that is to say, for Bichat – the continuity of all vital phenomena, corresponding to the requirement of vitalism and its assertion of the irreducibility of life to its physico-chemical conditions and, thereby, of the whole organism to its constituent elements.

What, then, does the metaphor of social *tissu* signify in Durkheim? In the first place, it is a colourful way of expressing the idea that forms the kernel of the Durkheimian conception of relations between the individual and society: the whole is irreducible to the sum of its parts. Durkheim rejects contractualist theories which view society as an artifice created by a decree of free and rational human will, the sign of the individual's founding power and his capacity to establish an order and decide the law. These theories conceive of social cohesion in terms of a mechanical, Newtonian model, which dominated the sciences of life in the eighteenth century. The social body is thought of as a juxtaposition of 'molecules' which preserve a separate existence in their association. The whole therefore has only an 'artificial individuality' resulting from the assemblage of isolated individuals.[7] Durkheim also criticizes the utilitarianism of someone like Spencer for whom society is no more than the establishment of external relations between isolated individuals, each pursuing their own interest and coming together to cooperate. In Durkheim the notion of community, rediscovered in the nineteenth century and central in romantic political thought, makes it possible to conceptualize the social bond. Far from being the fruit of calculation and human will, the community pre-exists the individual; it is the individual's condition of possibility and condition of intelligibility. The bond which joins individuals to each other is not rational or contractual but fusional.[8] From the very fact of association, the whole individual's form is irreducible to the sum of its parts and possesses specific properties which cannot be explained by those of its constituent units. The model which makes the society thus defined conceivable is that of the organism, in that the organism is precisely not a mechanism or assemblage of parts. As the article published in 1898 shows (1898b), Durkheim's social and political philosophy asserts the specificity of the social in the same way that vitalist biology asserts the specificity of the vital. Collective life and psychological life have the same type of relationship with their respective substrata – individual consciousness in the former case and nervous elements in the latter. Sociology is therefore no more a corollary of individual psychology than psychology is an epiphenomenon of organic processes. Representational phenomena are irreducible to the nervous elements which condition them. Mental life cannot be broken down into ideas individually associated with a distinct cellular vibration; it consists in 'a continuous flow of representations' such that we can never say where one begins or the other ends, 'They are mutually entwined' (ibid.: 25). What is involved here is a certain 'type of imagination' – the imagination of the discontinuous which underlies every atomistic conception and is unsuitable for accounting for the characteristic unity and continuity of representational activity. Psychical life is a *tissu sui generis* which certainly has a substratum in the nervous tissue, but whose properties are not explained by those of that substratum.

Secondly, the *tissu* metaphor refers to a conception of the social universe founded on what could be called a physics of fullness. In Durkheim, society abhors a vacuum, and the vacuum here does not only designate the absence of meaning which leads to suicide. When individual consciousnesses separate off from each other, when (extending the metaphor) holes appear in the fabric, this indicates the pathological condition of the social body. The normal state, on the other hand, is recognized by the absence of empty space between the constituent elements of society. This vision of the social world is present in Durkheim from his earliest works when he was assembling the materials he needed for the development of the theory: 'The individual is not separated from his fellows by a gulf', he writes in 1887, 'but all are so pressed up against each other that one cannot move without it being felt in some way by all the others' (Durkheim 1887c: 293).

The physics of fullness entails communication of the movement of one part to all the others. But there is also what could be called an 'imagination of fullness' in Durkheim, conveying the idea of continuity inherent to the metaphor of *tissu*, which paradoxically governs the explanation of the vacuum and solitude experienced by individuals. As we saw above, the sickness experienced by the whole is generally communicated to the parts from which it is formed. In particular, the loosening of the social fabric is the source of the emptiness which separates consciousnesses and produces the feeling of isolation. And do we not find this imagination of fullness again at the epistemological level behind the fundamental principle of the explanation of social facts formulated in chapter 5 of the *Règles*, according to which 'the determining cause of a social fact must be sought in antecedent social facts and not in individual states of consciousness'? What takes the form of a methodical prescription in the 1895 work was already stated in the 1887 article cited above. Durkheim disputes that the individual has the power to 'shake society'. Certainly, he may create habits, but a habit is not a social fact. The transformation of habits into accepted behaviour – that is to say, into customs endowed with authority and obligatory force; in other words, their crystallization into social facts – can only have its cause in the social itself. History shows that 'the origin of any social custom is another social custom', and 'in this uninterrupted sequence of customs generating each other, we never see the slightest empty space or the smallest join through which individual artifice could be introduced' (ibid.: 304–5). The requirement of continuity is also essential therefore to the explanatory approach, which matches, as it were, the texture of its object.

But the *tissu* metaphor is, precisely, a metaphor. It does not aid understanding the nature of social cohesion in itself. In a fabric, in fact, there is nothing but an intertwining of threads, in which warp and weft regularly and continuously interlace. In a society, however, 'strings' of social relations attach individuals to one another. Although irreducible to the sum of its component individuals, society is nonetheless formed from individuals and only individuals. The continuity of the weave is, as it were, punctuated or interrupted by these discrete entities, by these ultimate atoms-individuals between whom there is always a minimal distance. The irreducibility of the whole to the parts in Durkheim does not exclude resistance of the parts to the whole; the individual's requirements are far from necessarily coinciding with those of the social body.[9] What the metaphor expresses is much rather an 'ought'; it provides an ideal image of a society in which – if we take the metaphor, and the continuity it suggests, literally – there would be no rough patches.

Is such an idea realizable, and to what extent? Certainly, the individual could not disappear entirely. Without individuals there would be no society. Furthermore, the valorization of the individual personality in modern societies is the product of an irreversible evolution, a fact that the choice of therapy has to acknowledge. How is society's sickness to be treated? At the end of *Suicide*, Durkheim wonders whether education, as character formation, may be the most effective means for limiting the dissolvent action on society of the pessimistic tendency. But education is a social fact bound up with all the other social facts. It is a system of practices, institutions and ideas which reflects the structure and needs of society in its entirety; in that sense, it does not create anything, and reform of education would produce no lasting effects without overall reform. If you do not treat the whole, its disease is liable to make the medicine administered to the parts ineffective. So we always come back to the need for a social reorganization, whose content is developed in the *Division du travail social*[10] and the last chapter of *Suicide*. It consists in repairing the 'fabric' by tying the broken threads together and firmly fastening each part to the whole.

If the disintegration of society is in danger of plunging men into madness, leaving them no way out but an inordinate assertion of their individuality and abandoning them to unlimited desires which cannot be satisfied, men's madness acts in turn on the social bond, for the upsurge of egoism and the unleashing of ambitions accelerates its dissolution. There is no point in reforming education without reforming society. But it is just as idle to reform society without ensuring that the mental dispositions necessary for social cohesion penetrate the consciousness of individuals, shaping them so as to overcome their resistance. Political action gives stability to the effects produced by pedagogical action, but the latter is equally decisive vis-à-vis the former because it aims to reach into individuals at the level of their representation of themselves and their position within the whole. It thus guarantees a profound anchorage for social reorganization.

IV. Recalcitrant Nature

Le suicide represents the first application of Durkheim's sociological method to a social phenomenon. However, at the start of the chapter on anomic suicide, the method is subject to a distortion which straightaway reveals the tragic dimension of human existence. With the support of statistics and charts Durkheim establishes that the effect of every breach of equilibrium, of every crisis, even if it results in greater prosperity, is an increase in the number of voluntary deaths. Contrary to what we might think, sudden affluence pushes more men to kill themselves than an abrupt fall into poverty: 'How can what is generally seen to improve life take it away?' (Durkheim 1897a: 271). Durkheim says that the answer to this question calls for a detour through some 'pre-judicial considerations', which consist in defining the specificity of man as a being without any natural ability to limit his desires and needs. Neither his organic nor his psychical constitution contain a brake that can halt his pursuit of well-being: 'By itself, without a power governing it, our sensibility is a bottomless pit that nothing can fill' (ibid.: 271). If the pursuit of luxury and the desire to acquire material or symbolic goods are generated or exacerbated by society, the insatiability of the desire as such is inherent to the individual's constitution. What we should call human nature is invoked here to account for a collective phenomenon. Doesn't this go against the famous rule prescribing explanation of the social by the social alone, and is it not odd to see Durkheim resorting to the very method of analysis he denounces in Comte or Spencer?[11] Certainly, reading *Suicide* closely, Durkheim's approach seems more complex. Anomic suicide, like egoistic suicide, arises from the fact that 'society is not sufficiently present to individuals'(ibid.: 288) and is explained by economic and domestic anomie, that is to say, by a state of society, and so the rule is saved. But if this state can influence the number of voluntary deaths, it is actually because in the final analysis man is what he is. It is as if human nature is a sort of final cause which gives social factors the power to be in turn the cause of the phenomena studied.

Human nature requires an education therefore, since only an external moral force can stem the tide of passions. It is also, however, the obstacle on which any educational enterprise could stumble, or at least which may put up fierce resistance. *Le suicide* introduces a figure which is taken up and deepened in a later text (Durkheim 1914a: 322): that of the double man, divided between a physical being and a social being who pursues aesthetic, political, religious and moral ends which go beyond the strict necessities of organic life.[12] The severance of social bonds, the disintegration of the community, deprives the social being of his reasons for living and destroys the meaning of existence for him. This is the cause of egoistic suicide. When what binds man to society is loosened, his attachment to life is also loosened. Durkheim sees egoism as a product of society in the sense that it is society that gives birth to feelings relative to individuality alone. But like the insatiability of desire, egoism also has its roots in man's very constitution, so that every human being is thus torn between the individual and social poles of his existence. 'Society has needs which are not ours' (Durkheim 1897a: 380). It weighs on us, requires us to make costly renunciations, and the socialization of education encounters a formidable obstacle in this egoism. Can society contain the centrifugal force of the individual without exercising a form of violence?

If to the spontaneously egoist natural being education 'adds' a being 'capable of leading a moral and social life' (Durkheim 1911c(2): 552), we may wonder whether the first does not always subsist on this side of the second, like a sort of residue which offers no purchase for socialization. Durkheim's last texts lead one to think this, especially the 1914 article (1914a), which analyses what he sees as one of most specific human characteristics. It is the feeling of having a double being formed of two ontologically different substances, body and soul: on one side, sensory appetite directed solely on individuality, and on the other, moral activity, whose rules of conduct can be universalized, therefore presupposing the possibility of going beyond oneself. An analogous split divides the intellectual sphere. Sensation is intimately connected to the individual organism and as such is incommunicable to others, but the concept is necessarily common to a plurality of men and results from a social elaboration and expression of the community which employs it. The interest of the 1914 article lies in its treatment of this duality for itself, and from the point of view of the one who experiences it. Durkheim is trying to understand the cause of human suffering, of 'that universal and chronic state of malaise' (Durkheim 1914a: 322), which he thinks traditional philosophical explanations have left in the dark. Before giving his own analysis, he describes the forms taken by the internal strife caused by the duality of body and soul. The most evident distress is undoubtedly that of renunciation of the instincts, of the sacrifice involved in any moral action. But by its very nature, conceptual activity is also a source of distress. Sensory reality resists the rigour of the framework that concepts seek to impose on it. Trying to understand, that is to say, to violate reality, means irremediably altering and deforming that which one wants to understand. The concepts indispensable to communication are incapable of translating the sensations one wants to communicate: we can only express ourselves at the cost of a loss, of alienation. There is an insurmountable contradiction between 'knowing' and 'feeling', and the choice of one entails sacrifice of the other. 'We cannot understand things, therefore, without renouncing, in part, feeling their life, and we cannot feel them without renouncing understanding' (ibid.: 320). Durkheim turns to Pascal to describe man as a mixture of angel and beast, a being perpetually at odds with himself whose grandeur is equalled only by his wretchedness.

In a letter from 1907 Durkheim alludes to the reorientation of his thought after 1895, following his studies of religious history and his lectures devoted to the sociological analysis of religion. This path led to *Les formes élémentaires de la vie religieuse* in 1912. In the 1914 text, his solution to the problem of the duality of human nature takes note of the importance of the role of religion in social life. The dualism of soul and body is referred back to the separation between the sacred and profane, the basis of all religions, but also at work in unbelieving minds and a laicized society in which the human person and moral rules inspire a religious kind of respect. But sacred things are no more than collective ideals invested with a particular authority and fixed on material objects which are its symbolic expression and which make possible a communion of consciousnesses. Man's sense of his duality is not at all illusory – he really is double since he leads two lives, one individual, rooted in his organism, and the other social. So we come back to the problem of the relation between individual and society, which in this case is a form of the relation to the sacred. We know that elsewhere Durkheim stresses the ambivalence of this relation, the product of desire and constraint, love and fear. Here, he stresses the irreducible character of the antagonism, the pain generated by the sacrifices society constantly demands from the individual, in terms which foreshadow Freud's *Civilisation and Its Discontents*.

'The interests of the whole are not necessarily those of the part' (ibid.: 331), Durkheim remarks in the article's pessimistic conclusion. And there are no grounds for thinking that civilization will one day bring relief to human suffering. On the contrary, the malaise will grow together with the increasing importance of social being in human life, to the same extent, therefore, as man distances himself from the animal. At this point the conception of society modelled on an organism reaches its limits. Durkheim foresees society becoming a discordant and badly put together whole whose needs do not correspond to those of its constituent parts. Since they are not immanent to what they are supposed to regulate, social norms can only be imposed from outside. Far from socialization reducing the conflict between individual and society, the internalization of moral rules only exacerbates the antagonism between individual needs and social requirements. In which case, can education be anything more than the construction of fragile barriers, at most making possible the containment of the centrifugal forces of individuals within the social whole? It seems doubtful.

(Translated by Graham Burchell)

Notes

1. On the history of the concept of anomie, see Besnard (1987).

2. We wonder whether Durkheim reintroduces 'motives' without being aware of it. Charles-Henry Cuin sees this as the sign that Durkheim's explanatory approach is authentically comprehensive (Cuin 2000).
3. Cf. *Problem XXV*, that Seneca, Plutarch and Cicero agree on attributing to Aristotle. Our reference is to Jackie Pigeaud's translation, Aristotle, *L'homme de génie et la mélancolie*, Paris: Petite Bibliothèque Rivages, 1988. See also Rudolf and Margot Wittkover, *Les enfants de Saturne*, trans. Daniel Arasse, Paris: Macula, 1985; Raymond Klibansky, Erwin Panofsky and Fritz Saxl, *Saturn and Melancholy, Studies in the History of Natural Philosophy, Religion and Art*, London: Nelson, 1964
4. In what follows we adopt the expressions used by Durkheim himself to describe egoism and anomie.
5. We will come back to this figure of the double man that makes its appearance at this point in the analysis.
6. The French *tissu* can be translated into English as fabric, in the sense of the woven material of a textile and commonly used metaphorically in phrases like, for example, the social fabric, and also as tissue, in the biological sense of a coordinated aggregation of cells. In what follows the author draws attention to the nineteenth-century biological sense of *tissu* as the basis for Durkheim's metaphorical-sociological use of the term. Depending on the context, I use 'fabric', 'tissue' or the French *tissu* (the translator).
7. On the jurisdiction exercised by Newtonian mechanics on eighteenth-century political theories, see Canguilhem (1975).
8. This conception of the social bond is not incompatible with the affirmation of a practical individualism, inherited from the Enlightenment, on condition that it is not seen as a timeless principle and an eternal and immutable value but as the product of an historical development (see 1893b; 1898c).
9. Would a more adequate image be that of the net, which Elias employs to represent this configuration of interdependent individuals which, to his eyes, is a society (1998: 71)? The net does not have the smooth continuity of fabric (*tissu*), since it is made of knots which, at first sight, could represent individuals, but the substance of the knots is no different than that of the threads; they have no distinct existence apart from the threads that form them. Actually, Elias rejects any ontological caesura between society and the individual; the individual, for him, is nothing outside of the network of relations from which he is always already constituted.
10. See, in particular, the Preface to the second edition.
11. See, for example, 1895a: 98–99. Durkheim reproaches Comte with attributing progress, 'the dominating fact of social life', to 'the tendency which pushes man to develop his nature more and more', and Spencer with making the 'cosmic milieu' and 'the physical and moral constitution of the individual' the two determinant factors of social phenomena. For Durkheim, this way of explaining the social amounts to transforming sociology into an appendage of psychology, and thus deprives it of any autonomy.
12. 'In other words, if man is double, as it is often said, it is because social man is added to physical man' (1914a: 228).

Chapter 2

Suffering and Evil in the *Elementary Forms*

Massimo Rosati

Within Durkheimian studies the problem of evil has been neglected for a long time.[1] Even if, according to Durkheim, religion has primarily to do with communion, joy and shared emotions (see Pickering 2008; Watts Miller 2005), in this chapter I maintain that in the *Elementary Forms* one can find or reconstruct a thought-provoking 'phenomenology of evil'. In my further contribution to this volume, I will show how and why a Durkheimian approach to the problem of evil can be very useful in the context of contemporary reflections and debates.

Durkheim, to be sure, did not present the problem of evil in a direct way. However, my hypothesis does not only concern what I believe to be indisputable, namely, that the subject is present in his thought under other rubrics, such as the pathologies of the division of labour, suicide, anomie, egoism, infinite desires, deregulation, and so on.[2] What I would maintain is, first of all and more radically, that the problem of evil, if understood as suffering related to the role and nature of social norms, is an essential part of Durkheim's thought; secondly, that Durkheim understands evil as a social phenomenon, with the same characteristics of every other social phenomenon. As such he understands evil in a manner counter-intuitive for the modern mind.

In the *Elementary Forms* (1912a), Durkheim talks about evil and suffering basically in two sections, and broaches the subject once again in the conclusion to the book. First, he talks systematically about suffering in paragraph 2, chapter 1, Book 3, dedicated to the negative cult and particularly to ascetic rites. Secondly, he talks about evil in the famous paragraph 4 of chapter 5, Book 3, the one dedicated to the piacular rites and the ambiguity of the notion of the sacred. He refers to evil again at the beginning of the Conclusion (paragraph 1), stressing the *practical* virtues of religion.

We take a closer look at these points.

I. Evil as Ordinary Suffering

The discussion on asceticism is conducted in the context of analysis of the negative cults that are necessary to prevent the sacred and the profane from entering into contact with each other. Since the sacred and the profane cannot coexist in the same space and at the same time, negative cults constitute a system of religious interdictions, which separate all that is sacred from all that is profane. According to Durkheim, when these practices 'develop in such a way as to become the foundation for a genuine system of life' we are in the presence of systematic asceticism. Asceticism, in other words, is 'nothing more than a bloating of the negative cult' (ibid.: 316).

The systematic (one could say 'methodical' in Weberian terms) respect for a complex of interdictions 'is not a rare, exceptional, and almost abnormal fruit of religious life, as one might think, but quite the contrary: an essential element of it' (ibid.) The consequence of this centrality of asceticism must be that its effects are as essential as the role it plays in religious life. And what kinds of effects does an ascetic system of life produce? Durkheim's answer is clear:

> Abstinences and privations are not without suffering. We hold to the profane world with every fibre of our being. Our sensuous nature attaches us to it; our life depends upon it. Not only is the profane world the natural theatre of our activity; it enters us from every direction; it is part of us. We cannot detach ourselves from it without painfully clashing with our instincts. In other words, the negative cult cannot develop unless it causes suffering. (ibid.: 316–17)

Pain 'is the sign that certain of the ties that bind (the individual) to the profane world are broken' (ibid.: 320).

The very nature of religious life, namely, the necessity of keeping all that is sacred separate from all that is profane, consequently requires pain and suffering. In this way we are invited to see the religious meaning of suffering. Suffering, ironically, seems to be necessary in order to live in sacred time and to enter a sacred place; to abandon, in other words, those profane activities that make life 'monotonous, slack, and humdrum' (ibid.: 217). It means enjoying a life 'less tense, more at ease, and freer' (ibid.: 386). Leaving the world of the profane implies a painful act of self-transcendence:

> To serve his gods, he [the believer] must forget himself. To create for them the place in his life to which they are entitled, he must sacrifice some of his profane interests. The positive cult is possible, then, only if man is trained to renunciation, abnegation, and detachment from self – hence, to suffering. He must not dread suffering, for he can carry out his duties joyfully only if he in some measure loves it. If that is to come about, he must train himself to suffering, and this is where the ascetic practices lead. The suffering they impose are not arbitrary and sterile cruelties, then, but a necessary school in

which man shapes and steels himself, and in which he gains the qualities of disinterestedness and endurance without which there is no religion. (ibid.: 320)

Shifting our attention suddenly from religion to society, as in the logic of the *Elementary Forms*, Durkheim asserts that what is really important is that asceticism, and the interwoven suffering,

> serves more than religious ends. Here, as elsewhere, religious interests are only social and moral interests in symbolic form. The ideal being to which cults are addressed is not alone in demanding of their servants certain contempt for pain; society, too, is possible only at that price. Even when exalting the powers of man, it is often brutal toward individuals. Of necessity, it requires perpetual sacrifices of them. Precisely because society lifts us above ourselves, it does constant violence to our natural appetites. So that we can fulfil our duties toward it, our conditioning must ready us to overcome our instincts at times – when necessary, to go up the down staircase of nature. There is an inherent asceticism in all-social life that is destined to outlive all mythologies and all dogmas; it is an integral part of all human culture. (ibid.: 321)

So, there is inherent pain and suffering in all social life, because this is a necessary condition in order *to have* social life. Society, Durkheim writes again and again, is possible only at that price. Even our societies, that is societies that exalt the power of man, must often be brutal towards individuals. The point is that society is possible only if individuals are able to transcend themselves, to leave the world of ordinary and profane activities to gather together and leave aside ordinary worries and selfish interests. But the profane is so interwoven with our daily life that it is part of our being human. The breaking of all the ties with profane life is a matter of suffering and pain.

What is evil in this context? Evil, thus, takes the form of suffering and pain. It is inherent in all social life because it is actually a *constitutive* part of it. There is no society without evil-as-suffering imposed by the necessary self-transcending of individuals and of profane worries.

But what seems more troubling is a sort of systematic devaluation of everyday life. *If* the profane has to do with the ordinary, the everyday, *then* all that fits into the domain of private life has to be depreciated and associated with something evil. The problem is that in Durkheim the profane, as Pickering pointed out in discussing Stanner's contribution on this, appears only to be a residual category (Pickering 1984: 137–39). As a residual category it could be regarded as 'mundane', something neutral with reference to the religious, not something anti-religious. However, in order to be associated with evil (and to justify a painful self-transcending), it has to keep the strongest meaning of anti-religious and ritually polluted. When reading Durkheim, we must sometimes posit a third category, the ordinary, the mundane, the everyday, and it seems that the dichotomy between the sacred and the profane must be extended to a trichotomy. This is because parts of the activities that shape the everyday world that Durkheim appears to include within the profane do not have an anti-religious character. In other words, as we have a propitious sacred and an unpropitious sacred, it would be logical to find the same dichotomy within the domain of the profane. In this case we could identify evil with the unpropitious profane. Unfortunately, nothing in Durkheim's thought suggests that we can see things this way. There is no such inner articulation of the concept of the profane.

Obviously, we could try to defend Durkheim against the charge of devaluating private and everyday life (that is, after all, part of the modern-bourgeois mentality and values that most of us share, see Taylor 1989: Part III) in other ways. Mark Cladis studied the relation between public vision and private lives with reference to Rousseau, but in a way that may be adapted to Durkheim as well (Cladis 2003). However, at the moment it is enough to ask the reader to consider the equation of evil and suffering. What seems to emerge from the paragraph dedicated to ascetic rituals is unquestionably the existence of suffering as the primary condition to social life.

II. Evil as Collective States of Dysphoria

The other reference to evil made by Durkheim in the *Elementary Forms* is in the famous paragraph 4, chapter 5, Book 3. There, while praising Robertson Smith for his service rendered to the science of religion, Durkheim again stresses the dual nature of the sacred, and its ambiguity. 'Religious forces', he writes, 'are of two kinds. Some are benevolent, guardians of physical and moral order, as well as dispensers of life, health, and all the qualities that men value'. These benevolent religious forces 'inspire a respect that is full of love and gratitude' (Durkheim 1995c: 412). But 'on the other hand, there are evil and impure powers, bringers of disorder, causes of death and sickness, instigators of sacrilege. The only feelings man has for them is a fear that usually has a component of horror' (ibid.). As is well known, relations between these two classes of religious forces are complex. On the one hand, they are opposite and as radically antagonistic as the pure and the impure, so that any contact between them is forbidden. On the other hand, they are 'closely akin': first, they have the same relation with the profane (profane things must abstain from any contact both with the pure *and* with the impure); secondly, what is impure can now, without changing its nature, transform itself into a benevolent force later, and vice versa, depending on external circumstances:

> So the pure and the impure are not two separate genera but two varieties of the same genus that includes all sacred things. There are two sorts of sacred,

lucky and unlucky; and not only is there no radical discontinuity between the two opposite forms, but the same object can pass from one to the other without changing its nature. The impure is made from the pure, and vice versa. The possibility of such transformations constitutes the ambiguity of the sacred. (ibid.: 415)

At the base of this unity and diversity of sacred beings there is, as Durkheim explains, the unity and the diversity of social life. States of collective effervescence are at the base of both the lucky and the unlucky sacred. But as social life can cause the experience of states of collective euphoria and of collective dysphoria, so the religious forces that grow out of states of collective effervescence can be benevolent and evil.

> the two poles of religious life correspond to two opposite states through which all social life passes. The same contrast exists between the lucky and the unlucky sacred as between the states of collective euphoria and dysphoria. But because both are equally collective, the mythological constructions that symbolize them are in their very essence closely related. While the feelings placed in common vary from extreme dejection to extreme high-spiritedness, from painful anger to ecstatic enthusiasm, the result in all cases is communion among individual consciousness and mutual calming. (ibid.: 417)

What is evil here? Two things are worthy of note. First, evil here appears in a very different form from the one it takes in the paragraph on the negative cult. In that context evil had to do with the profane, on the one hand, and with the necessity of transcending it, on the other. Evil was related to the inescapable suffering implied by the breaking of all ties with the profane world. On the contrary, evil here has a much more demonic dimension. It is not the *ordinary*, even if strongly painful, suffering inherent in all social life, but it is an extraordinary evil; an evil that as the unlucky sacred is radically separate from everyday life. Evil, here, is *radical*, in the 'adapted' sense of Hannah Arendt of something that we 'cannot conceive' at least from within the horizons of an ordinary and profane life. Evil, here, is radical because it is connected to the radical powers of the unpropitious sacred.

The second thing to be noted is the social and collective nature of this kind of evil. Even if radical evil here has a *diabolical* character (ibid.: 413), it is nonetheless completely social. Pickering noted how the social character of evil forces is an enemy of Durkheim's logic: why, actually, should society create forces that threaten its destruction (Pickering 1984: 129)? Durkheim solves the problem by showing how religion creates evil powers responsible for collective ill being and, at the same time, how religion itself is able to neutralize them by means of piacular rituals:

> When society is going through events that sadden, distress, or anger it, it pushes its members to give witness to their sadness, distress, or anger

through expressive actions. It demands crying, lamenting, and wounding oneself and others as a matter of duty. It does so because those collective demonstrations, as well as the moral communion they simultaneously bear witness to and reinforce, restore to the group the energy that events threatened to take away, and thus enables it to recover its equilibrium. It is this experience that man is interpreting when he images evil beings outside him whose hostility, whether inherent or transitory, can be disarmed only through human suffering. (ibid.: 415–16)

So, even if the two kinds of evil are quite different (we could say ordinary and radical), both imply a necessary suffering, inherently social in its nature. Pickering notes that,

If it is so, then what is at the heart of Durkheim's system is really a theodicy and religion thus becomes a means of overcoming suffering in its various forms. He rejects one theory of naturism (Müller's), only to accept implicitly another, or at least to suggest that really the base of religion is suffering. (Pickering 1984: 129; see also Jones 1999: 296)

I find this to be a really striking judgement, but it is perhaps too fleeting. What I am trying to reconstruct here is, precisely, a sort of phenomenology of those forms of suffering most intimately related to Durkheim's idea of religion and, consequently, of social life.

So far, we have distinguished the two different ways in which Durkheim talks about evil in the *Elementary Forms*. The first one has to do with the ordinary but painful self-transcendence individuals have to practise in order to achieve and enjoy religious life; the second relates to collective states of dysphoria. Durkheim seems to give more importance to the first one. It is well known that the duality and ambiguity of the sacred is a topic that has been developed more extensively by the Durkheimians than by Durkheim himself. From Hertz to Bataille, Durkheimian sociologists and social philosophers have expanded this category and have attached more importance to the unlucky or left sacred than Durkheim himself, thereby relating it to Nietzschean philosophy (see Richman 2002; Riley 2005a; Ch. 7 here). According to Durkheim, ordinary evil was, so to speak, radical enough. As I tried to suggest, ordinary evil has to do with profane life, on the one hand, and with the suffering related to the efforts of transcending it, on the other. Durkheim believed that this form of evil is radical enough because it threatens the very existence of society. What is at stake in the everyday struggle against egoism and anomie and in favour of well-balanced regulation is the very existence of society. As Gianfranco Poggi rightly showed, Durkheim was totally aware of the contingency and fragility of society. This awareness justifies what Poggi called the Durkheimian 'pathos', the feeling of the dependence of society on something else, that is, on the individual's ability to transcend himself (see Poggi 2000: ch. V).

In the context of the *Elementary Forms* and when discussing Robertson Smith's analysis of sacrifice, Durkheim outlines his thoughts on what Smith considered as a sort of inadmissible contradiction, 'a piece of blatant illogic' (348), namely the fact that gods could depend upon men's religious practices (such as sacrifice). Indeed according to Durkheim,

> While it is true that man depends on his gods, the dependency is mutual. The gods also need man; without offerings and sacrifices, they would die … this dependence of the gods on their faithful is found even in the most idealistic religions. (Durkheim 1995c: 36)

What appeared to Robertson Smith to be an illogical circle appears 'quite real', to Durkheim, 'but nothing about it offends the intelligence. It arises from the fact that although sacred beings are superior to men, they can live only in human consciousness' (ibid.: 351). If this circle is real and is scientifically understandable, and given the symbolic parallelism between God and society,[3] the implication is that society itself is dependent on its members. Here a lengthy quotation is appropriate:

> But if, pressing the analysis further and substituting for the religious symbols the realities they express, we inquire into the way those realities behave within the rite, this circle will seem to us even more natural, and we will better understand its sense and purpose. If, as I have tried to establish, the sacred principle is nothing other than society hypostatised and transfigured, it should be possible to interpret ritual life in secular and social terms. Like ritual life, social life in fact moves in a circle. On the one hand, the individual gets the best part of himself from society – all that gives him a distinctive character and a place among other beings, his intellectual and moral culture. Let language, science, arts, and moral beliefs be taken from man, and he falls to the rank of animality; therefore the distinctive attributes of human nature come to us from society. On the other hand, however, society exists and lives only in and through individuals. Let the idea of society be extinguished in individual minds, let the beliefs, and aspirations of the collectivity be felt and shared by individuals no longer, and the society will die. Thus we can repeat about society what was previously said about the deity: it has reality only to the extent that it has a place in human consciousnesses, and that place is made for society by us. We now glimpse the profound reason why the gods can no more do without their faithful than the faithful can do without their gods. It is that society, of which the gods are only the symbolic expression, can no more do without individuals than individuals can do without society. (ibid.: 351)

I will not consider how well this passage (among many others) shows how society *is not*, in Durkheim's mind, a sort of Leviathan, as trivial criticism has affirmed over and over again. Rather, I stress once again that the ordinary suffering caused by the efforts of transcending oneself and the ordinary evil that a selfish attitude implies are of the utmost danger to a society. It can die as a consequence of the failure of those efforts as well as a consequence of those selfish attitudes.

On the other hand, there is also a justification on the part of the individual for this suffering. As we know, for Durkheim, a healthy life is a 'constrained' one: life is limitation. Individual aspirations must have a precise content and must be limited.[4] Otherwise, when the sky is the only limit, when the passion for infinity dominates, people suffer. The passion for infinity, an unrestrained tendency to comply with one's own temporary desires, can destroy both society and the individual. Not only society, but also men begin where the instincts and the unrestrained passions end. Social and individual integrity are, in modern societies, the outcome of a well-balanced equilibrium between the absolutization of the limits imposed by social norms, on the one hand, and the weakening of their regulatory force, on the other (see Paoletti 2003: 119 *passim*). Like Weber, Durkheim knew that the modern individual can die unhappy, dissatisfied, perhaps tired of life, but he cannot die full of life, satiated with life. Doing one's duties from day to day, as Weber also remarked, for Durkheim meant taming this – characteristically modern – superabundant and at the same time overwhelming thirst for life (see Rosati 2004a). Taming the tiger, pacifying the human soul, is society's task:[5] 'Society has no reason for existing unless it bestoys some peace on mankind – peace in people's hearts and peace in their normal activities' (Durkheim 1950a: 55).

So, as Robert Alun Jones noted some years ago, morality, discipline and social norms are conditions for happiness (Jones 1999: 269 *passim*). Limits that restrain people cause suffering just as they prevent an even worse evil. Giving a definite face to human aspirations and limiting them, on the one hand, and limiting the limits, on the other: the conditions of individual and collective happiness or, in the case of failure, the reasons for individual and collective malaise are all contained within this 'dialectic of the limits' (see Rosati 2004a). In any case, as we have seen, suffering is not only a consequence of individual and collective malaise, but also an essential part of the efforts to escape it.[6]

III. Evil and Expiation: Durkheim's Reluctant Modernism

But if suffering is in some way necessary and perhaps inevitable, religious life is also presented as a means of limiting and escaping suffering. In the Conclusion to the *Elementary Forms*, while pointing out the practical versus the cognitive value of religion, Durkheim maintains that men feel that they can be delivered from evil. Also, that they can overcome the miseries of the human condition only in those almost ecstatic moments of collective effervescence in which they live the experience of salvific religious forces (see Ramp 1998: 141–42). Social life is intermittent (Durkheim 1995c: 216 *passim*). Salvation comes only when social life becomes dynamic and people gather together to concentrate their vision on a single point. Durkheim writes:

> they [the believers] sense that the true function of religion is not to make us think, enrich our knowledge, or add representations of a different sort and source to those we owe to science. Its true function is to make us act and help us live. The believer who has communed with his god is not simply a man who sees new truths that the unbeliever knows not; he is a man who is *stronger*. Within himself, he feels more strength to endure the trials of existence or to overcome them. He is as though lifted above the human miseries, because he is lifted above his human condition. He believes he is delivered from evil – whatever the form in which he conceives of evil. The first article of any faith is belief in salvation by faith. (ibid.: 419)

This passage, and another one parallel to it (ibid.: 365), has been quoted by Susan Stedman Jones as proof of the prominence of beliefs over ritual in Durkheim's thought.[7] *Belief* in salvation is the first article of faith. On the same page, however, Durkheim maintains that the belief in salvation has to do with the communion of the believer with his god; namely, going beyond the believer's own errors, it has to do with the gathering of other people, with a communion with something external to the believer (ibid.: 420). Salvation is not within the individual soul. Salvation and redemption from evil are not a question of good intentions, of grace or of some secular version of it (as in Kant). From Durkheim's analysis of rituals, we know that 'there is no relationship between the feelings felt and the actions done by those who take part in the rite' (ibid.: 400). This is true not only of primitive religions, but also of Judaism and Christianity:

> If the Christian fasts and mortifies himself during the commemorative feasts of the Passion as does the Jew on the anniversary of Jerusalem's fall, it is not to give way to sadness spontaneously felt. In those circumstances, the believer's inward state is in disproportion to the harsh abstinences to which he submits himself. If he is sad, it is first and foremost because he forces and disciplines himself to be so; and he disciplines himself in order to affirm his faith. (ibid.: 403)

Here sincerity, namely the perfect correspondence of inner states with external ritual behaviour, is not the most important thing. Being part of a community of faith is the most important thing. It is from here that salvation comes. Salvation from evil and suffering is a collective drama, something that implies mutual responsibility, a shared destiny, a common past, common memories and projects for the future. Just as the proper dimensions of evil-as-suffering are exteriority and collectivism, the proper dimensions of salvation from evil are exteriority and collectivism. Evil and suffering, in other words, are social facts.

In a post-metaphysical world, Susan Neiman reminds us of the way moral theory approaches the problem of evil with categories such as good and bad, right and wrong (Neiman 2001: 29; see also Neiman 2002). From Kant to Arendt, modern moral and political theory rejects the theological foundations of evil and tries to translate them into secular terms. Part of this strategy consists in questioning the individual moral, social and political responsibilities for evil actions. From this point of view, the history of evil in modern thought is simply part of the general process of individualization that characterizes modernity. The modern vocabulary is one of guilt, not of shame. As Adam B. Seligman wrote,

> Shame, rather than guilt, leads us to a mode of relation with others that is far from the economistic or rational actor model of self. To feel shame for one's own acts (or even for those of others), one must be tied to others in ways beyond the contractual and in a manner that presumes more than simply material and causal links between our acts and those of others. (Seligman 2000: ch.3, especially p. 80)

There is no need to adopt an anti-modernist attitude to see the impoverishment implied in the loss of the vocabulary of mutual responsibility. What I am suggesting, and what the previous pages attempted to demonstrate, is that Durkheim's idea of evil-as-suffering, given its dimensions of exteriority and collectivism, goes against the current of modernity.[8] I believe that Durkheim's idea of evil is somewhat pre-Christian and pre-modern, in so far as the vocabulary of guilt is essentially Christian. Another sign of this difference from the Christian and the modern conception of evil is in the importance Durkheim places on collective rituals of the expiation of evil. In order to reach salvation, an inner and sincere feeling of repentance is not enough. What is needed is a public ritual. In Durkheim, rituals need *acceptance* more than *adhesion* (see Rappaport 1999). If modernity embraces the ideals of sincerity and inwardness, Durkheim insists, by contrast, on rituals and their performative effects.

What I am suggesting throughout this reading of the problem of evil and its characteristics, is Durkheim's rather disenchanted and bitter distance from the society of his time and from modernity: what I call Durkheim's 'reluctant modernism'. Poggi detects an increasing sense of estrangement regarding modern societies (Poggi 2000: 167), and Pickering puts forward the same hypothesis on several occasions. We have biographical evidence of this increasingly sombre mood, especially following the outbreak of the war and after André's death. On 19 March 1916, for example, Durkheim wrote to Mauss :

> In fact I feel myself detached from all temporal interests. But that also has its own happiness. It is the happiness of the ascetic who feels himself above everthing. It is a strong, melancholic happiness and certainly melancholy will be my way of life, as far as one can see. By nature I have an inclination towards it. But it does not frighten me. Without doubt I would have much preferred a more outgoing happiness but I reckon one can make something quite different of one's life. (Durkheim 1998a: 508)

It would be wrong to assume that it was only a personal feeling, related to his son's death, and that taking it into consideration is just a *coup de théâtre* that has no relation at all to theoretical issues. The *Elementary Forms* are, in some way, a bitter reflection on modern societies. We can try to imagine this man in his fifties bending over the pictures of the Haida tribe camp reproduced in Swanton's book, contemplating the 'scenes of the wildest excitement' described by Howitt, Strehlow, and Spencer and Gillen, or imagining the effervescence of the Arunta *Intichiuma*, and then pondering on the 'peaceful monotony' of modern, ritual-less life. If modern societies are ritual-less societies, Durkheim writes, it is because 'we are going through a period of transition and moral mediocrities'; 'the former gods are growing old or dying, and others have not been born' (Durkheim 1995c: 429).

Poggi, however, once again comments on Durkheim's pathos, his feeling of the contingency and fragility of society, and of modern society particularly, that is far from becoming 'bathos'. There is a sense of hope, after all, in his work not unrelated to the requirements of social life, as he revealed in the *Elementary Forms* (see also Watts Miller 1996). According to Durkheim, despite secularization, there is 'something eternal' in religion, since 'there can be no society that does not experience the need, at regular intervals, to maintain and strengthen the collective feelings and ideas that provide its coherence and its distinct individuality' (Durkheim 1995c: 429). And so, as a consequence of this scientific belief, comes the vibrant prophecy:

> A day will come when our societies once again will know hours of creative effervescence during which new ideals will again spring forth and new formulas emerge to guide humanity for a time. And when those hours have been lived through, men will spontaneously feel the need to relive them in thought from time to time – that is, to preserve their memory by means of celebrations that regularly recreate their fruits. (ibid.: 429–30)

According to Durkheim, the last time European societies experienced moments of collective assemblies was during the French Revolution. Perhaps a new revolution will come, or some other event, to rescue modern collective life from the profane everyday unravelling of the social fabric.

I believe this constitutes Durkheim's discourse on evil, at least in the *Elementary Forms*, where he associates evil with a sort of 'dialectic of limits'. Excessive or unjust limits are at the base of social malaise, under the rubric of the anomic division of labour and fatalism (see, for example, Besnard 2003; Paoletti 2003). Insufficient limits are an even worse evil. Society's life and individual peace and well-being are dependent on well-balanced, correct limits,[9] imposed by society in order to nurture our capability for self-transcendence. The capability for self-transcendence, nevertheless, is a matter, as we have seen, of suffering. So, at the level of ordinary evil, we are between two different evils: on the one hand, society's pressure is coercive and even repressive; on the other, society is the source from which we can shape and reshape our moral lives. Once we have participated in a recreational moment taking part in a collective assembly, and when we have fulfilled our ritual duties, we 'return to profane life with more energy and enthusiasm, not only because we have placed ourselves in contact with a higher source of energy but also because our own capacities have been replenished through living, for a few moments, a life that is less tense, more at ease, and freer' (Durkheim, 1995c: 386). This is, according to Durkheim, the promise that society makes us: a life that is less tense, more at ease, and freer. This is the hope that justifies the daily painful attempts at self-transcendence.

It is of course a very demanding ideal. 'It could be a wonderful life', as Robert Bellah once said,[10] if we could just provide contexts for gathered life to flourish. However, there are two 'buts'. The first one is that, even in the most flourishing of collective lives, suffering could not be completely eradicated. If, as we have seen, asceticism is inherent in all social life, suffering is, to some extent, something we have to live with, something from which we cannot be completely redeemed. It is simply inherent in all social life. Modernity from this point of view does not have a particularly rosy future. The more societies are civilized the more social pressure increases. Remember the Freudian tones of the last lines of Durkheim's *The Dualism of Human Nature and Its Social Conditions*:

> Therefore, society cannot be formed nor maintained without our being required to make perpetual and costly sacrifices ... we must ... do violence to certain of our strongest inclinations. Therefore, since the role of social being in our single selves will grow ever more important as history moves ahead, it is wholly improbable that there will ever be an era in which man is required to resist himself to a lesser degree, an era in which he can live a life that is easier and less full of tensions. To the contrary, all evidence compels us to expect our efforts in the struggle between the two beings within us to increase with the growth of civilization. (Durkheim 1960c: 338–39)[11]

Social solidarity and politics, from this point of view, could (and should) aspire to eradicate unnecessary suffering, not to establish heaven on earth (see Rorty 1989). Utopia is not part of Durkheim's thought. The ideal of bringing some peace into the heart of human beings and into their mutual relationships, the hope that justifies society's existence, according to Durkheim, is already utopian enough.

The second 'but' is that Durkheim, not surprisingly, is not inviting us to spend every day of our lives on the barricades in order to share exciting moments of collective effervescence that can render life less 'monotonous, slack, and humdrum'. Collective assemblies are, according to Durkheim's logic, the best way to experience society's *majesté*, but they are not the only ones. There are at least two other kinds of less exceptional circumstances in which we can feel the 'stimulating action of society' (society virtually never leaves us completely alone): first,

> In all kinds of acts that express the understanding, esteem, and affection of his neighbour, there is a lift that the man who does his duty feels, usually without being aware. But that lift sustains him ... because he is in moral harmony with his neighbour, he gains new confidence, courage, and boldness in action – quite like the man of faith who believes he feels the eyes of his god turned benevolently toward him. (Durkheim 1995c: 213)

It is not the case of the Hegelian honest conscience, completely conformist and absorbed within social roles (see Trilling 1972), but simply the case of every individual who needs to be recognized by others in order to acquire self-esteem (see Honneth 1992). Secondly, 'there are other forces congealed in the techniques we use and in traditions of all kinds' (Durkheim 1995c: 214) that come from society and that remind us, every day, of its power and benevolence.

However, there are no doubts that Durkheim's first concern was for macro-collective rituals capable of raising collective states of euphoria and of overcoming collective states of dysphoria. In the *Elementary Forms* his main example related to modern societies was, as we have already noted and as is well known, the French Revolution. A particularly interesting section in the 1912 masterpiece is the one dedicated to commemorative rites (Durkheim 1995c: 374–91). Even if what I have written is not concerned with current issues of our times, it is worthwhile noting that contemporary studies of rituals in modern societies show the importance of rituals of commemoration and reconciliation to expiate past evils. I cite only two remarkable examples, the Holocaust and apartheid in South Africa (see Alexander et al. 2004).

In my next contribution I will attempt to show in greater detail that the phenomenology of evil, as it is sketched out in the *Elementary Forms*, also proves to be useful for us. Above all, Durkheim's inner logic – namely, considering evil and suffering as social facts – proves to be a necessary counterbalance to the inner logic of modern Western approaches and interpretations of this everlasting topic of suffering and evil.

Acknowledgements

A previous version of this chapter has been published in *Durkheimian Studies*, 11, n.s. 2005: 67–85. I am grateful to the journal for permission to reproduce the article. I would also express my sincere thanks to Karen Fields in allowing me to use freely quotations from her translation (1995c) of *Les Formes Élémentaires*.

Notes

1. For the reasons why evil has been neglected in general in the sociological analysis, see 'Reflections on the Death of Emile Durkheim' and Chapter 9 in this volume.
2. For the ideas of evil and suffering in other writings by Durkheim, see other chapters in this volume. See also Wilkinson (2005: 69–76; 128–34).
3. Poggi talks about 'equation' between God and Society; Pickering shows how and why talking about parallelism is much more correct (see Poggi 2000: 162; Pickering 1984: 231–35).
4. I cannot face this question in this context, but I am stressing regulation over integration as the most relevant dimension of social legacy in Durkheim's intellectual development. (See Ch. 4 in this book.)
5. According to Steiner, religion is Durkheim's answer to the problem of regulation in his 'second program of research' (see Steiner 2005). Durkheim's idea of religion as a means to curb passions is strikingly echoed in Isaac Salinger's novel *Shadows of the Hudson*, for example, where religion is understood less as a matter of faith than as a matter of practices that have to tame the tiger of individual passions (see Epilogue). The knots of phylacteries are the symbolic expression of the regulatory function of religious practices. I hesitate, in this context, to enter the question of the relation between Durkheim and Judaism.
6. In her Introduction to the *Elementary Forms* Karen Fields talks about a 'tragic tension' within Durkheim's thought (see K. Fields 1995: li). I tried to stress this aspect in Rosati (2008).
7. See Stedman Jones (2001); the relation between rite and beliefs in Durkheim is at the centre of an ongoing historical/philological debate with important theoretical consequences. To be concise: if Susan Stedman Jones maintains the prominence of belief/myth over ritual, Robert Alun Jones (via Robertson Smith), Ivan Strenski (via Mauss – Lévi), Anne Rawls, among others, maintain the prominence of the practical dimension of rituals over beliefs; Pickering, basically, maintains the circular relation between them, perhaps with a slight prominence of the beliefs. See at least the essays in Allen, Pickering and Watts Miller (1998), and Idinopulos and Wilson (2002) (essays by Robert Alun Jones, Robert S. Segal and Ivan Strenski).
8. For an analysis of the usefulness of Durkheimian categories in the context of current debates, see Chapter 8 and, in general, Part II of this volume.
9. Greater insight into Durkheim's conception of evil would have to differentiate our analysis according to the various models of limits and limitation of the limits that Durkheim seems to embrace throughout all of his works. On the models of the 'juste milieu' and of 'l'équilibre' of contrasts, see the aforementioned works by Besnard and Paoletti. See Chapter 3 in this book.
10. See 'It could be a wonderful life', an Interview with Robert Bellah, http://www.cs.washington.edu/homes/kepart/bellah.html.
11. I believe that the parallelism with Freud is an important point for understanding the very nature of Durkheim's thought under various aspects. See Lukes (1973: 283, n. 40); Lacroix (1981); Bellah (1990: 21); Jones (1999: 83–84).

Chapter 3

Some Concepts of 'Evil' in Durkheim's Thought

Giovanni Paoletti

> Man could not live if he were entirely impervious to sadness.
> Durkheim, *Le Suicide*, p. 365

An inquiry into Durkheim's concepts of 'evil' presents some difficulties. In a sense, and despite his reputation as a 'sociologist of order and cohesion', the problem of 'evil' could be seen as a theme which Durkheim constantly took into consideration in all his main texts. However, we have to remember that the word 'evil' is not a Durkheimian term; on the contrary, he endeavoured systematically to translate it into other, more scientific, expressions. Therefore, if we wish nevertheless to speak of 'evil', how can we recognize where Durkheim is dealing with the concept of evil, without using the word? A further difficulty: the concept of 'evil' which occurs in Durkheim's texts is anything but simple. This is why I would rather talk of 'concepts' in the plural. These concepts can differ deeply from each other, and sometimes their theoretical implications lead to real contradictions. But Durkheim never drew sharp or explicit distinctions between them, and the notions he uses seem sometimes forced into problematic coexistence. Is it possible to bring some order into this conceptual family?

The scope of the topic would require a thorough analysis, which, as far as I know, does not yet exist in Durkheimian studies, and would largely exceed the dimensions of an article. Here, I will just make some preliminary moves in this direction, trying to define, within Durkheim's lexicon, the semantic area related to the problem of evil, and to put the notions included in it into a historical perspective.

I. In What Ways Could Durkheim Think about 'Evil'?

In general terms, Durkheim's discourse about evil – a discourse paradoxical in that it denies the reality of its own object – is part of a mainstream tendency in the epistemology of social sciences. As any dictionary or encyclopaedia of social sciences can clearly show, the project of sociology consisted precisely in translating the traditional vocabulary of evil into new and various terms, among which the very word 'evil' was no longer admitted, or at the most occurred, in an anthropological perspective, to designate a residue of a moral, theological, non-scientific culture. Because of his training and his enduring interests in philosophy, Durkheim was, of course, well versed in the classical theories about evil and in their conceptual schemes. His reflection on this subject owes a first level of meaning to the confrontation with this tradition.

It is therefore useful to recall briefly some elementary notions. In the last of his *Sens Lectures* (2004a: 312), Durkheim quotes Bayle's (and Leibniz's) distinction between three kinds of evil: (a) physical evil, i.e. suffering; (b) moral evil, including evils depending on human will (sin and, in general, all pains inflicted on men by other men); and (c) metaphysical evil, deriving from the imperfect and finite nature of all creatures, whose particular signs in human kind are ignorance, weak will, the power of passions and prejudices, etc. When we speak of evil in Durkheim's works, which of these kinds are we referring to? We can assume that, as a sociologist, he looked at this typology in quite a different perspective. It is worth noting that he continues to call physical and metaphysical evils by their proper names – suffering and natural finiteness, respectively. His translation effort was mostly concentrated on the notion of moral evil. Of the traditional meanings of moral evil, one – moral evil as sin – is obviously rejected from the equivalent Durkheimian notion, but the other one – evil springing from the relationships between men – is maintained. In his view, moral evil becomes 'social evil'. In what sense? For Durkheim this expression does not mean an evil *made by* society, as liberal thinkers, classical economists or Rousseau had believed, though in different ways. Durkheim, on the contrary, sees society primarily as something good – at least in the first instance – and not as a source of evil. In his view, social evil is an evil *inside* society, or afflicting it, and not an evil made by society. Nor does social evil consist for him primarily in the struggle between social groups (e.g. classes), and in the domination of one of them over the other, i.e. in social injustice. Internal conflicts and injustice do play a role in Durkheim's analysis of social evil. But society as a whole – rather than particular social groups – is his unit of measure. Conflicts between parts or injustices are forms or symptoms of a more general evil, they are not its causes. So, the most specific meaning Durkheim gave to his notion of social evil is that of an evil *affecting the social tie* (*lien social*). As he seems to have conceived the social tie in different ways in the course of his intellectual career, one can expect to find different conceptions of evil in his works, corresponding to different models of the social tie. We may also ask what the relations are between social evil and the other two traditional kinds and, in particular, if Durkheim's new conceptualization entails any changes in (or even the evacuation of) the notions of physical and metaphysical evil.

The philosophical classification of evils was part of the problem of rational theodicy – the justification of God's goodness, justice and omnipotence in the face of the existence of evil (*Si Deus est, unde malum?*, ibid.: 312). Some arguments, or families of arguments, were formulated by philosophical theodicy, whose general aim was to neutralize or relativize evil. The first consisted in regarding evil as a mere negative or privative notion, where evil is thought of as the simple absence of perfection or reality, and not something positive (force, activity, intelligence), existing on its own. Evil in this sense is a non-reality, or lack of reality (*privatio boni*).

A second argument was centred on the distinction between the whole and its parts: what appears as evil from a partial point of view could prove to be good from the standpoint of the whole. Some evil suffered at a certain moment or point of time could turn out to be something good in a longer timespan (or, at most, eternity); the harmony of creation could spring from single (but at any rate not too frequent) dissonance(s). In this sense, evil is only relative to a particular and limited point of view, and vanishes once we enlarge our visual angle.

Thirdly and lastly, there was the argument of finalism, presenting evil as a means to reach or realize good: for example, suffering as a means of moralization, expiation or redemption. In this case, evil is something real, but its harmful quality is neutralized by its positive function; evil is just a secondary, instrumental or subsidiary reality. A non-substantive notion of evil, and the dialectics between an individual and a general point of view are the conceptual elements shared by these arguments. Both are relevant to social science projects, and in this sense sociology has been said to promote a sort of secular theodicy (Pickering 1984: 128–29): the above-mentioned aim of translating away the word 'evil' has nearly always been pursued by replacing the archaic substantive concept of evil with relative or privative notions – deviance, absence of values, alienation, and so forth. The dialectics of particular/general was at the basis of well-known models of analysing social processes, like Adam Smith's 'invisible hand', by which private vices are turned into public virtues, and in general all social explanations based on the spontaneous combining of individual actions. As to Durkheim, we should ask: to what extent did he make use of traditional arguments of theodicy while rejecting the traditional notion of evil? Is his own notion of social evil a privative or a substantive one?

As a third feature of the philosophical discourse about evil, one has to mention another distinction – not equivalent to the first one, and eventually crossing over it – between two main representations that run through the history of our conceptions of evil: evil as guilt and evil as error or ignorance (Portinaro 2002: xiv–xv). According to the first representation, which is at the core of the Jewish and Christian traditions, a deliberate perversion of the will is responsible for evil – a perversion that requires pain, punishment, but, above all, a process of expiation. According to the second one – dating back, as is well known, to the Greek philosophers – evil is due to a cognitive deficiency, a lack of knowledge or reason, and not a positive determination of the will. The remedy then will not consist in expiation, but in increasing knowledge – understanding, consciousness, wisdom, science – and the removing of mistakes. This is what is called ethical intellectualism. Durkheim's approach to social facts, social evil included, explicitly refuses to grant any explanatory relevance to individual will and intentions. Does that mean a change in his position from an 'evil-as-guilt' conception – obviously related to his cultural roots – to ethical intellectualism? We are going to meet at least one truly intellectualistic moment in the development of his views of social evil. How does that ethical intellectualism fit with his oft-made affirmation of the unconscious character of social processes? In general, can we still be satisfied with an intellectualist solution to the problem of evil?

In order to answer these questions, we need to take a closer look into Durkheim's conceptual lexicon. Social evil, in the first meaning he gave to this expression, is a disorder affecting the social tie. In general for him, the social tie consisted in two variables or dimensions, one independent of the other, whose combination or parallel action is the condition for the very existence of a society. These dimensions are integration, 'the way in which individuals are attached to society', and regulation, 'how it regulates them' (1951a: 258). This general framework is clearly stated in many of his works and represents an element of continuity in his conception of society. The same cannot be said of the special features of the framework, i.e. the relation between the two dimensions and their relative importance, their inner nature – mere variables, positive forces, representations – and consequently, the nature of their action over individual minds and social behaviour. In fact, Durkheim did not conceive these features in a single, unvarying way. The changes that occurred in his conception of the social tie represent a deep and essential level of his intellectual development. Their history helps to distinguish and clarify, by way of contrast, Durkheim's concepts of social evil. In the perspective I have adopted here, conceptual analysis and historical reconstruction are but one and the same operation. This is why my brief enquiry follows a diachronic order, whose periods correspond to important shifts in Durkheim's theoretical attitude towards the problem of evil. The first period (about 1893–96), including the *Division of Labour* (1893b) and *The Rules of the Sociological method* (1895a), was marked by a rather radical strategy of neutralizing evil that made use of biological and medical models. In the second period, going from *Suicide* (1897a) to the Dreyfus affair (1897–99, approximately), Durkheim's discourse about social evil reaches its maximum development, and some different conceptual models, in particular a physical one, are tested out. Lastly, there is a reassessment of the whole issue, which Durkheim pursues in his later works, essentially the *Evolution pédagogique en France* (1938a), written between 1904 and 1905, and *The Elementary Forms of Religious Life* (1912a), by drawing on the philosophical model of representations.

II. The Neutralization of Evil (1893–96)

In Durkheim's main doctoral thesis, *The Division of Labour in Society* (1893b), the discourse about social evil has a definite place, i.e. Book III, about abnormal forms of division of labour. As Durkheim considers the division of labour to be the source of organic solidarity, in other words the kind of social tie typical of modern complex societies, everything that troubles the division of labour is a pathology affecting the social tie – social evil, in the proper sense of the expression. In Book III, Durkheim distinguishes three or four abnormal forms.[1] His exposition follows, for each of them, the same conceptual scheme: describing the abnormal form; finding out its cause or explanation; finally, and the most important one for our purpose, evaluating the nature of the cause, and, in particular, whether it is necessary or contingent.

The description of the abnormal forms is based on the two dimensions of the social tie. The social conditions of organic solidarity are, on the side of integration, (a) the existence of relations between organs of the social body and (b) awareness of these relations; on the side of regulation, (c) the existence of rules governing the relations, and (d) the justness of these rules. Abnormal forms are produced when one of these conditions is not satisfied: (a_1) absence of relations between organs defines the bureaucratic division of labour; (b_1) unawareness of these relations is typical of the fragmented one; (c_1) a lack of rules is equivalent to the anomic form and finally (d_1) unjust or arbitrary rules are the essence of a forced division of labour.

Once the abnormal forms have been defined, their cause has to be found. It is not possible to follow Durkheim's arguments in detail here, but we can at least point out some recurring explanatory factors. One of them is the social organization transformation processes: a certain amount of time is required to establish relations between organs (even more if relations have to be conscious); transformation entails crises (economic crises, for example); changes in 'the true state of affairs' (*la nature vraie des choses*, 1984a: 312) can make a rule or a system of rules obsolete. In all these cases, temporality plays a crucial, and ambivalent, role in the emergence of abnormal forms: social changes are inevitable, but they can be too abrupt or too slow; the various levels of social organization seem to move at different speeds, as in a lava flow. These effects of temporality, which in a sense are co-natural to every organized form of life, are more dramatic in the case of social organisms. This is a second general explanatory factor. Whereas a biological organism normally gives automatic and univocal answers to a temporary crisis of its equilibrium – until a fatal crisis inevitably occurs – the higher complexity of societies entails a higher contingency, both in crises and in the possible reactions, and that is precisely the space that allows the abnormal to originate: 'The field is open to trial and error and discussion, as well as being open to the free play of a host of causes that may make the individual nature deviate from its normal path, thus creating a pathological state' (ibid.: 310).

From these arguments, one could deduce the seriousness of the problem of social evil. Societies, because of their complexity, more easily lose their equilibrium, which is then more difficult to restore. Secondly, if we follow Durkheim's analogy between social and biological temporality, we have only to wait for time to exert over any single social group the same destructive action it has for every living organism. On the contrary, and perhaps a bit astonishingly, Durkheim used these same conceptual elements – complexity and temporality – to develop a strategy for neutralizing evil. Complexity means plurality of (contradictory) causes; in this plurality, essential and necessary causes have to be distinguished from unessential (accidental, contingent) ones, and Durkheim is careful to underline, for each abnormal form, that it depends on causes of the second kind (ibid.: 305, 321, 326). Thus, social evil is a non-necessary effect. Here the other factor, i.e. temporality, intervenes. In most of the concrete cases Durkheim takes into consideration, we are led to believe that the problems concerning integration and regulation will be spontaneously and necessarily solved under the action of time (ibid.: 306, 321–22, 326–27). Time, therefore, gives back what it has taken away.

In the *Division of Labour* we can observe at an incipient stage the two main strategies that Durkheim carried out in order to neutralize social evil. On the one hand, we are confronted with the construction of explanatory chains, where social evil proves to be just the contingent effect of unessential causes – I will call it neutralization by causes, or causal neutralization. On the other hand, neutralization is a logical consequence of the general conceptual model that Durkheim adopts to describe social reality, for example, a biological model, based on the analogy between society and an organism. Inside this model – which I will call neutralization by an underlying conceptual model, or conceptual neutralization – social evil gives way to other equivalent notions – like abnormality, pathology, etc. – and, in so doing, it loses reality. In Durkheim's doctoral thesis of 1893 to which we have constantly referred, the two strategies work together; but in most cases they act separately.

The *Rules of Sociological Method* (1895a)[2] offers an example of conceptual neutralization of evil in the famous Chapter III, about the normal and the pathological. The first reason of interest of this text for our purposes is that it sets the relevant limits of the sociological discourse about evil. 'For science', Durkheim says, 'good and evil do not exist' (1982a: 85), every fact having the same value as any other. If sociology conformed to this view, it could not say anything about what ought to be, and would lose any practical interest. On the contrary, for the theologian good and evil have a substantive reality: according to Durkheim, this fideistic position was expressed by pessimistic and irrationalist philosophies like Schopenhauer's and

Hartmann's (ibid. and see 2004a: 313–14; 1951a: 362: 'this is the preacher's language, not the scholar's'). The approach of the human sciences to this issue is situated somewhere between these two extreme solutions. What is difficult is to know exactly where. For the time being, the reader of the *Rules* learns that the conceptual binomial 'normal/pathological' is functional to a standpoint where evil is not an absolute reality, nor a mere non-entity.

If evil is real, but not an absolute reality,[3] it must be a relative one. When philosophers argued, in the perspective of theodicy, that evil was relative to a present and transitory state, to a particular point of view, or that it was a privation of good, they supposed an independent or absolute parameter, as divine providence or plans, or Good in itself. In the *Rules*, Durkheim seems rather to use 'relative' as a synonym of 'correlative'. The normal and the pathological, according to a widespread conviction in the biological science of his time, are just two complementary faces of the same reality. As a consequence, good and evil are correlative terms, and good is no more an absolute reality than evil. 'Nothing is good indefinitely and without limits' (1982a: 101; 93). It is a conclusion that seems incompatible with the conception of evil as *privatio boni*, and marks a striking difference between a sociological neutralization of evil and traditional theodicy.

However, Durkheim does not go far in this direction. As normal and abnormal virtually cover the entire domain of social phenomena, the extension of one notion is a function of the extension of the other. The definition of the range of the normalcy is therefore a crucial element in Durkheim's strategy for conceptually neutralizing evil. Now, the criteria of normality set by the *Rules* are quite flexible and comprehensive. Something can be normal even if it causes suffering, reduces the chances of survival, does not have any positive function. In other words, well-being or pleasure, adaptation, utility are far from being univocal signs of what is normal. Generality, or greater frequency, is all that allows for distinguishing the normal from the pathological. As is well known, the methodological function of this wide definition is to attract into the domain of the normal, and therefore of sociological explanation, some phenomena – crime or, as Durkheim is going to show, suicide – previously excluded from it. Criminologists and common sense, for example, agreed in conceiving crime as a sort of illness, caused by factors extraneous or external to the social body, like individual hereditary defects (ibid.: 98, 102–103) or the 'incorrigible', almost metaphysical, 'wickedness of men' (ibid.: 98). But as the area of normal/good widens, that of abnormal/evil is reduced in proportion. If, as to their intensions or conceptual properties, good and evil are placed at the same level, their extensions differ considerably, and the concept of evil progressively loses not its meaning, but its denotation, like a perfectly well-defined but empty set. We can assume that the stricter or more exigent the criteria for normality are, the more consistency the notion of evil gains. This is exactly what happens in *Suicide*.[4]

III. The Outbreak of Social Evil (1897–99)

When Durkheim published *Suicide* in 1897, something had apparently changed in his way of talking and thinking about evil. On the surface, the vocabulary of evil becomes richer and more diversified. Collapse or confusion, depression or discouragement, disillusionment, collective asthenia, social malaise (1951a: 213–14); torment, unhappiness, painful unrest, constantly renewed torture (ibid.: 247–48); a trail of weariness, a state of turmoil, agitation and discontent (ibid.: 271) – a crowd of synonyms, euphemisms and periphrasis of 'evil' gathers in some crucial pages of *Suicide*, provoking a dramatic climax in Durkheim's scientific prose. We can reasonably ask if this proliferation of new words to translate the old one is a symptom of a sharpened sensibility towards the problem. On a deeper level, there is a change in Durkheim's set of basic notions. The theme of limits (of human nature, ends, desires, rules, and so on), that was to be so typical of his thought, after being left in the background in his early works, emerges now in all its strength.[5] While the centrality Durkheim accords to the limits of human beings can remind us of the traditional notion of metaphysical evil, there is nonetheless a major difference. Whereas in the theological perspective, natural finiteness or imperfection is a cause of evil, in Durkheim's view what is finite is good and evil comes precisely from the absence or exceeding of limits.

How does this apply to the theory of social tie? The difficulty of *Suicide* is that Durkheim alternates between two different answers, whose compatibility has been seriously questioned (Besnard 1987: 81–98). In the greater part of his work, and especially in Books I and II, we see at work a conceptual model founded on a general biological principle, which could be called 'good measure' (GM stands for the good measure model): 'In the order of life, no good is measureless' (Durkheim 1951a: 217). When applied to the social tie, this means that the two dimensions of integration and regulation find their normal and well-functioning state in a middle degree, the distance from which, in the positive as well as negative direction, defines the nature and the gravity of social pathologies. Here specifically are the various kinds of suicide. So, excessive integration is related to altruistic suicide, while an excessively low degree of integration marks the egoistic kind; overly strong regulation goes with the fatalistic suicide, while anomic suicide is related to rules which are too weak, or absent. What makes the social tie depart from the good measure? Consistently with the biological origin of the principle, Durkheim finds an answer in adaptation mechanisms, which in the case of human (individual and social) organisms are, as we know, exceptionally complex. This can explain why the good measure is more easily lost by societies (ibid.: 216), and also why, in contrast to purely biological organisms, societies can no longer rely on spontaneous re-adaptation or an inner principle of self-organization. In this process, consciousness or reflection play an ambivalent role and they can be both toxic and healing, like in the ancient Greek word *phàrmakon*: 'The awakening of consciousness interrupted the state of equilibrium of the animal's dormant existence; only consciousness, therefore, can furnish the means to re-establish it' (ibid.: 248).

The other conceptual model is most clearly formulated in Book III of *Suicide*. The limit of the social tie, which was a matter of needs, adaptation and environment, is now described as the result of the checks and balances, or mutual opposition, between three (and not four) social forces or currents (*courants*) – egoistic, altruistic and anomic – on the basis of a mechanical principle ('a tendency does not limit itself, it can never be restrained except by another tendency', ibid.: 366) (I will call it EbF, equilibrium between forces model). When these currents 'offset one another' (ibid.: 321), we have a well-balanced social tie; if one becomes much stronger than the sum of the others, the balance is lost, and suicides make manifest the disorder of the social tie. In this simpler model, the three forces or currents are all that is needed to account for establishment of the social tie, its degeneration and the related individual actions. For this reason, EbF has been often criticized as an undue reification of social variables. But this is not at issue here. We are only concerned with the different implications that the two models respectively have on the conceptualization of social evil.

(1) In GM, the good or bad health of the social tie depends on the relationship between what is external to the social organism and its internal equilibrium (*milieu intérieur*), a relationship that can be more or less complex depending on the number and heterogeneity of the factors concerned – both social and non-social, internal and external *milieu*, hereditary antecedents, social influences (see, for example, 1982a: 100). Greater complexity means more chances for the social tie to be disrupted, that is, for social evil to break out (1951a: 216). Whereas in GM the social tie is an equation with 'n' variables, in EbF the distinction internal/external is not relevant, and everything seems to rest with the balance of three homogenous factors, in quite a simple way.

(2) In GM, interaction complexity implies that social transformation is an irreversible process. In a society's life, every substantial change in the equilibrium coincides with the creation and dissipation of a certain amount of energy.[6] It marks therefore, as in the second law of thermodynamics, a point of no return, beyond which new assessments are still possible but the former state can never be perfectly restored. This role and nature of social temporality is obviously a premise of Durkheim's later valorization of history as the ground where social evils are most likely to be created, understood and maybe cured. On the contrary, in EbF, equilibrium is a sort of algebraic sum of social forces, each of which intensifies while one or more of the others decrease. A perfect balance can be obtained again by replacing a certain weight in the pan of the scales from where it has been removed. In this case, at least on a theoretical level, temporality is reversible, as in classical dynamics.

(3) In GM, the turning point in the development of social processes and their difference from biological temporality corresponds to the rise of reflection or consciousness. Their role is ambivalent but decidedly relevant, as Durkheim will emphasize in his following works. EbF, based as it is on mechanical concepts or metaphors, tends to put aside (or even perhaps deny), any possible function of reflection.

(4) Finally, we know that the typology of suicides inspired by GM accounts for two defective forms and two excessive ones, depending on whether the social tie is too weak or too strong. The two excessive forms, however, though logically necessary, are far from the core of Durkheim's analysis. His commentary on fatalistic suicide, as is well known, is relegated to a final footnote, and the altruistic variety seems so strongly associated with the kind of integration typical of archaic societies that one can seriously doubt whether it is really ever a symptom of social disease.[7] If so, suicide is significant for the emergence of social evil only in its defective forms: evil here, as in the theological tradition, is mostly a matter of lack or privation of reality. On the contrary, in EbF the social tie is negatively affected when the strength of one social current prevails over the others. In this case, social evil derives from an excess of reality.

As a consequence of EbF, Book III of *Suicide* is probably the farthest point reached by Durkheim towards a substantive notion of evil. This could explain why, when Durkheim takes up again the neutralization of social evil, as he does in the last chapter of the book (III.3), he develops a remarkable battery of arguments. Some of the new arguments that he adds are taken from the traditional theodicy repertoire: social evil is just relative to time and point of view; if evil is a positive reality, then it has some 'perfection' and is therefore not really evil (ibid.: 362). Others sketch an interpretation of what could be called a 'social need for sadness', which Durkheim will fully develop only in *The Elementary Forms* (ibid.: 365–66). Furthermore, he makes a sharp distinction between normal social states, to which this conceptual neutralization of evil properly applies, and critical states, where the actual reality of social evil cannot be so easily denied. If suicide, like crime, must be considered in general as a normal social fact – and even useful[8] – it is no longer true when the suicide rate grows too high, as it was the case in his own time. So, the diagnosis of the social crisis of contemporary French society – 'the malaise from which we suffer' (ibid.: 386–87) – becomes more and more the centre of his concerns.

In January 1898, about six months after *Suicide* was published, the outbreak of the Dreyfus Affair could only make these concerns even more serious. But what the Affair revealed was a shocking social trouble, which did not perfectly fit with the conceptual framework of *Suicide*. It was not an anomic crisis, because the determinant factor had been, if anything, the application of excessively strict codes of rules, the army's or the *Raison d'état*. In Durkheim's view, the Affair was rather the symptom of a problem of integration, by which the nation was divided into two hostile parts: the question which for six months has divided the country so painfully (Durkheim 1970a: 261). However, he strongly rejects the opinion of anti-Dreyfusards who, like Brunetière, held that endemic egoism, i.e. a general lack of integration, was responsible for the crisis. Moreover, this painful social disease seemed to have some paradoxical corroborative effects, both on the 'good' side – the wide mobilization on behalf of Dreyfus, in which Durkheim was personally engaged – and, more disturbing to acknowledge, on the 'bad' or 'sinister' side, through the expiatory function of the Jewish captain's 'sacrifice' (Durkheim 1899d: 253).

In the two series of lectures Durkheim gave in Bordeaux in the academic year 1898–99 – on the *Physique des moeurs*, and on pedagogy, later published as *Education morale*[9] – the current social crisis is a central problem. In them the discourse about social evil is fully developed. Here even more than elsewhere, a detailed analysis would be needed. I restrict myself to summarizing some developments in Durkheim's position. First, the common points. Both *Education morale* and the *Physique des moeurs* refer back to the old biological model and converge in stressing the complexity of the factors making up social life and, consequently, how frequently and easily equilibrium among these factors will be thrown off (Durkheim 1957a: 40; 1961a: 39). As Durkheim had already suggested, but also implicitly disavowed by adopting the mechanical model of the equilibrium between forces, this complexity goes together with the irreversible nature of social temporality, and with the progressive emergence of reflection as a means of adaptation (Durkheim 1957a: 86–87, 89; 1961a: 42). What is now more clearly stated is that the loss of equilibrium – given its necessary derivation from complexity – is not evil in itself, but a perfectly normal component of social life. The symptom of a bad state of the social tie is rather the given society's incapacity to react to these unavoidable losses of equilibrium, that go along with its own development. A general decrease in a society's vitality or moral tone – this is now, in Durkheim's view, the major problem. In other words, between sins of commission, or active evils, and sins of omission, evils due to passivity or indifference, the latter appear more serious to Durkheim. He turns the traditional hierarchy upside down. Contemporary societies have but a 'life that is dull and gloomy', that frenetic and inconclusive surface activity is not sufficient to conceal (1961a: 70; see 1957a: 94). This could explain why, in both series of lectures, Durkheim's interest focuses on integration rather than regulation (Besnard 2003: 63). If the issue is how to reinforce feeble social vitality, only stronger integration seems able to carry out this task, because rules can do no more than channel and organize social energy that already exists. They cannot create it on their own.

From these common points, Durkheim draws two different developments. In the *Physique des moeurs*, he follows a causal *and* historical explanation of the crisis – the two terms gradually become synonyms – and sketches a sort of first draft of the great historical fresco he will paint in the *Evolution pédagogique en France*.[10] In *Moral Education*, he begins a conceptual reconsideration of the whole problem. In a few words,

Durkheim's operation consists in superimposing a third pattern on the biological and the physical models of the social tie. This third model, which will gradually replace or include the others, could be called psychological or more properly philosophical. It is centred, as is well known, on the notions of consciousness and, above all, of representations. In these terms, social integration is a function of the richness of the contents of a consciousness (Durkheim 1961a: 70, 72, 216–17), while well-determined object of representation, acting as a restraint and limit on needs and desires, is an essential element of social regulation (ibid.: 39). In other words, the more broad and developed our representational activity is, the more 'clear and distinct' our ideas are, the more socialized we are. Consequently, the social tie is troubled and social evil arises, if one's consciousness is empty or has little content and/or the objects of its representations are confused and indefinite. A 'painful' *void of consciousness* (ibid.: 216, 230) and the *mal de l'infini*, a cause of 'perpetual torment' (ibid.: 39–40), are the respective names Durkheim gives to these two elementary forms of social evil.

In the most Spinozan of his texts, the problem of social evil undergoes a double action: (a) *Radical ontologization*: the words 'good' and 'evil' – whether they refer to society, the social tie or individual consciousness – are but anthropomorphic names for an increase or decrease of reality (perfection, capacity for action). In Spinoza's *Ethica*, these basic ontological states correspond to two fundamental feelings, 'Joy' (*Laetitia*) and 'Sadness' (*Tristitia*):[11] Durkheim's insistence on these typical Spinozan terms, and especially the second one, when describing the social crisis (joy: ibid.: 92, 100, 234; sadness: ibid.: 40, 68, 72), is far from being a mere – and actually quite unusual – rhetorical effect that can only be understood by recalling their proper philosophical meaning. (b) *An explicit turn towards ethical intellectualism*. In a world strictly ruled by what has been named, 'improperly enough' (ibid.: 212), the principle of self-preservation, which is 'la tendance de tout être vivant à persévérer dans l'existence' (the tendency of all living beings to persevere in existing) or *in suo esse perseverare*,[12] 'evil' is not a matter of will or choice, but only of ignorance of the most proper means to preserve one's existence, and in general of the true nature of reality. Passions are the 'forme éminente' of prejudices (ibid.: 94), 'c'est la pensée qui est libératrice de la volonté' (ibid.: 118), freedom in general consists in giving rational assent (*adhésion éclairée*) to the necessary order of reality (ibid.: 115; see Durkheim 1957a: 91). By reactivating the link between integration and consciousness established in the *Division of Labour*, Durkheim is consistent in suggesting that reasoned belonging to the group is the fittest way to enhance both social cohesion and the reality of individuals. If so, association without consciousness – as in the blind, irrational and immoral effervescence of a crowd (Durkheim 1961a: 150) – or solitary thinking – this 'plaisir froid et pâle' (ibid.: 248) that cannot counterbalance 'les vents froids et violents qui soufflent dans ces immenses espaces sociaux' (ibid.: 248) – are just two specular kinds of social Sadness.

IV. History, Rituals and Symbolism after 1899

This striking intellectualistic turn in Durkheim's reflection about social evil may answer a double need: undertaking an objective representation of the social crisis, whose real gravity had not to be underestimated, without yielding to the temptation – actually quite widespread at the *fin de siècle* – of idealizing irrational forces as sufficient explanatory factors or, worse, as the core and the truly vital source of social life. What Durkheim was looking for, and for a while believed he had found in a Spinozan-like representation of social reality, was a concrete and complex rationalism, opposite to irrationalism, of course, but also different from the simplistic and individualistic rationalism epitomized by Descartes and his tradition (ibid.: 250). However, there are several unresolved problems. Even if we allow that wider consciousness is sufficient to improve social integration, how precisely can it perform this task? Can the great amount of movements and emotions that a large and complex society requires spring from rational ideas? Passions are the forces that move to action (ibid.: 94), but, as prejudices, they should have no place in an enlightened (*éclairée*) consciousness. Last but not least, is it not a typical Durkheimian thesis that social processes exceed by definition the range of individual consciousness?

The reconstruction of Durkheim's intellectual development after the turn of the century is particularly difficult, as is clearly shown by the *querelle* about the 'early' and the 'late' Durkheim. Our subject is, of course, no exception, even if, in a comprehensive view, one can say that the problem of social evil in this period no longer seems to have for Durkheim the same weighty, sometimes obsessive, presence as in the past. Here, I will merely focus on the two great syntheses that stand out from the wide and fragmented panorama of Durkheim's twentieth-century writings.

The particular interest for our purposes of the lectures on the *Evolution pédagogique en France* lies in the way Durkheim works on a new perspective on some aspects of his conceptualization about the social tie and social evil already familiar to us. The causal explanation of social processes is here completely developed in the form of a historical explanation, an explanation that includes some elements of what I called causal neutralization of evil. But the articulated system of causality he activates, distinguishing carefully between essential and accidental, internal and external causes, potential materials and social needs (see Paoletti 2005) is far from the somehow scholastic exercise of the book on abnormal forms in the *Division of Labour*, as well as from the oversimplified model of mechanical forces sketched in Book III of *Suicide*. Also, the biological model for the social tie, which was probably more deeply rooted in Durkheim's logic (Guillo 2006), is here subjected to a strategic criticism: by underlining the imperfect and non-automatic nature of *every* process of adaptation, not only the social one, Durkheim opens the conceptual space up to contingency – and therefore to social evil – even wider than in his former works. Once seen from the point of view of the whole, as traditional theodicy used to teach, the design that evolution shows is everything but providential: 'Here as elsewhere the struggle for survival has led to results which are only crude and approximate. In general it is the best adapted and the most gifted which survive, but as against that, this whole history is littered with a multitude of lamentable and unjustified triumphs, deaths and defeats' (Durkheim 1977a: 13). As he had already stated, but here he develops it systematically, when social and not only biological 'adaptation' is dealt with, two specific factors come into play: reflection or consciousness, and irreversible, that is, historical temporality. Hence, there is the double characterization of social evil we find in *Evolution pédagogique*. Behind every historical manifestation of social evil that Durkheim takes into account – the boarding school institution (ibid.: 117–18), the pedagogical and moral crisis at the end of the sixteenth century (ibid.: 219, 225–26), the first form of modern individualism with its simplistic conception of the relationship between the whole and its parts (ibid.: 275), the typically French excessive penchant for centralization (ibid.: 122–23) – he discovers two critical features. First, there is a defective comprehension of one's belonging to the group and of the real and complex condition of social life, that is, a lack of consciousness. Second, and following on from the first feature, there is the difficulty in managing the historical transformation of a society. Consciousness is in fact an essential condition for organization (ibid.: 40). The equivocal role formerly assigned to reflection in relation to life is here resolved to the advantage of its positive function, and a crucial element of the biological notion of adaptation is definitively translated into the philosophical model of consciousness and representations. Moreover, a wider consciousness means a far greater capacity to deal with the 'free' and unpredictable 'combinations of life',[13] a capacity that the non-reflexive immobility of routine, expressed primarily by overly rigid and uniform rules, can never give. That is how lack of consciousness is normally at the basis of the temporal form of social evil, that destructive tension between the old and the new, which Durkheim calls here – using once again a biological word –'hybridizing' (ibid.: 118, 210). In the light of this explanation, the transition crises that had attracted his attention for a long time, now become the paradigm of every social disease. Nevertheless, inside transition, Durkheim now distinguishes for the first time, at least so openly, the bad consequences of hyper-regulation from the potential creative power of hypo-regulation, that is, a beneficial social effervescence that accomplishes the integrating action of consciousness described in *Moral Education*.

When one comes to *Elementary Forms of Religious Life* (1912a), it is difficult to avoid the impression of a somehow changed atmosphere. Trying to capture the reason for such an impression is a classical exercise for Durkheimian scholars. Recent contributions moving in this direction have established some points relevant for our purpose. I will simply synthesize their conclusions and add a few remarks.

In all of Durkheim's major works, Book III seems to be the appointed 'unholy' place where thinking about social evil can develop. The *Elementary Forms* confirms this rule. It means that the problem of evil is discussed within Durkheim's analysis of religious rituals, a position that should not be underestimated if one wishes to understand the particular way the question is asked, and answered. Philippe Steiner has shown how the rhythmic alternation of profane and sacred phases in the life of Australian clans functions as a mechanism for perpetuating the social tie (Steiner 2000). During the long, grey, monotonous profane periods, mostly devoted to individual needs and economic purposes, the social tie is relaxed and progressively worn down. We have a chronic state of low integration and low regulation. This potentially morbid state is balanced by the beginning of the sacred phase, when, for a short but intense lapse of time – a crisis – the social tie undergoes a sort of ritual earthquake, i.e. effervescence. Society now experiences an odd critical state where the highest, near-ecstatic, integration coexists with the lowest regulation, in particular in conjugal and familial norms, sexual relations, incest. From this unleashing of social forces a new chronic state finally emerges where the social tie is firm enough, with high integration and high regulation, to face again the profane season of social life. So, starting from a state formally identical to the social disease of modern nations (insufficient integration and regulation, egoism and anomie), so-called primitive societies exhibit, via symbolism and positive rituals, such as the feast of *Intichiuma*, a performative way to convert possible social evil into a healthy social tie. In this mechanism, a central role is definitively granted to deregulation, according to a point of view typical of the late Durkheim. Moreover, one of the difficulties related to the intellectualism of *Moral Education* – how can consciousness generate integration? – is avoided by attributing a broader meaning to the term 'consciousness'. What really matters for the social tie is that shared representations or state of consciousness about society be produced, not that they be perfectly intellectual or self-conscious. In the logic of representations, consciousness-as-awareness is an important, but non-necessary feature.

This is in a sense a standard situation. The alternation of sacred and profane periods is the regular rhythm of social life. The wear and tear on the social tie is ordinarily related to the simple ongoing performance of profane activities, where we normally experience a weak regulation and integration. Actually, positive rituals prevent the social tie from being really troubled.[14] Starting from the pages of Book III where Durkheim talks about evil, Massimo Rosati in Chapter 2 here helps to point out what happens when the ordinary unwinding of social life is abnormally perturbed. First, there can be extraordinary threats, or threats felt as extraordinary, against the group's existence: a member's death, the theft of sacred objects, a bad harvest, a drought, aurora australis. Extraordinary events call for extraordinary responses – the piacular or 'sad' rituals. These rituals aim at restoring the harmed social communion through symbolic representations of the enemy forces, the 'unholy sacred', and the ensuing shared and compulsory states of dysphoria: grief, mourning, anger, 'a panic of sadness' (1995c: 404). And sometimes, as in the Dreyfus Affair, there is an expiatory victim. Then, there is the case when one of the poles of social life, say the profane, unnaturally departs from the other. When this happens, the weak intensity of the social tie normally associated with profane activities degenerates into actual social evil. From the point of view of individuals, the monotony of the profane life gives way to depressing isolation and anomic frenzy. From the point of view of society, we have that 'moral mediocrity' that Durkheim had described at length in his previous works, and which he deprecates again in the conclusion of *The Elementary Forms* as the social problem of his time. In this second case, social evil comes from within the profane – a sort of 'unpropitious profane', as Rosati suggests – and its ritual antidote could be found in negative or ascetic rites, whose aim is precisely to prevent the hypertrophy of selfish attitudes, by rudely educating the individual to 'sacrifice some of his profane interests' (ibid.: 320).

But why does the social tie degenerate in such a way? Supplementing or perhaps putting aside his former answers to this question, involving complexity, temporality and so on, Durkheim seems now to identify the source of this kind of social evil in the physiological needs of our individual life. The theory of human nature which he sketches in some of his last writings in introducing the notion of *Homo duplex* is a matter of debate. According to a common reading, the duality of human nature consists in the opposition between its social and its individual/biological halves. If so, one would think that negative rites aim at socially mortifying the purely biological side of our 'self'. But things are not as easy as that. For example, in Durkheim's impressive description, initiation rites consist in a radical and almost literal reduction of the neophyte to a bestial existence, i.e. the harsh destruction of a former *social* self and not of his 'natural' or biological one, in order to attain a new one.[15]

At any rate, this last point allows us to add to Steiner's analysis that not only deregulation but also temporary disintegration can have a positive function in restoring the social tie. So, Durkheim describes three ways in which the relation between social tie and rituals can take place. Positive ceremonies are the general sacred ritual counterpart of the normal relaxing of integration and regulation during the profane phase of social life. Piacular and negative rites are rather related to some particular sort of social evil, i.e. to actual afflictions of the social tie provoked by positive causes and not only by the rarity of social interactions. Negative rites prevent the dissolution of the social tie due to the 'unpropitious profane' to be realized. Piacular ones try to restore the social tie from some external harms that society represents as unholy or unpropitious sacred. *The Elementary Forms* provides a broad, sharp insight into the techniques by which a society can maintain, reinforce or rebuild its inner ties. These techniques can consist of joyful and sad effervescence, shared mourning or anger, asceticism and ecstasy, expiatory sacrifices, temporary deregulation and disintegration. All this presupposes (a) a relationship between the social tie and social evil that is more complex than the simple positive/negative opposition, because a ritual dissolution of that tie can be a prelude to its renewal; and (b) a positive function for individual suffering. It does not simply mirror the collective one – as in *Suicide*, for example – but can also be the means to reach a good social end, in a sort of secular version of the 'finalism argument' elaborated in theodicy. The traditional kinds of evil – physical experience of pain and suffering or metaphysical evil rooted in human nature – seem to find once again some place in Durkheim's last concept of evil. In the end, the question *unde malum?* remains. Durkheim's interpretation of unholy sacred and piacular rites seems to suggest that, in most cases, the causes of social evil are extraordinary, positive or active, and external to societies. Like all natural beings, societies tend to preserve their own existence, trying to escape from what moves them to sadness. However, the conceptual model outlined in *The Elementary Forms* leaves the way open for the other possibility. It is that the cause of evil, eventually revealed by piacular commotions, can be an ordinary or banal one, moving from inside society, and that common states of indifference, omission or everyday passivity can sometimes be worse than active deliberate evils. In this last sense, and in the light of the years to come, the final prophecy of Durkheim's masterpiece – 'A day will come when our societies once again will know hours of creative effervescence during which new ideals will again spring forth and new formulas emerge to guide humanity for a time' – sounds at the same time truthful and sinister (ibid.: 429).

Acknowledgements

My grateful thanks to Paola Volante, Amy Jacobs and Carol and Bill Pickering, who accurately read this text and improved it in different ways.

Notes

1. About the individuation of a fourth form (the 'fragmented' division of labour), in addition to the three that Durkheim analysed at length (anomic, forced, bureaucratic), see Besnard (2003: 23–35).
2. Durkheim (1982a: 102): 'crime must no longer be conceived of as an evil which cannot be circumscribed closely enough.
3. Durkheim (1982a: 102)
4. *Rules* add nothing to the causal neutralization of evil, as Durkheim does nothing more than evoke in a generic way the two general causal factors of the emergence of social evil already mentioned in the *Division of Labour* – temporality (1982a: 94) and complexity (ibid.: 100).

5. The theme of limits had been announced in the 1896 lectures on *Socialism* (1928a: in particular, 1958b: 200). This text occupies an interesting threshold position between two phases in Durkheim's reflection on evil, but there is not enough space to examine it here.
6. The notion of effervescence is foreshadowed here.
7. In fact, in the chapter on individual kinds of suicide, Durkheim will remark that people committing altruistic suicide are not sad or angry, but full of 'energy' and 'passion', they live their last moments with 'serene conviction', 'tranquillity' and 'calmness', or with a 'burst of faith and enthusiasm' (1951a: 283–4).
8. Durkheim (1951a: 362, 364). Durkheim introduces here again the criterion of utility, which was excluded from the *Rules*; in this sense, his notion of the normal is now more selective.
9. Besnard (2003: 55–64) persuasively demonstrated that the version we have of the lectures on *Moral education* was almost certainly the one of 1898 – 99.
10. Durkheim (1957a: 94–95, 106–109). The origin of the crisis is traced back to the sudden transition from the *Ancien régime* to contemporary French society: once the old corporation had been abolished, the social structure was oversimplified; the modern centralized state and growing individualism, which formerly were two complementary sides of the same historical process, were now face to face without any intermediary groups, giving rise to unmitigated and therefore harmful interactions between state and individuals.
11. Scholium prop. XI, pars III.
12. Prop. VI, pars III.
13. Durkheim (1977a: 141): 'les libres combinaisons de la vie', erroneously translated as 'elective affinities' (*sic*).
14. Essentially section 2 of the first chapter and section 4 of the fifth chapter, to which should be added sections 2 and 3 of the fifth.
15. Durkheim (1995c: 314–15): 'He [the novice] must withdraw from the society where he has spent his life until then, and from virtually all human society'… He must stay alone, in the bush, as it changed into a plant; he can only eat disgusting food, without touching it with his hand; he can not speak any words, nor move, he must remain 'lying on the ground, immobile, without clothing of any kind'.

Chapter 4

Suffering to Become Human: A Durkheimian Perspective

Mark S. Cladis

> *Keep your mind in hell, and despair not.*
>
> St Silouan of Mt Athos

I. Introduction: On Becoming Human

The trouble is that we are social beings dwelling in a mostly asocial universe. Since most of nature is silent, that is to say, does not participate in sociolinguistic forms of life, we find it difficult to describe our social nature in relation to the rest of nature. Perhaps this difficulty would largely disappear if we humans would consider ourselves part of the natural world and, by extension, consider everything we make and do as being part of nature. It is an illusion to maintain that humans are not part of nature, that humans do not necessarily dwell there. We must count ourselves in: we are creatures whose home, including our social home, is in and of nature. In this view, artistic, scientific and moral achievements are natural events. They may entail much effort, struggle, and even what some would call 'self-sacrifice'. But they do not entail placing the social against or above the natural.

This view, I will argue, is largely in agreement with Durkheim's perspective on human nature. He usually went to great lengths to underscore the fundamental position that social life is '*of*' and '*in*' nature (Durkheim 1953b: 94).[1] However, on occasion he did suggest otherwise, and making sense of this 'otherwise' is what much of this chapter is about. In particular, Durkheim sometimes claimed that individuals must sacrifice *natural* inclinations for the sake of *social* life. And he called such sacrifice a form of *suffering*. Perhaps the best example of this side of Durkheim is found in *The Elementary Forms of Religious Life*, when he claimed:

> Society is often hard on individuals: of necessity it demands perpetual sacrifice. It does unceasing violence to our natural appetites, precisely because it raises us above ourselves. So that we may fulfill our duties toward society, we must be prepared to violate our instincts at times – to go against the grain of our natural inclinations. Thus, there is an asceticism that is inherent in all social life ... it is an integral part of all human culture. (2001a: 235)

What are we to make of a quotation like this? Was Durkheim suggesting that humans suffer in so far as they experience a conflict between their natural and social selves? Was he suggesting that there is a perpetual conflict between 'the individual' and 'society' and that this conflict causes human suffering? These are large questions, and they contain large – and ambiguous – dichotomies that reach to the heart of Durkheim's work as well as to the core of modernity: 'natural' versus 'social', and 'individual' versus 'society'. Let's approach these large questions cautiously. Let us start with what we know.

What can we know about Durkheim? He held that to be a human is to be a social creature. Humans act naturally when they exhibit social behavior. This is not to claim that there are natural, innate, substantive social sentiments – compassion, for example. Rather, it is to suggest that humans naturally stand in need of sociolinguistic substance and sustenance. Humans are creatures that wither in the absence of social interaction and social education, broadly understood; humans are not naturally equipped with the results of these sociolinguistic activities and caring relations.

Just as humans need physical nourishment such as water, so they need social nourishment – which is also physical. This stance is basic to Durkheim's normative vision. It informed his work in sociology, pedagogy, epistemology and moral philosophy. If Durkheim spent much time investigating varieties of religious forms of life, it was because he held that religion profoundly exhibits deep and abiding social dimensions of human experience. Religion displayed how social life is written on the body (tattoos, for example), in the mind (categories and ideals, for example), and in the complex transactional relation between body and mind (rituals, for example).

Now, here is another basic Durkheimian claim that is less well understood, and that may initially sound like a paradox: humans need to *achieve* the social nature that is natural to them, and this achievement requires much effort. I can offer an analogy that I hope will make this claim seem less paradoxical and more like a natural fact of life. My baby girl struggles each day to become more fully human – that is to say, she struggles to become a more fully social, moral and mature human being. This struggle entails what some would call – and what Durkheim did on occasion call – *suffering*. Whatever we call it, the struggle in the process of becoming more fully human is ongoing.

In order for her to become socially competent, linguistically skilful, and morally wise in word and deed, she will often need to choose that which is difficult over that which is easy. If she is like her father, she will need to struggle to acquire reading and writing skills when part of her would prefer to play outside, watering the plants. If she is like her father, when hungry she will need to struggle to suppress her desire to reach immediately for the food in front of her and learn, rather, to wait patiently for others to gather at the table. If she is like her father, she will spend a lifetime struggling to subdue narrow, petty self-interests and pursue instead goals that connect her to larger goods and to greater purposes.

I have tried here to illustrate by analogy the claim that humans need to achieve their social nature. However, this analogy – my daughter's struggle in the process of inculturation – is also an *example* of the claim. Her journey to becoming more fully human is the same everywhere in this regard: it is by means of effort and toil that one becomes a social, moral creature. One works on becoming human. To be sure, the sociolinguistic and cultural material that a particular human inherits, internalizes, shapes, and amends will vary greatly – perhaps infinitely. But the training and maturation in one's social and moral universe will always entail some kind of work, and aspects of this work can be and have been characterized as a form of suffering.

Suffering to become human – it is this characterization of natural, human maturation that I will explore in this chapter. What does it mean for Durkheim – and for us – to claim that the ongoing process of becoming more fully human requires struggle and suffering? And what do responses to that question suggest about the nature of modernity and its portrayals of the self in relation to the social and to the natural?

Before I continue, I need to give some attention to the phrase, 'becoming more fully human'. 'Becoming' suggests an ongoing process with no endpoint. Maturation is continuous. I don't learn between the ages of, say, two to eighteen years, how to be moral and then simply live out that moral knowledge for the rest of my life. This is in part because the moral life, Durkheim never ceased to remind us, is dynamic. In the flow of life, we are constantly responding to new demands and circumstances. Moreover, even if life's circumstances were static, our relation to our sociolinguistic inheritance is dynamic. It provides an indeterminate resource that can be continuously mined. Language itself, Durkheim tells us in *The Elementary Forms*, is a living font that nourishes us and over which no one individual has complete mastery or control (Durkheim 2001a: 230).

So, 'becoming' in the phrase, 'becoming more fully human', expresses the dynamic aspect of one's ongoing relation to moral and social life. Acknowledging this process was central to Durkheim's thought. What, then, of the expression, 'more fully human'? Is this a helpful expression? Let me first say what I do not mean by it. I do not mean that somewhere out in the universe or in the recesses of the heart there is a gauge that places a life somewhere between 'full' and 'empty' on a human scale. Nor do I mean to allude to a Platonic or Christian or Navajo fixed paradigm of what it is to be fully human. Rather, by 'more fully human' I refer to the ongoing development of a variety of life skills, skills that can be continuously perfected. There are some sets of knowledge that can be mastered perfectly. Open-ended skills, in contrast, require constant effort if they are to be maintained and augmented. As humans mature they acquire thinking, speaking, acting, judging and emotional skills throughout their lives. They begin as infants possessing very few cognitive, social and moral skills. In time and space, they subsequently become more fully social, moral and mature human beings. This, then, is what I mean by becoming more fully human.[2]

This ongoing development, I have said, can take place in an infinite number of ways. Durkheim's account of human nature does not reduce humanity to a single, ideal human form, but rather highlights its sociohistorical indeterminacy. There are probably as many descriptions of human nature as there are cultures fashioning human natures. This is not to say that there are no constraints on human nature. The physical universe, including human genetic material, no doubt provides some constraints, some form. But within that form, whatever it may be, resides infinite possibility. There is nothing paradoxical or mystical about this claim. The sonnet is a poetic form. The form is a constraint. And the poems that can emerge within it are unlimited. So, too, is human nature and the process of becoming fully human.

In this chapter, I usually employ a narrow concept of suffering. By suffering, I mainly refer to the frustration, dissatisfaction or affliction that individuals experience when they adjust, curb or entirely suppress a variety of individual comforts, aims, and desires for the sake of public goals, loves and obligations. Such individual suffering is often said to accompany inculturation or socialization. One of the most famous accounts of this form of suffering is found in Sigmund Freud's *Civilization and Its Discontents*. In Freud's view, civilization is bought at the price of suppressing individual, instinctual desire. Such suppression causes profound unhappiness. Society hurts the individual by insisting that deep-seated natural needs and desires be stifled. Yet this price must be paid. Social ideals, accomplishments and stability can be achieved only if individuals are willing to accept personal suffering in the form of resisting natural inclination. The profound conflict between the needs of civilization and the needs of individual happiness is not, in Freud's account, a problem with a solution. It is a natural dilemma and it needs to be coped with variously and daily. The most that we as individuals can hope for is to minimize hysterical misery and thereby achieve everyday, common unhappiness. There is, then, no cure for this disease, for this painful condition of being both civilized and creaturely, social and natural, public and private, soulful and bodily.

This Freudian account is one of the more famous accounts of human dividedness. But there are others. Plato, Augustine, Rousseau, Kant, among other major theorists of human nature, all told some story of a profound struggle between our concern for ourselves as individuals – concern for something like private desire or narrow interests – and our concern for that which is larger than ourselves as individuals – for the good, the god or the group. I am painting here with large strokes in order to set up this question: to what extent did Durkheim, social constructivist par excellence, tell his own story of human dividedness? What does it mean, in Durkheim's account, to suffer from such dividedness? And what does our continued interest in such questions say about us today?

We typically talk of society over and against the individual, and of the individual sacrificing for the sake of society. Yet can we not also imagine suffering as the individual's public goals, hopes or joy being frustrated due to narrow, private desire and cramped self-interests? Can we think of that form of frustration as suffering? I suspect that we do not usually think of suffering in this way, because we assume that sacrifice always goes in the same direction: the individual relinquishing private desire for the sake of some social norm or obligation. But can we also explore the ways that limited private desire and self-interest can cause great unhappiness within the individual? And if forms of private desire can cause individual unhappiness, then we need to reconsider our habit of calling the relinquishment of private desire a sacrifice. Indeed, in many cases, relinquishment of private desire and narrow self-interests could be understood as a form of liberation and happiness, not sacrifice and suffering.

At the conclusion of this chapter, then, I will argue that we also need to pay attention to this other account of suffering – *suffering as the frustration, dissatisfaction or affliction that individuals experience when they adjust, curb, or entirely suppress a variety of public goals, norms, comforts and loves for the sake of narrow self-interests and self-absorbed goals and desires*. Moreover, I will argue that Durkheim was more interested in this form of suffering – egoistic and anomic suffering and the structural oppression and inequalities interrelated to them – than in the more conventional form of suffering, namely, suffering-as-individual-sacrifice. I will suggest that our continued emphasis on suffering-as-individual-sacrifice reveals a persistent feature of modernity, namely, the sacrosanct interiority of the natural, individual self and the odiousness of anything that would thwart it.[3]

II. Rousseau and Durkheim: The Social in Relation to the Natural

We stand to gain insight into the broad, fundamental questions at stake here, namely, Durkheim's understanding of the social in relation to the natural, and of the self in relation to society. We do so by looking at how Durkheim posed these same fundamental questions to Jean-Jacques Rousseau, a central figure in the genealogy of his thought.[4]

On occasion we come upon a short passage that manages to encapsulate the principal insight and perplexity of its author. The following passage – Durkheim's gloss on Rousseau's social and political writings – manages to capture not only much of Rousseau but of Durkheim as well:

> Though not necessarily contrary to nature, society does not arise from it naturally. To develop seeds which, though present, are infinitely remote from the act, and to find a form of development that is appropriate to them but does not conflict with the most basic tendencies of natural man, is bound to be a difficult operation ... To change man and at the same time respect his nature is indeed a task that may well exceed human powers. (1960b: 121)

The equivocation in this passage is dazzling: society is neither contrary to nature nor part of it; the seeds of the social life are present in nature yet remote from it. The ambiguity is as instructive of a tension found in Rousseau's thought as in Durkheim's. But is it the same tension?

Most interpreters of Rousseau insist that, according to him, the human entry into social life was a terrible and avoidable mistake. Yet Durkheim opposed this standard interpretation and claimed that 'social existence', in Rousseau's view, 'is not a diabolical machination but was willed providentially, and that although primitive nature did not necessarily lead to it, it nevertheless contained potentially what would make social existence possible when it became necessary'. Indeed, 'the social state is the more perfect one, though unfortunately the human race is only too prone to misuse it' (ibid.: 143).

Here Durkheim masterfully brought much nuance to offset the blunt caricature that had been affixed to Rousseau since the publication of his first *Discourse*, namely, that the *natural* human is happy and good, while the *social* human is miserable and corrupt. Challenging this cherished interpretation of Rousseau, Durkheim went so far as to claim that, according to Rousseau, social humans 'emerge naturally from the state of nature' (ibid.: 81).

Yet immediately after this helpful and novel interpretation of Rousseau, Durkheim appears to take it all back. Instead of stressing sociability as natural and the inevitable human journey into social life, Durkheim highlighted Rousseau's account of the accidental and artificial aspects of sociability. He wrote, for example, 'it was not man's original constitution that constrained him to enter into social life, the causes of which are outside of human nature, adventitious' (ibid.). Durkheim further claimed that Rousseau's belief in an ineluctable conflict between the natural self and social life accounts for Rousseau's profound pessimism. 'Rousseau's historical pessimism', according to Durkheim, springs from Rousseau's view that even as the self is engaged in social existence, the self can never be entirely transformed by society and will eventually direct itself against society. With this reference to Rousseau's pessimism, Durkheim completed his interpretive reversal. Having begun by claiming that Rousseau was not a pessimistic thinker because he did, in fact, manage to establish society in nature, Durkheim now concludes his lectures by asserting that Rousseau is a pessimistic thinker and precisely because Rousseau failed to ground society in nature. The 'concrete empirical individual who is the antagonist of all collective existence' emerges as the only real agent when compared to the ghost-like, 'abstract, general individual who is the agent and object of social existence'. Rousseau's fundamental failure, in Durkheim's view, was his inability 'to root social being in nature'. Hence Durkheim's final judgement on Rousseau:

> Herein lies the weakness of the system. While, as we have shown, social life for Rousseau is not contrary to the natural order, it has so little in common with nature that one wonders how it is possible .... So unstable is [social life's] foundation in the nature of things that it cannot but appear to us as a tottering structure whose delicate balance can be established and maintained only by an almost miraculous conjunction of circumstances. (ibid.: 137 – 8)

How are we to account for this interpretive reversal? Durkheim struggled to offer a faithful account of what he called 'the dual aspect' of Rousseau's thought (ibid.: 85). What is this dual aspect? 'The individualist principle, which underlies his theory of the state of nature, and the contrary principle (which might well be called the socialist principle if the word did not have a different meaning in the language of political parties), which is at the base of his organic conception of society' (ibid.). Although by the end of his lectures on Rousseau, Durkheim would conclude that Rousseau's social philosophy was fatally flawed by his inability to reconcile his individualist and communitarian sensibilities, during the course of the lectures Durkheim was more equivocal.[5] In some passages he suggested that Rousseau successfully reconciled the poles of the dual aspect, while in other passages he claimed the opposite.[6] Mostly, however, Durkheim presented Rousseau as attempting to maintain both (natural) individualist and (social) communitarian perspectives, yet, ultimately, unsuccessfully. In the end, Durkheim would place Rousseau in the camp that maintains that there is an unbridgeable gulf between the natural and the social, the individual and society.

Still, by claiming that for Rousseau 'social life is not contrary to the natural order', Durkheim brought to light, even at the conclusion of his interpretive reversal, a genuine ambiguity that reflects the complexity of Rousseau's position. Rousseau struggled throughout his lifetime to depict how human flourishing requires a robust social life and, at the same time, how that very social life will inevitably rob humanity of any happiness. Durkheim grasped Rousseau's attempt to characterize a conflict between the natural and social self that is neither ontologically necessary nor radically contingent. And it was precisely this tense stance that enabled Rousseau to indicate both the promise and the problem of the moral life, namely, *both our responsibility for ourselves and our powerlessness to radically transform ourselves*. Most of Rousseau's commentators had missed this central ambiguity: Durkheim, in contrast, highlighted it. If Durkheim could see what others failed to see, it was because the very ambiguity that troubled Rousseau's thought troubled his own thought as well. For, as we will see, Durkheim, too, struggled to capture the radical extent to which social structures shape humans as well as the abiding human responsibility for the shape of those social structures.

How Rousseau and Durkheim responded to the complex relation between the natural and the social is precisely what distinguishes them, especially with respect to their views on the moral life. For our purposes we can think of Rousseau as having two extreme responses to the precariousness of social life: denature the self by intensive socialization and immersion in the educative community; or else protect the self from social entanglements, thereby allowing it to experience the simple and sincere interiority of a natural, guileless existence. Such an existence would have minimum social involvements to disturb the self's profound but delicate happiness.[7] Durkheim, in contrast, never considered Rousseau's second option a viable one, namely, to dodge social engagement for the sake of private happiness. Durkheim was many things, but he was never a romantic individualist. He may have shared some of Rousseau's pessimistic, Augustinian sensibilities, but he never expressed such pessimism in the form of romantic escapism.

Rather, Durkheim embraced the first option, to initiate the self in the educative community, and he understood this initiation, this training, as a process of learning and growth that continues throughout a lifetime and that requires constant effort and attention. Durkheim, the professor of education, championed the merits and power of formal education in the classroom, but he also understood the limits of such education: it is but one piece of a lifelong process of work and growth as the self becomes more fully social, more fully human. And Durkheim increasingly came to see the process of becoming more fully human as entailing much in the way of moral struggle and effort as one works to achieve one's social nature, refining skills, gaining knowledge, learning to make judgements, developing attachments, and so on. Towards the end of his life, he increasingly described this work and struggle in grand, mythic terms, offering his own chapter in the Western, classic story of a cosmic, internal battle within the self.

But what *kind* of internal battle is this? What is this battle between or over? Unlike Rousseau, we have seen that Durkheim did not maintain the view that there is a fundamental antagonism between human nature and social life. His standard, normative position is that 'the characteristic attributes of human nature come to us from society' (Durkheim 2001a: 257). More particularly, Durkheim saw no *natural* barrier, no *natural* conflict, that would prevent the realization of a French Republic whose solidarity was built on progressive, democratic traditions that advanced social justice and the dignity and rights of the individual.[8] Unlike Rousseau, then, in Durkheim's view there is no natural egoism, no *amour-propre*, that imposes strict limits on what we can hope for in the way of collective achievements.

Nonetheless, Durkheim did identify barriers and conflicts that threaten to thwart shared, normative aims. He held that in order to achieve the ideals of the Third Republic, much would be required in the way of moral struggle, self-sacrifice, and other practices that we might call ascetic. Championing the rights of Captain Dreyfus, for example, could cost one much in terms of social status, salary raises and sleep. If power, money and sleep (health) are often common goals for individuals, then Durkheim acknowledged that a profound asceticism marks the obligations that accompany robust social, moral engagement. But such asceticism, or 'self-denial', is not the result of an innate conflict between things natural and social – a conflict that would otherwise curb our normative aspirations. The normative ideal that captured Durkheim's imagination and lifelong effort, *moral individualism*, as seen in democratic rights and virtues embedded in shared traditions and a common good, did not strike him as an oxymoron. It was not deemed a sociological impossibility, doomed to self-destruct into unprincipled, atomistic liberalism, due to an intrinsic conflict between the natural and social self. For Rousseau, in contrast, something like moral individualism or a communitarian liberalism could never endure because of an eternal tension between the natural and the social. Indeed, for Rousseau, *any* form of social life was destined to collapse under such a tension. It was this pessimism that Durkheim identified in Rousseau and excluded from his own moral vision.

III. Durkheim's Homo Duplex

None of this is to say that Durkheim was naïve about potential divergence between the needs and wants of the individual and the requirements of society, though he usually understood such divergence as the result of diverse spheres of conflicting *social* practices and norms. There are a thousand and one ways to talk about the individual's relation to social realms, including ways that include conflict. Durkheim knew this. He had studied a multitude of contingent conflicts that occur between individuals and the various social spheres in which they exist. When he made the strong claim that there is no antagonism between the individual and society, he was in conversation with such historical figures as Hobbes and Rousseau, on the one hand, and with such contemporaries as Brunetière and Bergson, on the other. All four held that there is a *fundamental* antagonism, even if each understood the consequences of that antagonism differently. Durkheim, we have seen, rejected the very idea of a single, basic, innate antagonism.

The problem, then, is how are we to interpret those texts in which Durkheim did seem to present something like a basic antagonism or tension between the natural and social self? This rarer facet of Durkheim's thought cut the deepest in one of his last publications, 'The Dualism of Human Nature and Its Social Conditions' (1914a). In this essay we find Durkheim claiming that 'society has its own nature, and consequently, its requirements are quite different from those of our nature as individuals; the interests of the whole are not necessarily those of the part' (Durkheim 1973a: 163). In this late essay, Durkheim described the human as *Homo duplex*. Humans possess two qualities, traditionally known as body and soul. The former is profane and refers to private sensations and egoistic propensities; the latter is sacred and refers to public concepts and moral norms. In so far as these two qualities are at war with each other, 'our joy can never be pure; there is always some pain mixed with them; for we cannot simultaneously satisfy the two beings that are within us' (ibid.: 154).

Many have interpreted Durkheim's 'homo duplex' along the following lines: the self is twofold: it is both a passive receptacle to be filled by society and a rebellious self, fighting against the mandates imposed by society. According to this view, Durkheim increasingly portrayed human nature sharply divided against itself, as an opposition between what comes from inside the self and what comes from society. In this interpretation he, like Rousseau and Freud, claimed that there is an innate conflict within humans between a natural and a social self: *we are destined to be divided, and that division causes suffering and pain*.

The difficulty with this by-now standard interpretation is that it is at odds with practically everything we know about Durkheim – his anti-essentialistic view of the self, his historicist view of human societies and their varied cultural productions, and his employment of a voluntaristic vocabulary of love, respect and desire to describe the individual's relation to social ideas and commitments. Nonetheless, we still need to make sense of those passages that seem to offer the most support to the standard interpretation. How are we to account for Durkheim's claim that 'all evidence compels us to expect our effort in the struggle between the two beings within us to increase with the growth of civilization' (ibid.: 163)?

Let us see if we cannot bring an *anti-essentialistic* interpretation to the very essay that seems to carry Durkheim's most essentialistic argument, namely, to 'The Dualism of Human Nature'. Durkheim began this work, as well as many others, with a reference to history: 'It is only by historical analysis that we can discover what makes up man, since it is only in the course of history that he is formed' (ibid.: 150). Note, then, that Durkheim began with a strong statement affirming his historicist approach. He did not simply make the claim of the historian, 'we *discover* human nature in history', but rather he made the more radical claim, 'human nature is *formed* in history'. Next, he stated that his historical studies suggest a duality in human nature. Actually, it would have been more apt to say 'dualities', since Durkheim went on to mention more than one, and claimed that some are more prominent than others, depending on whose history is being told.

A generic dichotomy is described in the vernacular, 'the body and the Soul'. This body – soul antipode symbolically represents a host of dualities. Durkheim identified three. There is dualism number one: private sensations (like seeing red) versus public concepts (like *Homo duplex*). There is dualism number two: private activity (quenching my thirst) versus moral activity (providing water for the refugee). Later in the essay Durkheim introduced another generic dichotomy, the profane and the sacred, and with it dualism number three: mundane personal preoccupations (washing the dishes) versus extraordinary public occasions (the French Revolution).

Not one of these dualisms is absolute. Durkheim often qualified the first dualism, arguing that individual experience requires collective representations even as collective representations require sense experience. Durkheim qualified the second dualism of private activity versus moral activity, by claiming, 'it is an error to believe that it is easy to live as egoists. Absolute egoism, like absolute altruism, is an ideal limit which can never be attained in reality' (ibid.: 153). Here Durkheim rejected the very idea of radically private or egoistical activity. And finally, Durkheim tempered the third dualism by noting that between daily routines and singular, public occasions there are a host of periodic 'public festivals, ceremonies, and rites of all kinds' (ibid.: 161).

We can think of the three dualisms as ideal types (in the Weberian sense). Durkheim crafted these conceptually precise polarities in order to highlight sociohistorical events and developments. When he applied these polarities to concrete, empirical realities, he softened the contrasts. To fail to note this, to fix one's attention on the ideal types alone, is to miss Durkheim's nuanced interpretations of history and modern society. It is to offer a literalistic interpretation to dualisms that were intended to be ideal and operate in a heuristic manner.

The three dualisms, then, are 'ideal' in a Weberian sense. They are not, however, illusory. Durkheim dismissed those theories, such as empirical and idealistic monism, that attempt to remove what these dualisms represent by simply denying them. Durkheim sided, rather, with 'the great religions of modern man' that insist on 'the existence of the contradictions in the midst of which we struggle' (ibid.: 156). Durkheim was no sanguine optimist. He understood the importance of not underestimating the struggle of (what I have been calling) becoming more fully human. In this regard, he belonged to William James's *sick soul* category, for he did not possess the sunny attitude of those in James's other category, namely, the *healthy-minded*. For the healthy-minded, the world is basically good and harmonious. If we do find ourselves experiencing suffering and conflict, we simply need to adjust our mindset. A rather extreme example of this is the mental healer who tells her patients, 'there is nothing but Mind ... as a man thinketh so is he' (James 1985: 104). In this view, there isn't any actual suffering, struggle or conflict in the world. It's all in our head, and with proper instruction, we can wish it away. This is one of the types of *monism* that Durkheim rejected and offered instead a variety of *dualisms* in order to highlight human struggle and conflict.

James contrasted the healthy-minded with those whom he called the *sick souls*. For the sick soul type, the world and our lives in it are fundamentally flawed: all is not well, and we stand in need of a basic change. In spite of the name, sick souls in James's view are in fact healthier than the healthy-minded. Again, Durkheim would have shared this view. Unlike the healthy-minded, who deny struggle, whose basic starting point is that there are not genuine conflicts that confront humans, Durkheim believed that struggle and conflict were simply part of what it is in the ongoing process of being human. To think otherwise could lead to moral slackness and to social and individual unhappiness in the form of anomie or egoism.

I am suggesting, then, that we think of Durkheim as a sick soul in so far as he used the language of struggle and dividedness to remind us that life is difficult and the attempt to dodge the challenge and work of human maturation is to court a different kind of difficulty. This 'different kind of difficulty', to which Durkheim gave much attention, is the vain exertion of seeking to live always on the sunny side by denying what Durkheim and 'the great religions' seek to affirm, namely, 'the existence of the contradictions in the midst of which we struggle'. To live in such a state of denial is as painful and exhausting as it is futile.

Let us return, then, to some of the chief passages in which Durkheim seems to claim that there is an innate conflict between a social and a natural self. Let us see if we now have new eyes with which to see the conflict and struggle that Durkheim is attempting to locate in the drama of being and becoming human. We will begin with 'The Dualism of Human Nature'.

Of the three dualisms that I identified, dualism number two (private activity versus moral activity) is the most likely candidate to suggest that Durkheim was positing an innate conflict between 'the natural' and 'the social', specifically between natural inclination and social norms. And this dualism, in fact, is the one that Durkheim the moral philosopher worried about the most. His worry, however, was not about the private side per se; that is, he did not deem private activity to be intrinsically immoral. Rather, his concern was over those forms of life characterized by systematically placing private activity and desire above public goals, loves and obligations. He did not, then, deplore everyday, utilitarian activity; rather, he deplored what he called egoism. Egoists, those whose loves are centred excessively about themselves, and who are often captivated by such external goods as wealth, power and status, lead lives that conflict with the social obligations and loves that we associate with moral activity. The egoist, in Durkheim's view, is unhappy and is alienated from both self and society in so far as the egoist lives over and against prevailing social ideals and normative practices that constitute a portion of one's identity.

Of course, the tension borne by dualism number two is not reserved for egoists alone. We all experience it. It is, in Durkheim's view, a feature of human existence. I love long drives in the countryside and I desire to reduce my consumption of fossil fuels. If I forgo the drives so I can achieve my environmental goals, I am, as Durkheim claimed, making a sacrifice, even if I desire it: 'We can accept this sacrifice without resistance and even with enthusiasm, but even when it is accomplished in a surge of joy, the sacrifice is no less real' (Durkheim 1973a: 152).

No doubt Durkheim is correct. In placing one love above the other, I have lost my pleasant country drives. But I have not lost myself. I have not lost my natural self to my social self. I have, rather, placed a more public, inclusive love above a more private, exclusive one. And this could be described as a Durkheimian view of what it is to have made a small step in the process of forging a moral self as I become more fully human. This is not to denigrate private activity or everyday, utilitarian acts. It is only to say what both Durkheim and Kant agreed on: if there *is* a conflict between private, narrow goals and public, inclusive ones, do the right thing: act for the public good.[9]

My argument, then, is that we take this central dualism in 'On the Dualism of Human Nature' to represent the predictable conflict between more or less public and private activities, and not between social and natural selves. This is the appropriate interpretive stance for understanding what amounts to Durkheim's own summary of the essay: 'society has its own nature, and consequently, its requirements are quite different from those of our nature as individuals; the interests of the whole are not necessarily those of the part'(ibid.: 163). When Durkheim refers here to society's own nature and to a set of requirements differing from those of the individual, he is referring to different spheres of being that the individual inhabits, not to different ontological substances or selves that inhabit the individual. The manner, goals and obligations of public spheres are 'naturally' different from those of a variety of private spheres. It is also true to claim that sociolinguistic scaffolding informs *all* realms of existence and interpretations of those realms, including the very distinctions, public/private, soul/body, and so on.

When public and private spheres conflict, the individual experiences the suffering of what is often called an 'internal' struggle. Internal, here, simply means that individuals experience forms of dividedness as they attempt to navigate conflicting sets of legitimate goods. Such internal struggle is daily, and it can be quite acute. Durkheim the moral philosopher, I have said, was eager to acknowledge and express this struggle, and towards the end of his life he employed the classic vocabulary and narrative of body and soul caught in eternal battle.

But there is more. Durkheim, along with Kant, also maintained that the future would bring more, not less, internal struggle. This was not a dire or pessimistic prediction. It was, in fact, premised on the hopeful prospect of public and moral reasoning spreading to encompass what was once considered more or less private realms. The hope was that members of society would increasingly shed parochial prejudice and narrow self-interests as they adopted more humane perspectives and publicly inclusive aims and goals. Yet with this expansion of public, moral reasoning would come increased obligations, including the demand that individuals be willing to relinquish claims on domains once considered private. Examples are: willing to accept taxes on private property and wages for the sake of public benefit; public control of the schooling of one's children for the sake of egalitarianism; regulation of such 'personal' choices as work hours, driving speeds and the consumption of alcohol; public mandates that one not discriminate on the basis of race, religion or sex; public prohibitions of 'hate speech'. These are but a few cases illustrating the diverse ways that individuals are required to 'sacrifice' what were once private belongings and prerogatives for the sake of entry into a more inclusive public, moral existence. Increasingly, then, becoming more fully human will require more of us, including more effort and struggle. It is for this reason that Durkheim wrote, 'all evidence compels us to expect our effort in the struggle between the two beings within us to increase with the growth of civilization' (ibid.: 163).

IV. Back to the *Elementary Forms*

Having looked closely at Durkheim's perplexing essay, 'The Dualism of Human Nature', let us now turn to the *Elementary Forms* and address those passages in which Durkheim seemed to have suggested that individuals in society are required to sacrifice natural inclinations for the sake of social life. We will begin with the passage that appears to pose the greatest challenge to my interpretation – the same passage that I cited at the start of this chapter. While discussing the negative cult, Durkheim claimed:

> Society is often hard on individuals: of necessity it demands perpetual sacrifice. It does unceasing violence to our natural appetites, precisely because it raises us above ourselves. So that we may fulfill our duties toward society, we must be prepared to violate our instincts at times – to go against the grain of our natural inclinations. Thus, there is an asceticism that is inherent in all social life ... it is an integral part of all human culture. (2001a: 235)

Is this not a clear and unambiguous assertion of the social self against the natural self? Is this not but a version of Freud's *Civilization and Its Discontents*, in which civilization requires nothing less than the suppression of the individual's natural, instinctual desire? Does this passage not support the standard interpretation of Durkheim's 'On the Nature of Human Dualism and Its Social Conditions'?

Yet if we answer in the affirmative, how do we also acknowledge that the very language of *social versus natural* is alien to what is most fundamental in Durkheim's social theory, namely, that humans act *naturally* when they exhibit *social* behaviour? Such acknowledgement should give us pause and lead us to revisit the context in which the above passage rests in the *Elementary Forms*.

Let us begin by noting how Durkheim used the terms 'nature' and 'natural inclination' immediately before the challenging passage just cited above. In the process of approaching the sacred and distancing himself from the profane, the worshipper, Durkheim claimed, 'has been purified and sanctified by detaching himself from the base and trivial things that were *weighing down his nature [alourdissaient sa nature]*' (ibid.: 230). If nature is what must be overcome to achieve the social, then why did Durkheim claim that it is the individual's *nature* that needs to be released and set free from 'base and trivial things'? Here, nature stands for that which needs to be liberated from narrow self-interests. Durkheim's fundamental argument, then, is that *in order to achieve one's nature, that is to say, in order to enter the more challenging and robust religious and moral life, one sheds narrow self interests ('base and trivial things') by means of ascetic acts of self-sacrifice.*

What of 'natural inclination'? What does the context suggest about Durkheim's use of this key term? When describing the ascetic character of all prohibitions, Durkheim claimed, 'To abstain from something useful, or from a form of activity that, since it is habitual, must answer to some human need, is of necessity to impose discomfort and renunciation on oneself' (ibid.: 231). What is this 'natural inclination' that needs to be thwarted and sacrificed? Is it a form of natural, innate propensities universal to all humans and which stands in opposition to the particularity of the social? Durkheim did not employ such a thick and metaphysical notion of the natural. Rather, 'natural' in this context stands for that which *comes naturally* to individuals, that is to say, it stands for that which is useful and habitual for humans in their daily activities.

Again, then, Durkheim is not juxtaposing the natural to the social, but rather narrow utilitarian and now habitual action to broader, associational, moral action. Also, Durkheim rightly understood that to halt useful and habitual activity, even briefly, can cause distress and suffering. By definition, the utilitarian is that which serves human need in all its diversity. The habitual is that which brings routine and comfort to the dynamic flow of life. It is therefore a form of self-sacrifice and suffering to relinquish that which advances daily, utilitarian interests and that which brings comfort in the form of routine. Hence Durkheim's claim, 'pain is the sign that certain ties that bind him to the profane world are broken...'

(ibid.: 234). The mark of the religious believer, then, is not the ability to suppress natural instincts for the sake of social norms, but rather to suspend 'easy living' and 'ordinary pleasures' for the sake of greater social goals (ibid.: 235). It is, moreover, this very break in ordinary, daily activity that sets off and marks extraordinary, 'sacred' events.

In sum, my argument is that Durkheim did not present to us a grand metaphysical account of humans caught between natural, innate instincts and social, artificial – and hence painful – social norms. Rather, he presented a more historicist view of humans and their struggles. It is still a grand story, and it taps into the drama of similar stories or accounts told by Plato and Kant. In Durkheim's account, humans navigate various spheres of being that often collide and conflict with each other. Some spheres are more goal-oriented in the pursuit of narrow self-interest; others, more publicly oriented in the pursuit of larger, shared projects; but none of these spheres can be facilely described as 'natural' as opposed to 'social'. Rather, if any one polarity or dualism did capture Durkheim's imagination and animate his dramatic narrative, it is the epic story of individuals torn between their private, utilitarian pursuits and their public, moral pursuits.

None of this is to say that, in Durkheim's view, the moral and religious life disdains and denigrates narrow self-interest. What could that possibly mean? Are humans morally and religiously obliged to belittle or oppose systematically the occupations and requirements of ordinary, daily life? Extreme asceticism might seem to suggest such hostility towards the ordinary. But Durkheim used the extreme cases of asceticism to illustrate a more general and far-reaching argument, namely, that the religious life works to relativize private pursuits by insisting that: (1) they are not to consume one's life; and (2) they ultimately draw their meaning and significance by being linked to a greater public, moral life.

With this interpretation in mind, let us turn to one last passage in the *Elementary Forms* that would otherwise seem to support the standard metaphysical interpretation of Durkheim's *Homo duplex*:

> To serve the gods, he must forget himself; to make a proper place for them in his life, he must sacrifice his profane interests. The positive cult is possible, then, only if man is led to practice renunciation, abnegation, detachment from the self, and consequently suffering. He should not dread suffering – he can even accomplish his duties joyfully if he embraces it to some degree. But to do this, he must be fit for it, and ascetic practices exist to this end. The sufferings they imposed are not, therefore, arbitrary and sterile cruelties, but a necessary discipline in which man is shaped and tempered, in which he acquires the qualities of disinterestedness and endurance without which there is no religion. (ibid.: 234 – 5)

In this passage, and in Durkheim's work more generally, we discover a profound and fundamental normative stance: the sacred – the religious life – demands that humans become characters similar to Nietzsche's 'overman', that is, one who is engaged in the constant struggle of overcoming one's narrow pettiness and confining self-interests. Such 'overcoming' requires much in the way of 'endurance' and 'disinterestedness', that is to say, it requires the constant struggle of becoming more fully human as one increasingly identifies with goals, aims and projects that reach beyond the petty self and its narrow concerns.

This has much to teach those of us who are attempting to understand the nature of modernity and its relation to religion (and those asking such questions were among Durkheim's intended audience). The process or struggle to become more fully human, which can be understood as a moral or religious task, does not entail the attempt to become free *from* nature, but rather to become free *in* nature in our socially pleated, natural existence. For the vocation of the scholar, this Durkheimian notion of freedom entails conducting sociohistorical investigations that reveal to us the social traditions and practices that are shaping our formal and informal institutions in order that we may subject them to critical reflection and critique as we work together towards achieving a more humane future. Correlated with this notion of Durkheimian freedom, that is, to work felicitously and conscientiously within our sociohistorical environment, is the obligation to combat *genuine* suffering. By genuine suffering, I mean the unnecessary harm that is caused by callousness, cruelty, unjust institutions, economic and social inequalities, and devastating war.

Perhaps Durkheim, late in life, exhausted physically and emotionally by the personal and public loss exacted by the First World War, moved towards Rousseau's pessimism (see Chapter 1 here). Durkheim inescapably inhabited a moral universe informed by Plato, Augustine, Kant and Schopenhauer – thinkers who advanced some notion of human dividedness. And 'dividedness' no doubt marked much of Durkheim's personal universe as he approached his own untimely death. What is remarkable, however, is how Durkheim modified his inherited moral universe and in some ways stood it on its head. The grand battle described in Durkheim's narrative is not ultimately about taming 'the natural' or 'nature', but about the constant work of transforming the social to furthering moral aims and human flourishing. And social transformation, Durkheim understood, also entails personal transformation, the moral cultivation of the self. His language of effort and struggle was an attempt to convey aspects of this process of human maturation.

V. Conclusion: Suffering and a Condition for Joy

Durkheim's fundamental concern was not about the pain of relinquishing various private needs, wants and desires, but rather about the pain caused by unjust institutions and deleterious social forces. This is what unites Durkheim and Rousseau. Rousseau understood suffering as the private and collective pain caused by the triumph of *amour-propre* (narrow self-interest) over public goods and inclusive, humane goals. Durkheim understood suffering as the private and collective pain caused by the triumph of utilitarian egoism and anomic desire – on both an individual and a collective scale – over the more inclusive and expansive public goods as expressed by progressive democracy. And both Rousseau and Durkheim drew on master narratives of deep-seated dividedness to express the conflict and struggle entailed in the battle in and against injustice, violence and exploitation.

Unlike Rousseau, however, Durkheim also held that the battle against social injustice and social pathologies requires strenuous and sustained moral effort and self-sacrifice of individuals. In Durkheims view, to deny such effort (as Rousseau often did), and the sacrifice and pain that it entailed, would undermine efforts to mitigate genuine suffering.

Keep your mind in hell, and despair not. These words of St Silouan of Mt Athos have something to teach us about Durkheim of Paris. It captures much of his approach to his life and work. Let us start with, 'Keep your mind in hell'. This speaks to the importance of acknowledging, as Durkheim did, the difficulties of life – that we be not deceived and think living a life worth living is easy and without suffering and conflict. Indeed, the attempt to *deny* this struggle is likely to cause all the more pain.

Yet what about the second part, 'and despair not'? If not for this, St Silouan, and by extension, Durkheim, would be simply a grim pessimist. But St Silouan added, 'despair not' and thereby became a person of hope. But this is no easy optimism. This is not an instance of wishful thinking or healthy-mindedness. The tone is not, 'Cheer up! It's not so bad!' Rather, the words come to us as a sombre imperative – *despair not*. We are charged first with acknowledging pain and struggle and next with not being crushed by it. How to obey this twin imperative? I don't claim to know the way in St Silouan's Eastern Orthodox tradition. But Durkheim's way, as I have been arguing, is to accept the suffering of 'self-sacrifice' – the suffering of becoming more fully human – while experiencing the buoyancy and moral wherewithal of the very communal life for which one is becoming more human.

To be cut off from this communal source of life is to be deprived of resources for individual happiness. Durkheim, like many of his contemporaries, described acts of self-sacrifice as a form of suffering. This was standard practice. But Durkheim also acknowledged and investigated a very different form of individual suffering. The individual who, due to anomie and egoism, is incapable of participating in public goals, ideals, and hopes is destined to experience much suffering. The extreme form of this suffering leads to anomic or egoistic suicide. About this form of suffering, Durkheim wrote and cared much. This is why I suggested in my introductory comments that we need to pay attention to suffering as the frustration, dissatisfaction or affliction that individuals experience when they adjust, curb or entirely suppress a variety of public goals, norms, comforts and loves for the sake of narrow self-interests and self-absorbed goals and desires. No doubt, this form of individual or private suffering, in Durkheim's account, is intimately connected to collective forces, structural dynamics and institutional pathologies. Most of the time Durkheim focused on the need for rigorous sociohistorical investigations of our institutions for the sake of transforming them. But he also sought to remind us of the personal effort and self-sacrifice that such transformation ultimately entails. In this regard, Durkheim does not fit our caricature of the Enlightenment philosopher who holds that knowledge alone is sufficient to bring about progress. Moral struggle and 'self-sacrifice', and the pain and suffering that accompany these, are also required, in Durkheim's view.

This language of moral struggle and self-sacrifice may sound quaint today. Modernity is still perplexed by, and even rebelling against, the idea that the self cannot create itself by itself, free from social influence. And scholars in the social sciences still insist on focusing on the pain of 'disciplining' or 'socializing'the self. This focus reflects a tacit and persistent reverence for the sacrosanct interiority of the self and its presumed ability and right to create itself freely, autonomously, without encumbrance. Durkheim, however, spoke in a different language, expressing a different vision. It is a language and vision that drew from Kant while also anticipating Foucault. *Social structures shape us (Foucault) even as we remain responsible for their shape (Kant)*. Durkheim's language attempted to reveal the logic of the close connection between social training and social revision, challenging the very training and forms received. This Durkheimian voice has much to offer us today, as we are increasingly torn between polarized options that either deny the subject, on the one hand, or else, on the other, assert the subject over and against historical and institutional forces.

I end on a note that was sounded at the beginning. If you have spent any time with children, you know their cry and their smile belie the idea that the subject is a fiction. Achieving maturity will require much work and struggle on the part of the children. This work – this becoming more fully human – will continue long after they leave their parents' arms and homes. And they will be shaped not only by parents, teachers and peers, but also by a myriad of tacit beliefs, ideals, customs, symbols, rituals, prejudices, hopes, fears and interests that criss-cross here and there and form a weave that holds and shapes their lives. But in that weave they need not be passive. Maturity requires that they spin their own strands and knit them to the weave, creating a new shape (I know this for a fact: my daughter is already shaping me). This shaping and being shaped does entail suffering. It is also a condition for joy.

Notes

1. Here, Durkheim was referring not to social life in general, but to social ideals.
2. I am here highlighting the dynamic aspects of what it is to become fully human. My claims are made in the context of understanding the role of effort, struggle and suffering in human acculturation and socialization as discussed in the work of Emile Durkheim. My claims here are not meant to serve as a judgement about who is and who is not (fully) human. So, for example, if my daughter Sabine had been born with severe disabilities that prevented her from developing complex social, linguistic and moral skills, I am not suggesting that such limitations would in any way reduce her dignity and worth as a human being.
3. The opposite emphasis, namely, disciplining or reining in private desire for the sake of achieving personal and public human flourishing, is also a persistent feature of modernity. In this chapter, I try to show how Durkheim reworked both of these modern traditions (suffering-as-individual-sacrifice and suffering-as-individual-intemperance) by insisting that the struggle and effort of becoming human is *natural* to social creatures.
4. Throughout his life Durkheim discussed Rousseau, but his most systematic treatment is found in his turn-of-the-century Bordeaux lectures. These have been published with his Latin thesis on Montesquieu under the title, *Montesquieu and Rousseau: Forerunners of Sociology*. These lectures on Rousseau deal principally with *The Social Contract*, yet they also give evidence of Durkheim's tremendous mastery of Rousseau's writings, for he peppered his lectures with quotations from *Emile, Letters from the Mountain, Essay on the Origin of Language*, the second *Discourse, Political Economy, The Geneva Manuscript*, various fragments, and even from Rousseau's personal letters.
5. I am substituting 'communitarian' for the term that Durkheim employed but was unhappy with, 'socialist'. It is clear from the context that Durkheim wanted a concept that opposed 'the individualist principle', that is, that humans are naturally self-sufficient and do not stand in need of sociolinguistic community and training. Think of communitarian, then, as opposing the individualist principle by maintaining, normatively and descriptively, that sociolinguistic community is a natural, inescapable condition for humans.
6. Compare, for example, pp. 85, 90 and 143 to pp. 81, 84 and 137.
7. There is a third, more complex response that Rousseau made to the precariousness of social life. I refer to this as Rousseau's tense middle way in my book of 2006, *Public Vision, Private Lives*, pp. 187–213.
8. For my arguments on Rousseau's and Durkheim's communitarian liberalism, see Cladis (1994: 11–28; 2006: 220–22).
9. By 'private, narrow goals' I am not referring to such profound and compelling individual goals as obtaining medicine for one's own sick child.

II.
The Durkheimian Legacy

Chapter 5

Robert Hertz on Suffering and Evil: The Negative Processes of Social Life and Their Resolution

Robert Parkin

I

Within the Durkheim group, the life and work of Robert Hertz (1881–1915) occupies a unique position for a number of reasons. First, of all the members of the group who died in the First World War, he is perhaps the most regretted, due to his perceived brilliance and promise. Secondly, while the influence of his published work over later anthropology is clearly eclipsed by that of Durkheim and Mauss, it has still been considerable, but unlike theirs it has been primarily limited to anthropology. Thirdly, there is the intellectual focus in most of his work on the negative aspect of social life. This relates to the rent in the social fabric caused by death, the negative symbolism of the left hand, and – most centrally in his own conception of his work – the notion of sin and its expiation. In expiation, inner conviction draws the malefactor back to submission to social authority. This is not to say that Hertz was at odds with Durkheim's generally positive view of social life (see below, Sect. III). It is, however, this focus that makes Hertz's corpus suitable for consideration in a volume devoted to suffering and evil in the Durkheim school. Fourthly, there is the heroic nature of Hertz's own life and death. In life, he was permanently torn between the groves of academia and the desire to devote his life to the betterment of society through both teaching and political action. It is to Durkheim's credit that he managed to convince Hertz that academic scholarship could also contribute to this aim. As for Hertz's death in the First World War, it was not merely a matter of him being killed, as were millions of others, but of his growing and perhaps calculated readiness for sacrifice in the war. Since sacrifice clearly suggests suffering, we need to take Hertz's personal life and death – as well as his academic and political work – into account, if we are to arrive at a comprehensive view of his ideas on these topics.

Before turning to these ideas in detail, however, I offer my own brief interpretation of work on suffering in the sociology of Hertz's time and later, up to the present day, as well as in anthropology, which is my own discipline (Section II). Section III discusses the background mapped out by Durkheim, and then follows Hertz's own contribution, which is assessed in more detail in Section IV. The fifth and final section crystallizes the basic underlying position I adopt throughout this chapter, namely that the Durkheimian approach to social life, in emphasizing its fundamentally positive aspects, does not lend itself easily to a comprehensive, *existential* theory of suffering of the type developed more recently and mentioned in Section II. Even for Hertz, who opted to study what Mauss called 'the dark side of humanity' (Mauss 1925b: 24), negativity was merely symbolized by the left hand, or else resolved. The double burial remakes society as the sinner finds his own way back to God. Education and political activity ease the social conditions of the poor, while self-sacrifice in war ends the evils against which the war is being fought.

II

There appears to be a current perception that up to now the themes of suffering and evil have scarcely been addressed in the social sciences. Indeed, it is only very recently that a book on the sociology of suffering has appeared (Wilkinson 2005, on which I draw freely). Nonetheless, as Wilkinson himself remarks, there are reasons for arguing that a great deal of what the social sciences have studied is related to suffering of one sort or another. Evil is never far behind, at least implicitly. Wilkinson argues first and fundamentally that all social life is stressful. People are constantly faced with obligations and other pressures that they would prefer to avoid, but which cause them suffering, even of a physical or mental kind. Secondly, the academic social sciences have always aimed to give a voice to those who lack one. For example, one can point to people who are generally economically or politically disadvantaged, or both, whether because of class, gender, ethnic identity, disability, mental or physical illness, juniority, etc. The focus on economic disadvantage is especially associated with Marx, but it also occurs in a great deal of subsequent social science. These disciplines have increasingly addressed issues of communal conflict and violence throughout the world. They are associated with atrocity research, as well as an increasing focus on forced migration, refugees and asylum-seekers.

The traditional emphasis on positivism and objectivity in the social sciences does not help in writing on these topics. In the view of many writers, their respective disciplines should not simply explain or contextualize suffering, but should suggest how it might be ameliorated or prevented altogether. Coupled frequently with this position is the argument that, whatever they write, social scientists can never be neutral but inevitably assume, if not express, politically oriented positions: even silence about the horrors of conflict therefore reflects a political bias. In general, Wilkinson appears to associate himself with such views. But further, in this literature suffering is addressed not only in terms of its underlying reasons, proximate causes, potential for alleviation and mechanisms for restitution, but is also considered under the aspect of *experience*. This makes it an existential condition and not simply a set of more or less mechanical processes or an inevitable concomitant of normal social life.

This 'hands-on' position, adopted by Wilkinson and those who think like him, though attractive to the humanity in us, has attracted considerable objections on both intellectual and methodological grounds. This theme is too vast to be pursued further here, but is merely stated to alert the reader to the argument in this chapter that, despite a degree of convergence with the view that the social sciences can be useful – which contains within it all the hopes and disappointments of the seducer – Durkheim and his colleagues, including Hertz, never produced an *existential* account of suffering and evil of the sort just mentioned.

III

Positions like Wilkinson's, which characterize much social science, represent a fundamentally negative attitude to social life. Yet social life can also be regarded as positive, as improving our conditions beyond what our lives in isolation would give us. It is in any case an inescapable aspect of our humanity. This is essentially the position of Durkheim, Hertz's teacher and senior colleague, reflecting the influence ultimately of Jean-Jacques Rousseau.[1] Despite Durkheim's misgivings about the atomization and relative lack of collective feeling in modern industrial society, with its division of labour and class system, this attitude emerged in France as part of the anti-revolutionary reaction of the early nineteenth century. It certainly was not Durkheim's invention. For Durkheim, suffering is really little more than anomie, usually conceived as the progressive failure of modern society to bind the individual to itself. Here is one reason for suicide.[2] Durkheim also occasionally emphasizes the stress, already noted, that can arise from undertaking social obligations that conflict with our instincts as biological individuals. Yet he also argues that punishments have become less severe in the modern world, which has also acquired a greater degree of sympathy for the culprit as well as the victim. But anomie can be only a temporary state. Durkheim hoped that a basic sympathy for other individuals would be reformatory in itself. There is a parallel between Durkheim's position and that of Wilkinson: for Durkheim sociology could provide the intellectual framework for improving social solidarity in particular cases, such as the Third Republic. Among other things, Durkheim used this argument to attract Hertz to his circle.

Durkheim's strong and positive attitude to social life was clearly shared by Hertz, despite the latter's focus on what he saw as its inevitably negative aspects. This is different from Durkheim's theories of the anomie produced by the growing division of labour in human history, especially in the modern industrial economy. In effect Durkheim treated these as contingent, historical events, unlikely to be repeated, though hopefully capable of reform. The phenomena Hertz dealt with – sin, death and religious polarities – fall into the area of process and its repeatable structures rather than history in the above sense. They recur frequently as part of the normal operations of social life and are therefore essentially replicable: they are not seen as altering either the structure or the basic values of society.[3] Of course, sin and negative religious polarities can be regarded as values in their own right, since they appear to be culturally determined. The notion of sin is questionably universal, while the ideas and objects that are loaded symbolically with negativity depend equally not only on the society, but very frequently on the social context also. As for death, although it can be seen as universal physiologically, it is certainly not regarded in the same way in all societies. Such variations can be compared and synthesized synchronically. This is what Hertz does. For Durkheim, as already noted, anomie is treated as a trend in world history, in effect, if not by design.

Like Mauss, Hertz can be seen as a proto-structuralist, more so than Durkheim himself. Hertz's ideas concerning religious polarity form an abstract model of opposition which, as the famous 'binary opposition', became the basis for Lévi-Strauss's later structuralism. Similarly, like van Gennep (1909), whom Hertz may have influenced, ritual, here death ritual, is not only a sequence of phases. Their very sequence has a clear, generally repeatable structure, although some of the phases may be merely vestigial, as is often the case in the modern world.

This is a development of Durkheim's treatment of ritual as the privileged site for reinforcing the bonds between the individual and society. It is achieved by stimulating a sense of collective unity and harmony, which itself is created through the circulation of significant social knowledge in both symbolic and explicitly linguistic form. Ritual also represents for Durkheim the meeting of sacred and profane, as well as a phase between stretches of ordinary social life, which is given significance. Durkheim's account is therefore a dynamic one or one of process. This, however, does not relate to the ritual itself. This is partly Hertz's (and van Gennep's) contribution, though it extends, not contradicts, Durkheim's own account, which Hertz accepts in full.[4]

IV

As already noted, Hertz's own contribution, to which I turn in this section, is focused on the negative aspects of social life. As a result there is, perhaps, a strain of pessimism in his work that one detects far less in that of Durkheim or Mauss. In general, however, Hertz fitted in with the intellectual project of the school, specializing in one aspect of social life rather than contradicting the central theoretical precepts of his colleagues and master. I shall now discuss the three main texts in the order in which they were published (and largely composed), namely death, the right and left hands, and sin.[5] I then briefly discuss Hertz's educational, political and wartime activities, and his death in the war.

Death

The long essay on death is basically concerned with a number of interconnected themes that can be regarded as both reflecting Hertz's Durkheimian intellectual roots and pointing to structuralism in the future. Its essential points are the following. First, death is a social phenomenon that causes a rent in the fabric of society through the loss of one of its members. Secondly, a ritual is required to mend the fabric. This ritual is therefore not primarily held to assuage feelings of loss on the part of the bereaved but, in accordance with Durkheimian theory, produces *social* sentiments and *social* knowledge to bind the members of the society together as a collectivity. Thirdly, the ritual has a structure which is interpreted by Hertz mostly in terms of two different mortuary rites. The first of these is concerned with the temporary disposal of the corpse, the second its permanent disposal, perhaps years later. In addition, the structure includes the period in between the two rites, during which the corpse, the soul and the bereaved are all in limbo. The corpse is physically changing, the soul is in transit to its final home, and the bereaved are in symbolic, though not usually social isolation. The second rite has as its main function the ending of this period of limbo in all three cases. In particular, the corpse is finally laid to rest, perhaps in a collective site with other ancestors; the soul finds its final home, perhaps in a similar, spiritual location; and the bereaved cease their mourning.

Clearly associated with these ideas are notions of suffering and evil. The very fact that society has lost a member may represent both. In Western terms, death is a source of suffering for the bereaved, but in other societies, where deaths may be routinely attributed to mystical attacks, such as witchcraft, it may also be a source of evil. As a consequence, the bereaved may be restricted in their social activities, may not be able to cook for themselves or even dress normally, or move physically for long periods, let alone remarry. They may be regarded as shunned by the gods – a situation that may even prove permanent, as with high-caste widows in India. This may be linked to ideas that, unless the bereaved mimic the deceased in some way, the latter will resent it and afflict the former. The bereaved may also attack one another, or even themselves, with weapons in an outpouring of symbolic anger, for example, in the way Durkheim describes Native Australians (1912a).

Another source of evil for Hertz is the corpse itself. For example, in Borneo the coffin may be sealed completely during the decay of the corpse, not for hygienic reasons, says Hertz, but to protect the survivors from mystical dangers – not, he is careful to point out, the soul itself here – arising from the putrefaction of the corpse. Elsewhere, as in many hunter-gatherer societies, the corpse is simply abandoned, perhaps for similar reasons. Conversely, the corpse may attract evil influences, such as spirits, rather than simply being the source of them. It therefore has to be protected, either physically (by washing, being dressed, closing its bodily orifices) or with spirit-scaring tactics (noise, fire etc.). The soul is potentially a danger to the living also, since it may cause them harm or alarm until it has found its final home. It may even try to leave it, missing as it does its 'other half', its old body. It is also likely to be confused, resentful, not fully aware of the loss of its body, seeking food in vain. Hence the food and drink left for it by the living, as well as the specific rites, such as keening or playing music or singing songs to it. These are designed to encourage it on its way. However, the experience is also one of suffering for the soul. Such is the reason for its danger to the living, and it may even suffer further from the very act of the flesh separating from the bones. Even greater suffering is attendant on souls who never, for some reason, find their final home, but who turn into ghosts and are destined to wander for ever. This may be either because something goes wrong with the ritual, or else relates to cases of accidental deaths, deaths away from home, suicides etc., when the body and soul may both be lost or destroyed prematurely. In these cases, says Hertz, there can be no second rite of disposal. Therefore the soul remains in permanent limbo, possibly much feared ever after by the living. Finally, the soul may be delayed in its path to its final home or rejected from it altogether, because of a need to purge sins incurred during its life on earth, or because it has not acquired sufficient goodness (religious merit, purity) to continue its existence.

Hertz is also keen to stress, however, that mourning is principally a social obligation incumbent on the bereaved that must be observed, regardless of one's real feelings for the deceased. Connected with this, the elaborateness of a funeral is generally linked to the social importance of the deceased. Thus, a ruler may receive a very elaborate funeral, an infant none at all because its death is devoid of even negative social consequences where the emotional loss felt by its parents is irrelevant for society. A practical consequence, which itself may cause suffering, especially of the often greater, communal, second rite of disposal, may cripple a family financially. One reason for this, a more significant one symbolically, is that the second rite may involve elaborate sacrifices of many expensive animals, and even of humans (slaves, war captives), whose killings may be brutal and long drawn-out, as if the suffering of the corpse, the soul, the bereaved and society itself is transferred on to them. Thus the Dayak of Borneo slowly spear sacrificial captives until they collapse, whereupon they are swiftly dispatched.

The latter aspects aside, however, the evil and suffering that arise from death, though in one sense infinitely repeatable – everyone dies and possibly more than once, where there is a belief in reincarnation – are also temporary, since they are resolved symbolically and ritually. This contrasts with the suffering of victims of oppression and conflict studied more recently, where suffering may continue throughout their lives and which medical cures may never, in fact, be able to alleviate fully. By contrast, death rituals offer hope in terms of the renewal of life for the soul after death in another place, as well as closure and certainty that this has been achieved for the bereaved and for society as a whole, in ways that the cures of medical science never can. And as Hertz himself points out, other worlds, including those of the dead, are subject to the unfettered collective imaginations of the living as paradises, as the location of the continuous acting out of collective ideals, or as the home of the sacred, where souls are united forever. It is hardly any wonder, then, that death is seen as an initiation, and that religious belief has survived the coming to prominence of scientific thought in the modern world. For science, there is nothing beyond death but physical decay; for many religions, there is the promise of revival or continuity of life in another world, in a different form, and permanently. Ultimately, then, Hertz's view of the consequences of death is of a positive kind.

Right and left

When we turn to Hertz's work on the polarity of the hands, right and left, we find that evil is far more prominent than suffering (Hertz 1909, 1973). Indeed, 'suffering' is not mentioned once (though 'misery' occurs twice), while 'evil' occurs eight times, alongside 'death' (mentioned six times), and occasional appearances of 'maleficent, wicked, devil, hostile, destruction', etc. Yet even so, evil is hardly the central focus of his article, which is really about the use of the human body as a vehicle for expressions of cultural symbolism. Indeed, the most radical argument here has nothing to do with evil or suffering, but is that, far from the physical asymmetry of the hands being the determinant in this relationship, society itself has reacted on the organism by giving privilege to the right hand for symbolic reasons. It has thus stimulated the major internal division in the brain between the two hemispheres. In other words, the left hemisphere, which controls the right hand as well as speech and voluntary movement, has developed more than the right hemisphere because of the socially determined symbolic dichotomy between left and right, which gives privilege to the latter.

Where does the dichotomy come from? Hertz rejects naturalistic explanations, such as religious attitudes to the sun, the different use of the two hands for offence and defence in primitive warfare, or the body itself. For Hertz it is clearly related to Durkheim's famous dichotomy between sacred and profane, in which the sacred is not only threatened by the profane, but is itself divided between pure and impure, which are themselves antagonistic to one another. The profane is therefore joined to, indeed fused with, the impure sacred as a threat to the pure sacred. Throughout most of the article there is no ambiguity, as in Durkheim's case, over whether the profane is within the social or just represents the selfish actions and interests of the individual. Both of Hertz's poles stand clearly within the social. They have, however, been modified by some later writers into auspicious/inauspicious, or positive/negative. It is only towards the end of the article, when Hertz briefly refers to man as *Homo duplex*, that he alludes to the opposition between individual interests and those of society. This occurs when he discusses the moral aspect of the dichotomy and sees in the physical restrictions on the use of the left arm an expression of the will animating man to make the sacred dominate over the profane, to sacrifice the desires and interest of the individual to the demands felt by the collective consciousness, and to spiritualize the body itself by marking upon it the opposition of values and the violent contrasts of the world of morality (Hertz 1973: 21).

The left hand, in Hertz's article, therefore certainly stands for evil in some measure, though this is expressed in many different ways, not all of the same intensity, and may not be implied at all. Thus the values of impurity, clumsiness, being low (in space), the feminine, for instance, all occur, as well as treachery, perjury, sorcery or fraud. These taken together can be considered inauspicious or negative, though not necessarily evil. Moreover, evil is not considered further. There is no theory of evil, save a discussion of its symbolic representation through the body. As for suffering, although it is not mentioned specifically,[6] it is implicitly present. First, evil itself causes suffering. Secondly, Hertz ends by pointing out that the restrictions replaced on the left hand mutilate the organism and restrict human capacities. Here implicitly, therefore, is a source of suffering. As a result, they are challenged by the modern world, which, in being more 'liberated' (Hertz's word), is not only seeking to equalize the symbolic use of the hands, but in order to do so, is having to separate their physicality from the moral and symbolic baggage with which non-modern societies and human history have burdened them.

Sin and expiation

When we examine the text on sin, we find that the relative emphasis between evil and suffering described above is reversed (Hertz 1922, 1994). 'Evil' is mentioned only twice, 'suffering' occurs thirteen times, 'misery' five, and 'distress, despondency, torments, despair, pain, affliction' and 'trouble', between one and three times each. Broadly speaking, we may say that, while the act of sinning can clearly be considered to be associated with evil, suffering comes from the malefactor's separation from God, or some other representation of the collective. Since the sinner cannot survive this for long, he seeks redemption through unconditional submission to authority and the latter's readmittance of the former into the moral community. Thus the sinner in the Catholic confessional is contrite, but also feels guilty because of the sin that he has committed. The sinner should therefore confess everything to the priest, who in return both absolves him and imposes a penance. Absolution is an act that is required for the sinner to rejoin the Church. Although ostensibly private, the confessional box is usually situated in the public space of the church. In any case, sin, if only in the form of evil thoughts, is an ever-present danger into which the believer may fall at any time. Finally, it is the operation of belief, through conscience, that draws the sinner back to God. The belief system is thus internalized by the sinner so that he himself is induced to seek redemption. Indeed, given the secrecy of the confessional, it is hard to see what other element of compulsion there is, at least in the modern world. There is therefore no external compulsion to force the sinner to divulge all his bad deeds in the confessional. For Hertz, what is at work is an awareness of sin and its awful consequences.

Sin therefore implies a particular form of evil because it depends on the sinner's belief in a moral and religious system which he is conscious of having violated, and therefore of having become separated from it in ways that are deleterious to his very existence. In this way, for Hertz, it is different from risk taking, crime and loss of honour. Risk-taking involves folly, or possibly heroism, but it is not a fault of a moral or religious nature. The essential difference between sin and crime is that, in the latter case, commission of the fault does not produce an internal change in the conscience of the criminal by which he is led to seek redemption. He is punished, but he simply suffers his punishment or seeks to minimize it. He does not try to make his peace with the judicial authorities in a religious manner. Despite attempts to reform criminals, the relationship between a condemned criminal and the authorities is ultimately one of power rather than religious belief or morals. Indeed, in the overwhelming majority of cases the punishment is inflicted on the criminal without a path of redemption being made available to him. All he can do is to avoid reoffending. Nor does the criminal himself generally internalize the moral precepts and beliefs that inform the judicial and penal systems.

Hertz is less satisfactory in seeking to distinguish sin from loss of honour. The chief differences in his view are that sin involves religious belief represented by a church that is ideologically egalitarian. Loss of honour is purely this-worldly and involves hierarchical social relations. However, as with sin, loss of honour arises from the commission of a moral fault against a collectivity. Authority in a collectivity may be more diffuse than in a church, but may nonetheless be represented by public opinion, and expressed in the form of gossip and social rejection. As with sin, honour relies on the internalization of social values, which make one recognize one's faults as a delinquent and seek to accommodate oneself to public opinion in a socially approved way, assuming this to be possible. Moreover, subsequent ethnographies have not indicated any necessary connection between honour and social hierarchies: on the contrary, honour is more usually seen as a test of equality among men, since one of its usual features is the ability to assert oneself as an equal in the company of other men. It is the loss of honour that deprives an individual of status. Except *within* a social stratum, honour cannot coexist with systematic inequalities, that is, the socially approved subordination of some men to others.

Hertz's text also raises the question of whether sin is a universal category. Anthropologists have frequently pointed out that a good many offences are magical or mystical rather than moral in kind. Further, social authority, even if framed in religious terms, might not be concerned with offences so much as the individual's conscience or his relations with God or with his relatives. Nonetheless, in his work here, Hertz went considerably further than his colleagues or even than did Durkheim in describing the consequences of sin for the sinner in terms of the suffering it produces. In this sense, there is perhaps a greater convergence with existential studies of sin, that is, suffering of the sort with which Wilkinson is more concerned. However, since the suffering that comes from sin is self-inflicted, it can be ended through the sinner's own search for redemption. Indeed, in the modern world, suffering inflicted by others has tended to become even more divorced from the religious sphere. This is because physical and mental suffering is treated by the medical profession. It is not the confessor to whom one goes but to the doctor or the psychiatrist. The latter may, in fact, have less success in curing the sufferer than the confessor. The confessor at least can offer certainty, provided the proper steps are followed. As with death, so also with sin: unlike medical science, religion offers continuous life, largely through the possibility of renewal after death – which, in a broad sense, sin is.

Life and death

Hertz certainly thought he encountered suffering in real life in the way Wilkinson implies in his definition of the word. In alleging that the influence of Nietzsche's thought can be found in Hertz's writings and even Durkheim's, Riley comes close to seeing the Nietzschean superman or hero in Hertz's sacrifice of himself in the First World War (Riley 1999). I now turn to both these aspects of Hertz and draw freely from my own study of him (Parkin 1996a, especially ch. 1).

Throughout his life, Hertz was affected by an attitude common among social thinkers in France in the century between the Restoration of 1815 and the outbreak of the First World War. This deplored the allegedly antisocial individualism and egotism that the Revolution of 1789 had allegedly created in economic, political and social spheres. Among other things, it had led to a persistent search during these decades for a secular cult of man or society or the nation that could replace the Catholic belief that the Revolution had allegedly undermined, while providing a focus for social harmony. This can be found in some shape or form from Robespierre via Saint-Simon and Comte to Durkheim and Hertz. Because of his sharing in this attitude, Hertz was an uneasy academic, torn between life in study and activity outside it, such as in politics or education. In converting Hertz in late adolescence to his project, Durkheim had had to convince him that one way to understand such problems was to examine the individual's formation by way of society's ideas and concepts in religion, morality and the judiciary. This, however, was never enough by itself for Hertz, nor, it should be remembered, for others in the Durkheim group. Politically, most of the latter were parliamentary socialists, and many pursued political activism of some kind, although this did not apply to Durkheim himself. As for many of these men, Hertz's path to socialism owed much to his contact with Lucien Herr, the socialist librarian of the Ecole Normale Supérieure, which Hertz entered in 1901. Even before then, in his school days, he had become friendly with Lawson Dodd, a leading British Fabian.

Hertz's brief intellectual career was therefore supplemented and sometimes interrupted by politically inspired activism. Thus in the 1905–6 school year he went off to teach in the *lycée* in Douai out of a sense of duty. This caused much concern to Durkheim and Mauss, who wanted him to continue his ethnographic studies, and indeed feared losing him altogether. In the event, however, the indifference and indiscipline of many of his pupils evidently left Hertz disillusioned; after a year, under pressure from Durkheim to complete the study of death rituals, he left Douai on long-term leave, never to return. However, Hertz's wife, Alice – a professional educationalist, with a specialty in the then newish concept of the kindergarten – and some of his last letters to her from the front indicate that he was thinking of abandoning sociology and taking up teaching permanently again after the war, had he survived.

Another extracurricular activity of Hertz's was the foundation, in March 1908, of the Groupe d'Etudes Socialistes, a small debating society bringing together socialist intellectuals, mostly, it seems, Durkheimians and activists. They met to discuss policy issues in areas such as cooperatives, trade unions or alcoholism. The talks given at these meetings were published in a specially created series, the Cahiers du Socialiste, to which the Webbs contributed by means of translation (Parkin 1997, 1998). Hertz contributed a talk and pamphlet on depopulation, which he regarded as an evil threatening France itself (see Parkin 1996a: 50–56). Since France was the most civilized of nations, its decline would be catastrophic for humanity as a whole. Among the evil consequences of this decline were the need for immigration (of less civilized peoples, like Italians and Poles, who would compete with Frenchmen for jobs) and France's declining military strength compared with that of Germany. Hertz's remedies included immediate reforms to the tax system and improvements in public health, coupled with poverty-reduction policies in the longer term. His targets for blame were the middle classes, who postponed having children or failed altogether to have them in an effort to create wealth for themselves. Their attitude was fundamentally antisocial. Although a socialist, Hertz's arguments were distinctly chauvinistic in tone. All these activities, however, both educational and political, represented Hertz's desire to ameliorate what he saw as the depressing nature of French society. He was certainly motivated by the gulf he felt existed between his own, relatively privileged background and the lives of millions of French citizens. All this he saw as being characterized by social and economic deprivation and therefore by suffering.

Hertz was by descent Jewish. This, perhaps above all else, helps to explain why he saw his impending death in the war as a sacrifice. In his few months of service at the front, he seems to have been more and more influenced by the circumstances in which he found himself – the camaraderie, the feeling of the Durkheimian concept of solidarity, into which he could immerse himself. This was coupled with a feeling that it was his duty to give more of himself than others did and to embrace death and sacrifice if he encountered them. The aim of giving more was of the nature of a return, first for the relatively privileged life he had led thus far, seen in social and economic terms, and also because, as a Jew, he felt gratitude to France for having given Jews a refuge from oppression or disadvantage elsewhere in Europe. In short, he owed France his life, which he was prepared to give back to her in her hour of need. The pity is that the attack in which he perished never stood a chance of success and was totally devoid of military consequence. In addition it was, of course, far from unprecedented, replicating an act committed and a fate suffered by millions on all sides in that war. But here, if anywhere, we have Riley's Nietzschean Hertz, the Hertz who willingly pays with his life for a France that is both suffering from, and combating, the evil of German aggression.

V

Despite a degree of convergence between Wilkinson and Hertz, it cannot be said that either Hertz, or his mentor Durkheim, produced any comprehensive, *existential* theory of either suffering or evil. By such a theory, I mean one that purports to explain not only the causes and consequences of suffering, but also its actual experience. Considering experience encourages a phenomenological or existential approach, describing symptoms rather than explaining causation, which may even be taken for granted if, for example, there is a clearly identifiable conflict. Such approaches are remote from either Durkheim's critical rationalism or later Lévi-Straussian structuralism. More particularly, for both Hertz and Durkheim, suffering is seen as a consequence of a more central concern in their respective writings, whether that be the division of labour, death or sin. These are all seen as producing negative effects on society, but these effects are mostly asserted or taken for granted rather than explained. The focus instead is on how to overcome or reverse them. One of Durkheim's main problems is how society binds its individual members to itself so that together they form more than just a collection of individuals. A leading corollary of this is that evil and suffering result from individuals pursuing their own particular and selfish interests, regardless of or contrary to those of society. Although Durkheim recognized that individualism itself is ideological and essentially modern, and that modern law is more and more inclined to protect the rights of the individual, he assumed rather than proved that any manifestation of the individual was necessarily an antisocial phenomenon. He certainly did not draw a theory of suffering from it. Conversely, the notion of anomie, which certainly causes suffering, appears to increase as society abandons the individual rather than the reverse. It is a functional breakdown of collective bonds rather than the operation of the individual's will against either society or other individuals in the Nietzschean sense. Nonetheless, although the problem is sufficiently revealed to allow a remedy to be envisaged, no existential account of anomie as suffering is attempted.

Similarly, Hertz, in the article on death, focuses on the disturbance death has on society, though we are left with a hint that rebinding the wounds left by a death represents an assertion of its opposite, life itself. Here also death is not used as an approach to a theory of suffering; nor is sin, which is simply an expression of the individual's temporary self-centredness. As far as evil is concerned, though it can clearly be seen as both a cause and a consequence of suffering, in effect all we are told by Hertz is that it *may* be symbolized by the left hand, along with all sorts of other negative values. Again, the experiential, existential dimensions of evil are lacking.

It is not my intention to promote existential explanations to the detriment of Durkheim's sociology, only to try to identify some key differences between the two positions. Reasons are not hard to find for Durkheim's choice of approach. There appear to be three of particular importance. First, for Durkheim and his school, approaches such as phenomenology and existentialism were effectively ruled out as explanations by Durkheim's consistent rejection of psychological explanations of social facts. This is fundamentally because psychological facts – including experiences of evil and suffering – relate to the individual human being and are simply too variable *within* a collectivity, let alone between them, to inform its collective representations.[7] Secondly, there is the expectation in Durkheim's sociology – unlike those of Marx or Weber – that, on balance, social life is and should be positive in its effects. Negative aspects were recognized, but mostly as pathologies, not as normative, and therefore as requiring remedies, not comprehensive intellectual explanations or theories. These aspects aside, individuals benefit overall from being social. Durkheim's sociology is hostile to the contract theories of, for example, Hobbes or Rousseau, but he agreed with the latter that individual freedom is illusory, and is, in any case, eclipsed by the advantages of social life.

Thirdly, Durkheim and his school scarcely addressed conflict at all in their academic writings, though it is a key context of suffering and of evil, both symbolically and experientially. This is clearly related to the previous point concerning the positive attitude of Durkheimians towards social life. It has been a long-standing criticism of this school that social harmony is stressed far too much at the expense of structured differences in attitudes within a collectivity,[8] let alone individual agency, mere personal scepticism regarding particular collective representations, or conflict. There are some rather marginal exceptions regarding the latter. In *The Gift* (1925a), Mauss concedes that exchange may entail antagonism, even violence, as in the potlatch or in feuding, as much as in material objects or ritual services. Bouglé's account of the caste system also emphasizes its conflictual aspects in serving primarily the interests of the Brahmans (Bouglé 1908). In his study of the cult of St Besse, Hertz uncovered conflicts between the villages involved in it. It also showed that the shepherds, the church and the local antiquarians all had different views about the cult's origins, part mythical, part historical (Hertz 1983). This demonstration may have caused some misgivings among Hertz's colleagues and was certainly at variance with the Durkheimian doctrine that rituals produce a sense of harmony and unity in the collectivity they bring together (see Parkin 1996a: ch. 7). But these are really occasional deviations from a sociology that assumes that social life has an equilibrium between the different perspectives of the different sub-groups in a society and, overall, benefits the individual. It is not a sociology that stresses orderly social change, let alone the disruption and suffering caused by revolutions and other conflicts.

Despite their evolutionism, therefore, the Durkheimians were not historians but functionalist social scientists. The particular events that historians traditionally concentrate on, as in the case of particular wars and revolutions, were therefore of less interest to them than the principles and processes of maintaining a stable and harmonious social life. This included discovering the means of remaking social life if it had become seriously disturbed. Discarding history as an explanation means turning to some form of sociological analysis and theory. To see conflict, evil and suffering as inevitable concomitants of social life, and therefore in a sense as normal, clearly offends a sense of order and of stability. But it also requires a deeper appreciation of history. Marx and Weber both had the latter and, in varying degrees, both recognized the former. Durkheimian sociology was not equipped for this, for it was an approach to sociology in which conflict, evil and suffering were part of 'normal' society.

Notes

1. I am relying here mainly on accounts in Lukes (1973) and Wilkinson (2005).
2. I am aware of arguments that anomie does not appear as a unitary phenomenon in Durkheim's writings, whether deliberately or because of his own inconsistency in using the term, but I am not concerned with this issue here. See Besnard (1993) for a detailed account.
3. This difference might also be found in the distinction made by Durkheim between chronic anomie and acute anomie. See Besnard (1993: 180–82).
4. However, Hertz did not treat the St Besse ritual dynamically, his text focusing much more on myth and history in connection with the cult. See Hertz (1983); Parkin (1996a: ch. 7).
5. Where they exist, I cite only the English translations here.
6. Except where Hertz says, towards the end, that 'neither aesthetics nor morality would suffer' from the development of physical ambidexterity.
7. This is despite the fact that, *as categories in a classification*, psychological states may themselves constitute collective representations.
8. This, however, is recognized as an aspect of societies with a division of labour, while Hertz, in his field study of St Besse, drew attention to the different explanations for the cult held by different social groups (the Church, the local shepherds, the local folklorists and historians, different villages). Also, the groups' political writings often recognized conflict, but they were polemical rather than sociological or academic in type, as with Hertz's pamplet on depopulation.

Chapter 6

Le Malin Génie: Durkheim, Bataille and the Prospect of a Sociology of Evil

William Ramp

> An excessively blinkered attempt to present theories in all their period colour, to scrupulously present them solely in the terms in which their inventors formulated them, may sometimes mean that their true significance is misinterpreted ... . If, on the other hand, one systematically and methodically compares the present with the past, so as to illuminate the former by the latter by a kind of reverse effect, the present may itself sometimes project on the past a light which shows it up in a new way. A question which seemed quirkish, which could be put down to some peculiarity of the period or the author, then assumes a significance which would otherwise have gone unnoticed.
>
> Durkheim, 'Préface', in O. Hamelin, *Le Systeme de Descartes*, p. 122

Several topics once deemed quirkish or marginal to Durkheim's purposes have been revisited productively in recent scholarship. They displace the image of the sober theorist of order and function with one anticipating a latter-day avant-garde: the Collège de Sociologie and, in particular, the preoccupations of Georges Bataille (Richman 2002).[1] The Collège may have owed as much to Nietzschean readings of Mauss and Hertz as to Durkheim (Gane 2003; Rosati 2004b), and attention paid to Bataille may unjustly neglect Collègiens such as Caillois (Riley 2005b). Nonetheless, it seems intuitively apt to examine Durkheim's and Bataille's references to suffering and evil in light of each other. Suffering as a civilizational burden haunts the pages of *Suicide* (1897a) as does violence the description of piacular rites in *The Elementary Forms of Religious Life* (1912a). The various provocations of Bataille – advocate of de Sade's 'use value', alleged proponent of murder or self-sacrifice, writer of astounding pornography, trenchant critic of fascism – promise a fruitful, if unsettling, comparison.

But closer attention reveals complications, beyond the already complex and mediated relations between these figures and their respective circles. Durkheim did not treat evil explicitly as a topic in its own right; his readers must supply the explication. Bataille's more shocking formulations deliberately flout conventional morals but serve a *hyper*-morality, a particular vision of truth. The trials of defining evil in the work of Durkheim and Bataille also reflect a broader difficulty marking the culture in which they wrote and we read (Cabrera 2001; Neiman 2001). We may recognize evil intuitively but still have trouble theorizing it or discerning its conceptual boundaries. The following discussion does not pretend to resolve these difficulties, nor to describe exhaustively the historical links between Durkheimians and Collègiens. Instead, in a preliminary way, it explores the development of certain discussions of evil, tracing selected affinities and divergences among them. This is not to claim Durkheim for Bataille nor Bataille for Durkheim, but to see how (and how successfully) each addressed this resistive and perplexing topic, and thereby to project on their legacy 'a light which shows it up in a new way'. The history of philosophy, properly construed, said Durkheim, could become 'an instrument of philosophical culture' (Durkheim 1911d). An historical look at theories of evil and suffering might similarly illumine prospects for a contemporary sociology of evil and so sharpen questions about its cultural status and moral purpose.

I. Durkheim's Descartes: Cosmic Indifference and the Ascetic Pursuit of Truth

In the preface to Octave Hamelin's posthumous *Le système de Descartes* Durkheim praised Hamelin's pedagogical devotion and nuanced approach to the history of philosophy (Durkheim 1911d). However, he said little about the substance of Hamelin's work, save for one brief reference to Hamelin's interpretation of a quirkish Cartesianism, the 'evil genius' hypothesis:

> The hypothesis of the evil genius has generally been considered by historians as a dialectical subtlety, a product of Descartes' somewhat strange imagination. It will be seen how, by rethinking it and comparing it with concepts which are still topical, Hamelin succeeded in interpreting it in a completely new way, and one which illuminates several aspects of Cartesian philosophy. (ibid.: 122)

This hypothesis formed part of the procedure of systematic doubt in the First and Second Meditations (Descartes 1970[1641]: 148–57) by which Descartes first dismantled the comfortable furniture of the taken-for-granted, before rebuilding, from the proposition *cogito ergo sum*, a logical assurance of his existence as a rational being, of a benevolent God, and of the sensible world. What, he asked, if even the most evident features of everyday life were but deceptions of an evil agent? His response was that such a demon might deceive him even about his bodily existence but could not rob him of the certainty of thought itself. How can I think and not *be* a thinking entity? Hamelin, however, lingered over the question of deception, noting that,

> We are contingent beings and, according to Cartesianism, finite beings. As limited beings, we are subject to foreign influences; our thought is not pure and master of itself, it is dominated occasionally by exterior circumstances which dictate our judgments, to which, from that time onwards, it remains only an appearance of rationality and therefore they can be fundamentally irrational. The evil spirit is nothing other than a personification of the violence to which the possibly irrational nature of the universe perhaps subjects the mind. (Hamelin 1921[1911]: 119)

Hamelin noted that the evil genius argument could be used to suggest some essential falsity in human intelligence, but denied this to be Descartes's intent. Reason is beset, not by an enemy within, but by an 'external pressure' which menaces it unceasingly. However, reason has an ally in the will, which empowers us to refuse or suspend belief in doubtful things (ibid.). If this is the passage Durkheim admired, it is an interesting choice. The reference to a 'personification of violence' invites comparison to Durkheim's allusions, in *The Elementary Forms of Religious Life*, to dramatic acts and personifications of violence in piacular rites; responses to injuries sustained by the collective, such as the deaths of its members. The violent actions of participants respond to violence visited upon them which they cannot, ultimately, control or forestall, and which continues to menace them. The cosmos, though mapped and made sense of in collective representations (Durkheim and Mauss 1903a), can escape and turn on such representation. The arbitrariness of death renders the cosmic order presented in myth and ritual as a collective home, momentarily *unheimlich*, unfathomable. If, for Durkheim, society is somehow God, this god is also vulnerable, or perhaps has an enemy.

We moderns still face such cosmic indifference, though we trust science to confront or even tame it more effectively. In Durkheim's vision of science, religious responses to cosmic unpredictability themselves become another kind of arbitrary externality, impurities expelled with difficulty from the process of rational inquiry:

> The mind is so naturally disposed to disregard [the truth of the existence of social facts] that one will relapse inevitably into the old errors if one does not submit oneself to a rigorous discipline, of which we will now formulate the principal rules, corollaries of the one preceding.
> 1. The first of these corollaries is: It is necessary systematically to rule out all preconceived ideas [*prénotions*]. ... The methodical doubt of Descartes is nothing, fundamentally, but an application of this corollary. If, at the

moment at which he sets out to found science, Descartes makes a rule for himself to place in doubt all the ideas which he has previously received, it is because he does not wish to employ any concepts save those which are scientifically elaborated; that is to say, constructed after the method which he institutes. All those ideas he holds which have another origin must therefore be rejected, at least provisionally. (Durkheim 1901c: 31–32)

The web of *prénotions*, once stripped from the apparatus of scientific understanding, ceases to be a threat to it. Instead, as factual objects of inquiry, the subject matter of a sociology of knowledge, *prénotions*, like natural phenomena, can yield evidence of regularities. In this sense, Durkheim denominated himself (and by implication, any scientist) a Cartesian.[2] However, his new philosophical anthropology also owed much to Kant (Nemedi and Pickering 2005), and thus we commence with a brief contextualization of both Cartesian and Kantian ideas about evil, before examining how the cognitive and moral dimensions of a Durkheimian approach to the topic (the possibility of true knowledge of good and evil, and of a clear and practical distinction between them) might engage each other.

II. Out of the Garden: Knowledge of Good and Evil

The narrative drama of Judæo-Christian sacred history is marked by certain key binary distinctions which structure its traditions and order the lives of believers.[3] These, however, develop and shift in the course of the scriptural record. In Genesis, God calls into being a cosmos of ordered distinctions, unified in goodness by its Source and rendered symbolically as a garden, a place of delight for its human inhabitants. But, tempted by a serpent, Eve persuades Adam to eat the fruit of the tree of the knowledge of good and evil. When God next addresses them, they are immediately aware of their nakedness and hide, *knowing themselves* now as beings divided from God and as having acted in opposition to God. Evicted from the Garden, they fall into mortality, toil, pain – and sin. It is a condition in which one of their children murders another. Against a created order transparent of God's goodness appears another binary – a division between good and evil, the outworking of which occupies chroniclers, prophets, psalmists and evangelists. God sees evil acts and intentions alike, but humans repeat the primordial attempt to cover and dissemble, hiding their fatal knowledge from God and themselves. The dramatic power of this story is unquestionable, but its subsequent elaboration has provided no philosophically clear and distinct basis for a definitive 'theory' of evil, theological or otherwise. Christianity and Judaism developed as often-fractious communities of interpretation, not as propositional derivatives (Forsyth 1987; Wright 2006: 44–47). Debate raged for centuries over the meaning of evil, or of the Fall into sin. Did humankind fall alone? Is the indifference of the cosmos a sign that all creation is estranged? Was the creation of a universe inhabitable by evil, a good act? Is evil substantial rebellion or abstract negation? Are we tempted into it, or is it the result of free choice, and was original sin (Milton's 'happy fall') an inauguration of ethical autonomy? Is evil what we do (or neglect to do)? Is this what happens to us? Or is it what recruits or possesses us?

Similar dilemmas haunted the Western philosophical tradition, even in its secularization. Descartes's hypothetical *génie*, an inverse of the Anselmian definition of God, also recalls the 'deceiver of the whole world' in the book of Revelation. Here is a demon, 'not less powerful than deceitful' usurping 'that God who is supremely good and the fountain of truth' (Descartes 1970 [1641]: 148). Hamelin and Durkheim proposed that this demon, even if a human creation, still had substance, personifying collective experience of unfathomable calamity. Such calamity might include the violence we do to each other; it certainly includes the idea of 'natural' evil which engaged intellectual discourse after the Lisbon earthquake of All Saints' Day, 1755. Two centuries earlier, this event might have been interpreted as an instance of divine wrath, however inexplicable. But in the hands of Voltaire (who noted sardonically that churches collapsed while whorehouses survived), and Kant, who wrote no less than three pamphlets on its causes and characteristics, it gained another significance. It was no longer a sign that revealed the divine will, but rather a phenomenon of nature. It was now an object of study and amelioration which, however arbitrary and terrible, presented opportunities for risk reduction (the use of seismic engineering in rebuilding Lisbon) and scientific inquiry (Kant's postulation of subterranean causation). In place of God as Subject and Other now stood Nature – a field of objects which, if still other to the understanding, was now potentially subject to that understanding.

However, Kant is most commonly associated, not with the idea of natural evil, but with that of radical evil (Kant 1793), which is defined in terms of a capacity to choose freely between alternative courses of action (*willkur*). This evil resides not so much in actual suffering caused by human action, as in the quality of intentions according to which actions are carried out. It is often said that evil acts follow from evil influences or inclinations, but Kant does not let us off so easily. If we are conscious of and capable of reasoning about our actions, we are capable both of deluding ourselves and – taking the place of the God of Genesis – also of seeing through our own dissembling. In short, we have a conscious capacity to establish good or evil maxims governing our actions. Our present choices may subsequently dispose us to good or evil, but every subsequent choice recapitulates the primal drama of the will. To choose the good morally is to choose it because it is good, not because we are so inclined (Bernstein 2001: 61 – 62). Radical evil, ultimately, is the inverse of the free choice of good. It is a free exercise of a capacity to choose evil, not because it brings pleasure, but for its own sake. Kant did suggest, in a secularized reprise of the doctrine of original sin, an inherent human tendency to choose evil (ibid.: 71) and interpreted the Fall as a sort of anomic infinity of choice leading to restlessness and disillusion. One could see in these suggestions, echoing Hamelin, a sort of phenomenological intuition that the violent indifference of the universe finds an analogue in apparently wilful tendencies to choose atrocity repeatedly, for arbitrary reasons.

To a legacy of metaphysical conundrums about evil, Kant added questions about human as well as divine will, about natural as well as spiritual calamities. Durkheim's discussion of reason and will, though still recognizably Kantian, interpreted forms of perception and categories of the understanding sociologically,[4] and construed the categorical imperative as a social one, as a focus of moral duty but also a repository of collective and emotional force.[5] We would therefore expect him to treat questions of good and evil as indications of the social condition of humanity, anticipating a post-metaphysical approach to the topic (Ferrara 2001).

III. Durkheim: Suffering and Evil in the Social Condition of Humanity

Rosati suggests two different senses in which Durkheim treated the problem of evil (2005: see also Chapter 2 here): (1) the profane as a focus of ascetic renunciation; (2) the negative sacred, experienced as an actively malign force or power. One can expand this typology to identify at least four types of 'evil' in Durkheim's writings. First, we might define as evil (at least in their consequences for individuals, the social fabric and justice) an anomic attenuation of moral significance or an egoistic exhaustion of social energies in unrelieved profane or everyday life. Here also perhaps is the burden or 'effort' imposed by civilization (Durkheim 1914a) or the ennui consequent on the dualism of human nature. These are to some extent inevitable counterparts of modernity. Durkheim sought their mitigation, but also suggested that their historical significance was not always negative. Second, if we define evil in terms of suffering, it is possible to argue that privation arising from service to an ideal – refusing easy or pleasurable commerce with profane things – involves a kind of evil inherent in social life. 'Because society lifts us above ourselves,' Durkheim wrote, 'it does constant violence to our natural appetites' (1995c: 321). As Rosati says, 'there is inherent pain and suffering in all social life, because this is a necessary condition in order to have social life'(2005: 72). But from the standpoint of the sufferer, the duty of privation in itself is not evil. The Cartesian (and Durkheimian) pursuit of truth involved ascetic refusal of a 'natural inclination' to fall into the sleep of *méconnaissance*, but it is sleep, not sleep deprivation, which is to be condemned. However, there is nothing inherently evil in profane things either; it is the act of renunciation which identifies their depreciated moral status. The profane itself causes no suffering, no direct violation of the social fabric. It is simply a designation of ordinary aspects of human life not set apart in time or space, nor emblematic of the collective. However, Rosati also suggests that, just as Durkheim divides the sacred into positive and negative sub-categories, so too, the profane exhibits two tendencies. On the one hand, it is a necessary dimension of social life. Everyday routine provides respite from the emotional transport of collective celebrations, and it is in the everyday that we live, work and perpetuate ourselves. On the other hand, profane routine weakens the social *élan vital* – the regulative and symbolic force of the collective dissipates in everyday life. The profane is both counterpart and enemy of the sacred.

Third, in both a conventional and a sociological sense, acts forbidden by the collective could be called evil. But regulation constraining them is not simply superimposed on a naturally selfish or transgressive 'human nature' (Durkheim 1914a). The will or passion to transgress is a consequence of sociality. Specifically, it is the loss of instinctual regulation that accompanies the latter. Further, individuality, passion, desire, transgression and limit have significance only in a sociocultural matrix.[6] Thus, the disposition to transgress, the definition of particular acts as transgressive, and the 'suffering' which accompanies the duty not to transgress, are all in some sense social. If evil resides in them, it cannot be separated from the social capacities of individuals, nor from the particular collective conscience to which those capacities are oriented. For Durkheim, the social condition of humanity, the burden it imposes, and the transgressions it defines, incites and punishes, are given facts.

The fourth guise of evil, the negative or left sacred (Durkheim 1995c: 392–417), involves things set apart as fearful, disgusting or abhorrent, associated with a malign force construed as actively evil in some phenomenological sense.[7] Here is an evil with substantive power; here is Satan himself (ibid.: 423). Durkheim's anthropological reach extended beyond the abstract formulations of Descartes and Kant to something they still hinted at but could no longer maintain without philosophical embarrassment: that evil is a power in the world or in us that can be both feared and desired. His is a Levitical account of evil; attractive and repulsive forces attach to the existence and transgression of social categories. These are not simply epiphenomena of regulative systems as a functionalist account might suggest; they are experienced by believers in relation to a priori categories, as *transcendent powers*, defining and shaping the ontological character of their cosmic existence.

However, in Durkheimian comparative anthropology, things, places, times or people are defined as malign only in terms of a particular cosmos as represented by a particular collective. There are, Durkheim comments dryly, 'no immortal gospels' (ibid.: 430). All cultures classify, but even those which classify in terms of an explicit good/evil binary cannot be expected always to do so in the same way (Douglas 1978). It remains an open question whether all cultures have a concept of evil or if one is read into them by scholars familiar with a particular religio-philosophical tradition. Did Durkheim develop any notion of a malignancy transcending particular moral or cosmological categories? Despite the specificity of his examples, he did note certain continuities apparent in the Australian cases he studied:

> Funeral rites – that is, the ritual attention given the corpse, the manner in which it is buried, and so forth – vary from tribe to tribe and within a single tribe, according to the age, sex and social rank of the individuals. But the ceremonies of mourning itself vary only in detail, repeating the same theme everywhere ... the same silence punctuated by wailing, the same obligation to cut the hair or beard and cover the head with pipe clay, ashes, or even excrement; everywhere, finally, there is the same frenzy of beating, lacerating, and burning oneself. (Durkheim 1995c: 395–96)

In these ceremonies, the souls of the dead transform into malevolent forces, returning to benevolence only at the end of mourning. Durkheim linked this malevolence to a sense among mourners that the death of a member of the group not only removes an individual from it, but threatens the vitality of the collective itself – a threat personified in the temporarily malevolent soul. The agitated responses of mourners demonstrate, in a sort of counter-violence, the continued vitality of the collective in the face of death:

> The extraordinary violence of the displays that necessarily and obligatorily express the shared sorrow is evidence that, even at this moment, society is more alive and active than ever. In fact, when social feeling suffers a painful shock, it reacts with greater force than usual. (ibid.: 405)

It is hard to know if this was an implied reference to universals, or if Durkheim simply followed where his evidence led. Death has different faces in many cultures, just as diminution of the collective can be represented in different and often indirect ways. But Durkheim's description hints that, in the Australian societies he studied, deaths of members were in some sense always apprehended and represented as violence done to the fabric of social life and of meaning. These assaults had then to be reincorporated into a meaningful cosmos after first being ceremonially repeated and given a specific and intelligible malevolent force. In this sense, Durkheim's discussion of piacular rites represents his own version of Hamelin's *malin génie*. It is a collective experience of the violent indifference of the universe to human life and to meaning. 'Everywhere' it incites renewed efforts to narrate and to live representations – myths, legends, theologies and philosophies – which reincorporate an alien cosmos into a human one. But can any of these representations of evil – or, for that matter, representations of the good – be said to indicate something true beyond given cultural boundaries? Is anything we represent to ourselves as good or evil, true or false (or anything which violates such representations) necessarily recognizable as such in all cultures? Or in a Cartesian converse, can something *falsely* represented as good or true by an individual or a collective be discovered and judged according to a standard not just specific to its own or some other universe of meaning, but in some sense ultimate and applicable to all? A cultural-relativist Durkheim would demur. But the Durkheim who noted continuities in mourning rites might suggest differently, as might the Durkheim who privileged scientific over religious knowledge, perceiving in science a way to make cross-cultural sense of the basic elements of social life.

Durkheim appears at times to anticipate post-modern sensibilities, noting in a work devoted to the scientific study of religion that science itself bears marks of its religious origins and is itself organized in terms of religion's elemental forms (ibid.: 421 – 40; Ramp 2003). But this indicates kinship, not identity. For Durkheim, science accomplishes what religion cannot by methodically identifying and explaining mechanisms which religion itself merely enacts. Science is a collective process, but is the highest development of the *conscience collective*, the pinnacle of 'consciousness of consciousness'. Its work is not 'illogical or alogical, inconsistent, and changeable', but aims at 'things only in their permanent and fundamental aspect' (Durkheim 1995c: 445). Social science has the additional task of developing a universalizing counterpart to philosophical culture – a *culture sociologique* through which society might become aware of that part of itself to which, Durkheim says, religion blinds it. But practitioners of this culture confront two limits. The science Durkheim envisaged could truly apprehend the social experience of humanity only from beyond the standpoint of the individual *cogito*, for whom the social must always in some sense necessarily constitute a transcendental dimension of its own conscious existence. Social science is irreducibly collective not only in its practice but also in its epistemology. The warrant for its universality lies beyond the grasp of the individual practitioner. But in that 'beyond' lies a second limit – the universal viewpoint of science would still only be a viewpoint of the common human culture which produced it. That culture would still suffer, and respond in its suffering, to the injuries and assaults of an indifferent cosmos, taunts of a *malin génie*.

The Augustinian asceticism which René Descartes applied to a secular pursuit of knowledge also marks Durkheim's version of a discourse on method. Although social facts, like physical facts, impose themselves on our minds, to recognize and acknowledge them properly entails a disciplined setting-aside of preconceived understandings. The resistance offered by 'things' to the imagination is a salutary obverse of the indifference of the universe to the human subject, impressed on us by events which happen whether we wish them to or not. Our vulnerability to this indifference, and to the temptation to misrepresent it, shadows our ability to inquire into and act upon the causes of earthquakes, or atrocities. To assert that social facts exist as things, demonstrable as such by their resistance to our imagination, is not the same as to claim that we can know absolutely that what we say about those facts is true. This, and cosmic indifference, may have constituted for Durkheim a philosophical limit beyond which science need not peer. Human existence may be ultimately and irreducibly contingent, but one's obligation within its limits is to pursue the possible in service of enlightenment and of the collective milieu in which one finds oneself. Durkheim's ascetic devotion to scholarly duty in face of the unspeakably arbitrary loss of his son is a poignant example.

IV. Bataille: Evil and Truth

Georges Bataille's acknowledged debt to Durkheimian sociology appears clearly in his discussion of the charged oscillations of homogeneity and heterogeneity, which echoes Mauss's description of the alternation between everyday routine and collective effervescence (e.g., Bataille 1989 [1973]: 123). The sacred – its negative manifestations especially – also reappears, associated with heterogeneous energies. Like Durkheim, Bataille noted that left and right sacred, though opposed, share similarities and can switch polarities. The left sacred in itself can be both repulsive and attractive, inciting fear of transgression but inviting transgressive fascination. Its forceful malignity, which Durkheim discussed almost in passing, became central to Bataille's anthropology.

For Bataille, the ordered homogeneity of everyday life – roughly equivalent to what Durkheim termed profane – is marked by sites, times and things in which its heterogeneous inverse erupts, or within which it must be contained (Bataille 1988b [1979]; 1988c [1979]). Production, conservation, regularity, economy, order and integration call out their opposites in Bataille's evocative examples. The bucolic routine of village life revolves around a parish church situated in a graveyard filled with mouldering horrors. The calm order of the Christian liturgy refers to death, sacrifice, even apparently to cannibalism – one might add (without necessarily contradicting Bataille) that the resurrection it celebrates is also excessive, shattering the bonds of ordinary death. Solemn funerals evoke the disorder of tears, stifled laughter and sexual arousal. Capitalism encourages disciplined work and strict accounting of time and money and depends on political and legal stability, yet it generates prodigious waste. Museums, archives and recycling struggle ineffectually with its overproduction.[8]

It can be argued that both homogeneity and heterogeneity are necessary to human existence, much as Durkheim and Mauss could claim that everyday particularity is both transcended and revitalized in effervescent assemblies and in ceremonial encounters with the sacred. However, Bataille's fascination lay with heterogeneity and its sacred manifestations, typically represented in violent and abhorrent terms. This was not simply a personal idiosyncrasy. In the political and economic order of his day, Bataille saw an exhausted but totalizing homogeneity embodied in moral legislation, worship of economy and production, hypostatized individualism and obsession with national stature. Its denial of heterogeneous energies presaged their Freudian return in violent colonial or working-class uprisings (not a Marxian transcendence of the old order, but its immolation),[9] or their diversion into totalitarian violence and spectacle (1985a [1970]) with its couturier-designed uniforms and declamations about war as liberation. In response to bourgeois homogeneity, Marxist class war, or the shackled heterogeneity of fascism, Bataille proposed various provocations and incitements. They were not to carve out a mere niche for the subversive, nor to impose heterogeneity in totalitarian fashion or monumentalize it in a moral or political philosophy, but to energize social and political engagement. To do so by privileging the left sacred made sense in a context in which positive expressions of awe and veneration had been reduced to a marriage of religious and cultural convention, to technological spectacles for the masses, to nationalist or authoritarian mysticism, or to an aesthetics of force.

However, Bataille's emphasis on violence and horror was more than a response to a political context. Heterogeneity, like the Durkheimian sacred, energizes the social, but Bataille claimed that it is also necessarily repulsive to ordered social existence, and that similar polarizations define both natural life and individual consciousness. In nature, animals are impelled to congregate and reproduce, but also to fight, kill and consume. Like the natural world, individual human consciousness is not an orderly machine nor an inherently unitary Cartesian 'thing which thinks', but a *'realité composé*, an effect of a *mouvement communautaire* of representations and sensations (1988a: 80 [1979]). The contingent and composite character of consciousness evokes its necessary and heterogeneous opposite: decomposition and disintegration. The passion of individual consciousness is given not simply by a positive desire (for the other, for sensation, for wholeness, for immortality), but also by horror of oblivion, a fate indifferent to any conscious effort at self-maintenance and thus abhorrent to consciousness. Where Descartes had posited the *cogito* as a foundation from which to reconstruct faith in the world and in God, Bataille envisaged a subject which thinks and acts in passionate but doomed defiance of its own end. This defiance takes a double and even self-contradictory form; on one hand, the conservation and preservation of self against death, and on the other, a prodigal exercise of will or of desire that dares violence and obliteration.[10] As with the body, or with consciousness, so also with society. There is a resonance here with Durkheim's suggestion that the violence of piacular rites is a revitalizing response to the threat of collective dissolution. But the emphasis is quite different. In this universe, violence and indifference have a place more central and more explicit than they did for Durkheim. Biological excess is the prodigious, unceasing but indifferent gift of the sun. Consciousness is invested with passion fed by the sensed imminence of its own destruction. Awareness of this imminence – analogous to a Cartesian awareness of finitude and contingency – is, for Bataille, a consequence of encounters with others. But these encounters are wounding violations. Our integrity as self-conscious beings is assaulted in the moment it is established.[11]

It is difficult, nonetheless, to define this uncaring, violent cosmos, or the horror central to individual and social life as evil. Certainly it is not necessarily so as Bataille might define evil. The human situation – indeed the cosmic situation – involves suffering, but suffering is also generative. Rather than a fallen realm, Bataille's universe is what it is: an explosive collision of passion and indifference which fuels life and consciousness. Violence and horror are malign, for Bataille, not when acknowledged as a source of passion, but when denied and bound over in service of an order which, by consequence, becomes monstrous. This monstrosity is the world as it might be if created by a *malin génie* who built into the very conditions of life and consciousness a reigning tendency to individual and collective self-deception. This tendency is an affinity for illusion, embodied in a denial or misrepresentation of excess, of the *part maudite*, the fatal gift of the sun to the cosmos.

Against such denial, Bataille asserted a hyper-morality beyond the good-and-evil conventions of homogeneous morals (Bataille 1973 [1957]: 10). He argued, like Kant, that doing good for intrinsic or extrinsic reward is in some sense evil and is not a sovereign exercise of will. But where Kant pitted a pure will to choose good against radical evil, Bataille defined sovereignty (*souveraineté*) as a free capacity to choose either good or evil for its own sake. An act was merely loathsome if done out of desire or lust but for Bataille it was more honourable if done freely for the sake of doing evil. Morality captured by prosaic homogeneity is neither authentic nor sovereign, and fails to recognize that homogeneity cannot be sustained (without becoming monstrous) apart from heterogeneity. Bataille latterly sought to exercise this sovereignty in a type of literary 'communication' quite different from a Habermasian emancipatory dialogue. It was rather 'the gamble, the risk, the danger' of hazarding words and self in potentially wounding and fatal encounters (ibid.: 16).

Taking full measure of human contingency and cosmic indifference, Bataille concluded that the passion of all life derives from and drives towards death. The authenticity of sovereignty, as he defined it, has no ultimate end nor persistence beyond moments in which one consciousness confronts another. The collective is not God but an acephalous milieu in which we are formed and wounded, and out of which we spill words ending in nothing. Instead of 'clear and distinct objects, intelligible or thought to be so', Bataille attended to 'moments when subjectivity seems unintelligible'; when 'what 'is', for us, is scandal'; when 'scandal is the same thing as consciousness' (ibid.: 171). Bataille's atheism, neither comfortable nor rationalist, necessitated a courage close to despair. It delivered him from certain types of delusion: for example, that the collective can take the place of God in any but a contingent, anthropological sense. Nor does it allow one to take any ultimate comfort in being self-made, or to imagine without irony remaking the world in our own image. But it also expels any assurance of our deliverance from ultimate delusion – assurance that 'sovereignty itself' may not be misled. This, perhaps, marked a limit beyond which Bataille could not go.

V. The Possibility of a Sociology of Evil

Recently, Jeffrey Alexander has invoked Bataille in calling for a sociology of evil (Alexander 2001). However, Bataille's lonely, occasionally almost inarticulate championing of an anthropology, politics or economics of heterogeneity appears to give it scant encouragement (e.g. 1985b [1970]). Alexander himself stresses the perennial nature of good-and-evil binaries, appearing to reference a general cultural condition rather than a particular research programme. But he rightly points out two impasses for a sociology of evil. One is to propose that evil derives from an 'absence of values', a proposal which fails to recognize that certain values themselves might be evil, and the basis of an evil political community. The second is to suppose that a community of values in itself inoculates against evil. As Alexander notes, communities are constituted not only by what holds them together but by what they exclude. Echoing a Durkheimian point that society is a structure of limits, he suggests that limits also provide a logic in terms of which violence against the 'other' can occur. A sociology of evil is needed to map out how what we revere and what we abhor are intertwined, logically, symbolically, and in action. But does such mapping itself have a moral compass which can direct a further understanding of evil?

As Milbank has noted, Durkheim inspired various comparative philosophical anthropologies concerned with violence in social life (Milbank 1995). These include Girard's discussions of mimetic violence and scapegoating (e.g. Girard 2001), and even alternative explanations of violence critical of both Durkheim and Girard, such as that of Bloch (1992). Bloch identified a social mechanism he termed 'rebounding violence', which can be seen, for example, in ceremonies by which the Orokaiva of New Guinea mark the transformation of children designated as 'prey' into adults who are 'hunters'. These ceremonies recapitulate the mortality and vulnerability of children and animals – and by extension, of all humans. Children are driven from the village to 'die' and undergo activities involving some risk which render them part-spirit and at least partly invulnerable to death. On return, they celebrate this partial triumph by hunting pigs which, as prey, stand for the vulnerable, mortal aspects of embodied life. The arbitrary violence of death 'rebounds' in the organized violence of the returned 'hunters'. Like Durkheim's examination of piacular rites, or Bataille's fascination with the individual and collective horror of decomposition, Bloch focuses attention on cultural responses to arbitrary and inescapable injuries visited on the collective (as well as on individuals) by mortality. Even Girardian mimetic violence could be interpreted as a response, however mediated, to an intimation of mortality provoked by confrontation with an other who is 'like me but not me'.[12] These ventures indicate less a new sociology of evil than variant discourses about an elemental drama – confrontation with death. In concert with the anthropologies of Durkheim and Bataille, they suggest that violence (or, for Durkheim, social forces manifest in violence) indicates something basic to the human condition. But like suffering, violence in itself is not necessarily defined as evil. It may be evil in some contexts, but directed against evil in others.

Bataille, as Alexander notes, locates evil in terms of conventional moral polarities specific to given cultural circumstances, embodied in positively or negatively sacred things. Sovereignty lies beyond these polarities, in the realm of hyper-morality. But sovereignty, as noted above, invokes as its own opposite the possibility of a more radical evil, a sovereign delusion haunting the freedom to choose good or evil, that is, to borrow Bataille's phraseology, a hyper-evil. This might be said to reside in a denial of the ultimate contingency of human existence and of the expressive oscillations defining the human condition – attraction and repulsion, conservation and waste, order and excess.[13] Such denial, unlike the piacular rites of Durkheim's Australians, seeks not to respond to and reincorporate death, but to render itself as if invulnerable, immortal, self-sufficient. This evil, if evil it is, was a constant threat to Bataille's struggle to articulate his unsettling message, without thereby rendering it as a homogeneous system – at once neutralized and totalitarian. Could that struggle still usefully inform a Durkheim-inspired sociology of evil?

One might expect such a sociology, more than an exercise in philosophical anthropology, to define evil through rigorous comparative conceptual clarification and to generate knowledge of it as something real and observable, resistive of imaginative fictions. For Durkheim, the great gift of Christianity to Western culture had been to surrender the material world to the sphere of the profane, making it available to scientific inquiry, and to the arts of amelioration by which the depersonalized and now indifferent forces of nature – 'fortuit, absurde, amoral' – could be subdued by civilization. Additionally, the power of science to test and displace religion would become 'ever more extensive and effective, without any possibility of assigning a limit to its future influence' (Durkheim 1995c: 431, 433; 1902b: 381). Bataille, though he employed ethnography less for comparative analysis than for dramatic examples, also characterized his work as scientific, at least some of the time, and in the idea of *souveraineté* one can glimpse a distant practical analogue to the Durkheimian notion of scientific enlightenment. But Bataille's understanding of consciousness confronted him with its 'scandalous' contingency, and conversely, its capacity to deceive itself about that contingency. With the ability to deceive comes the ability to imagine *being* deceived, a dark gift of a *malin génie*.[14] Durkheim's passing appreciation of Hamelin's treatment of this demon might lead one to wonder if even his optimism about civilization's conquest of nature and about the explanatory power of science was momentarily arrested by an intimation of limits to that power, and perhaps also of a malign capacity beyond particular cultural anti-gods. Something colonizes human consciousness, entering through its vulnerability, and then becoming transparent, even apparently earnest, in its subsequent wilful denials of its own contingency, and in actions which it is fully capable of representing as 'good'.

Among those who still take their measure from Durkheim, Jean Baudrillard has most explicitly defined evil as a condition entwined with the struggle to understand. The clear implication of his references to the 'transparency' of evil is that conventional sociology may be powerless against its manner of apparition.

> One finds oneself within the virtuality of goodness, of positivity, whereas, on the contrary, within such a system evil transpires everywhere. And that is the trans-apparition of evil. Evil is not that through which one sees, but that which sees through everything, which goes through, transpires through Good, as well. And at that specific time, one notices a perverse conversion of all positive effects, of all political constructions which finally, through some perverse and magical effect, become evil ... And I do not understand evil as suffering, as pain. I define it, rather, as negativity, as the diabolical nature of things when they are reversed into their opposite, so that they never reach their finality, nor even go beyond it and thus become, at that specific time, monstrous. A good part of monstrosity, in our banality, is just that – all phenomena become extreme. Because of the media, our scientific means, our know-how [I suspect Baudrillard had 'savoir' in mind], progress all takes an uncontrollable, inhuman dimension. Evil, for me is just that form. (Baudrillard 1995; see also 1993)

This 'reversal' echoes Bataille's descriptions of totalizing homogeneity. The banal 'monstrosity' of things that 'never reach their finality' also resonates with morphological social pathologies identified by Durkheim as absolutism (Durkheim 1901a), and an 'inflation and hypertrophy of the state' (see Durkheim 1951a: 379–80, 389; also Ramp 2000: 92) in which the latter abandons its moral debt to the collective it governs, enthroning itself 'above' society to 'protect' it and to institute by measures seen and unseen an exaggerated and invasive stasis. Baudrillard's caustic remarks on present-day obsessions with national and international security would seem to indicate that he thinks of its operation in an analogous manner – a deluded and deluding nullity imagining itself to be everything reasonable – save that he acknowledges no 'social' reality in which to anchor a resistive sociological analysis or moral/political response. His discussion of evil is located but not grounded, informed by a sort of stoic irony that carries him far from Durkheim and also from Descartes, whose sense of his own contingency did not prevent him from reconstituting a faith in his God, his world, and his assurance of intelligible Good. Ironically, however, it does echo an ancient Christian idea that evil can take the form of a transparent, even apparently 'rational' possession.

Kant proposed that we have a tendency, having chosen evil once, to choose it again. Bataille also noted a tendency of evil to build on itself, which he distinguished from 'honourable' sovereignty. In a sober assessment of more recent atrocities, Dan Stone sees a genocidal association between collective effervescence and ecstatic community which licenses indulgence in 'frenzied transgression of norms and laws' (Stone 2004). Wars now supplant festivals as opportunities for a 'total break with the normal functioning of society', and a 'long-inhibited joy of destruction' which feeds on itself. Stone's reference to an 'innate desire to transgress the law (thereby reinforcing it) and [an] equally innate capacity to kill' parallels a capacity for transgression that Durkheim located in the social dimension of human nature and the social circumstances of its expression (ibid.: 59). Durkheim, Bataille and Caillois thus might still provide insight into the social conditions of genocide. Stone does not suggest that sociological understanding might eradicate the capacity for genocide, but that it could inform our capacity to refuse to add evil to evil, and our attempts to limit its proliferation. But it is not only ecstasy which releases the capacity to kill. So does assumption of an invulnerable and self-sufficient right to kill, a sovereign delusion which may appear both methodical and reasonable.

In light of events of the last century, discussions of evil as ecstatic transgression, totalizing transparency, or deluded responses to personal and social contingency all have moral and practical immediacy. Evil is manifest not merely in a philosopher's *malin génie*, but in present history. The contemporary wish to measure progress, especially in defining and addressing evil, seeks to recruit social science to its ends. But what do we measure, against what, and how? Descartes employed methodical doubt to arrive at certainty, but some might argue that doubt in the form of a conversation with self, corroding moral and existential certainties, has disarmed us before the moral tragedies of our age. Others shudder at fundamentalist reassertions of such certainties. But we can perhaps no longer be as certain as Hamelin that the evil genius resides outside the capacity to reason – or outside the will. In another age, classical Stoic drama once held a mirror to Rome, reflecting back to its audience an image of itself, but it could not guarantee the truth of the image (Bartsch 2006). Today, can a Cartesian capacity for laborious wakefulness, refusing belief in doubtful things, alone ensure clear and practical moral distinctions between fascist pageantry, Orokaiva ceremonies, Christian celebrations of resurrection, or the ameliorative projects of applied science? Perhaps, some might say, there is no difference. Or perhaps discernment lies in the degree to which individual and cultural responses to contingency involve either wilful denial of vulnerability, or attention to its mystery. The former, both an enemy to and a simulacrum of moral sovereignty as Bataille envisaged it, enslaves to illusion. The latter, more Augustinian than Cartesian, appears to be sovereignty's inverse but is perhaps its unexpected ally in Bataille's sense of the term: a patient, vigilant refusal to refuse contingency. Neither faith nor atheism provides a comforting response to dilemmas posed by evil, nor does either offer easy reassurance to the sociology which must address it.

Acknowledgements

I should like to thank T. Will for helpful suggestions concerning clarity and style, and T. Pope for advice on matters of translation. Any errors of translation and style nonetheless remain my responsibility.

Notes

1. For present purposes, Richman exemplifies such reinterpretation, but others include Jeffrey Alexander, Jonathan Fish, Mike Gane, Michel Maffesoli, J.-C. Marcel, Philip Mellor, Stjepan Meštrović, Ken Morrison, Frank Pearce, Anne W. Rawls, A. Tristan Riley, Massimo Rosati, Chris Shilling, and W. Watts Miller; see also Riley (2005a); Smith and Alexander (1996); Alexander and Smith (2005).
2. See e.g., Jones (1994).
3. A classic anthropological interpretation of such binaries is Douglas (1999).
4. On affinities between Durkheim, Kant and Renouvier, see, variously, Allen (2000), Pickering (1993), Schmaus (2004), Stedman Jones (1995, 1998), Tekiner (2002).
5. The latter appears closer to Kant's idea of *wille* (volitional force) than to *willkur* (a capacity to choose between alternative courses of action).
6. Arguably, accounts of the origins of self-consciousness, domination and strife, whether biblical, Hegelian or ethnographic, redescribe in narrative form an always already social condition of humanity.
7. As Durkheim noted, violation of distinctions between sacred and profane, or left and right sacred, could release deadly force.
8. The heterogeneous excess of the so-called 'Protestant ethic' is consequent on an *unlimited intensification* of rational, disciplined labour as an ethical end in itself.
9. In response to rioting in French cities in 2005, Michel Maffesoli wrote that a 'grande fantasm of social antisepsis', culminating in a fantasy of 'zero risk', had sought 'to evacuate the vertiginous shadow from the individual and collective body'. This led to 'a

dead society, in which security and well-being are purchased with the certainty of dying of boredom'. In 2005, the evacuation reversed, appearing on the nightly news as 'juvenile rebellions, political disaffectations, terrorisms, archaic beliefs, diverse symbolisms, integrationisms, and fanaticism on all sides', leading to 'suspension of all of the good intentions of the ambient moralism' (Maffesoli 2002: 288).
10. Conservation or preservation can themselves become prodigal obsessions, and intellectual prodigality, like its social or political equivalents, can be diverted into monument building.
11. To resort to biblical imagery: Adam was wounded by the making of Eve; and both Adam and Eve discovered themselves to be mortal, and naked, at the moment at which they were called out by a God who had become, in time, and for them, Other.
12. In the Genesis account of the first confrontation with God as other (in which hiding nakedness indicated knowledge of self-exposure and of separation), the expulsion of Adam and Eve from the Garden into mortality was, perhaps, necessary in a Girardian sense to the structure of the narrative – if they had stayed, they would have had to kill God, being made in God's image.
13. In this sense, the bourgeois culture of 1930s France could be called evil, as could Nazism. Whatever Bataille's distaste for for the former, this would be a disturbing equation to make without qualifying both the degree of evil (or its consequences) and its type.
14. One of Sade's literary characters proposed a universe ruled by a malevolent deity.

Chapter 7

Evil and Collective Responsibility: The Durkheimian Legacy and Contemporary Debates

Massimo Rosati

I. Evil, Sin, Expiation and Responsibility within the Durkheimian Tradition

It was observed in a previous chapter that in the *Elementary Forms* evil emerges as a social fact more associated with collective forces than with individual agency (Chapter 2). Consequently, salvation from evil (and suffering) is a collective drama, implying mutual responsibility, a shared destiny, a common past, common memories and projects for the future. Salvation, like evil, is a social fact.

In the *Elementary Forms* (1912a) Durkheim shows how the social forces that are at the basis of evil have religious overtones. Accordingly, rescuing oneself and a community from evil implies a ritual process of expiation. In his *Division of Labour in Society* (1893b) Durkheim highlights the social character of punishment and particularly its religious nature in primitive societies. Punishment is a social reaction against the offence to collective sentiments. For Durkheim, 'punishment is a passionate reaction of graduate intensity that society exercises through the medium of a body acting upon those of its members who have violated certain rules of conduct' (Durkheim 1984a: 96). In this context, punishment (penal law) is, in primitive societies, a form of vengeance. Durkheim emphasizes clearly the nexus between collective *conscience*, punishment and expiation, namely, the religious overtone of punishment:

> Since these sentiments are collective, it is not us that they represent in us, but society. Thus by taking vengeance for them it is indeed society and not ourselves that we are avenging. Moreover, it is something that is superior to the individual. We are therefore wrong to impugn the quasi-religious

character of expiation, making it some kind of unnecessary, parasitical trait. On the contrary, it is an integrating element in punishment. (ibid.: 57)

In other words, given the religious nature of collective conscience in primitive societies, crime in penal law is equal to sin (see Cotterell 1999). In modern societies, according to Durkheim, this religious nature of crime never completely disappears. Even in modern societies, punishment still maintains a connection with vengeance. In modern law, says Durkheim,

> we have remained true to the principle of talion, although we conceive of it in a more lofty sense than we once did. We no longer measure in such material and rough terms either the gravity of the fault or the degree of punishment. But we still consider that there should be a balance between the two elements, whether we derive any advantage or not in striking such a balance. Thus punishment has remained for us what it was for our predecessors. It is still an act of vengeance, since it is expiation. What we are avenging, and what the criminal is expiating, is the outrage to morality. (ibid.: 47)

Crime and expiation are still, at the end of the day, religious phenomena – social facts.

This is not to say that punishment today is equivalent to what it was for our predecessors. In 'Two Laws of Penal Evolution' Durkheim attempts to combine his 'reluctant modernism' with the values of modern societies (Durkheim 1901a(i). In the essay he formulates two theories or 'laws' on how punishment changes as societies develop (see Cotterell 1999: 79). The first is: 'the intensity of punishment is greater in societies that are of a less advanced type and where centralized power is more absolute in character' (Durkheim 1901a(i): 65). And the second: 'punishments consisting of deprivations of liberty and liberty alone, according to periods of time relating to the seriousnes of the crime, tend to become increasingly the normal type of subjection' (ibid.: 78). What explains this evolution in terms of less intensity and milder forms of punishment is the importance that modern societies accord to human dignity. In modern societies, what criminal law and punishment have to vindicate and protect are individual life and dignity. So, as Cotterell correctly maintains, 'the vast collective consciousness of earlier times, imbued with traditional religious overtones, has been reduced to a small but important modern compass. The modern value that underlies penal law and punishment is *the value of human dignity and the protection of the security of persons and their property*' (Cotterell 1999: 79, emphasis in the original). However, the cult of the individual notwithstanding – or rather, given the social nature of the cult of individual – modern penal law in fact retains its social nature and its original religious overtones.

The strict relation established by Durkheim between crime, punishment, expiation and religion, namely the understanding of them as social facts, is emphasized by other Durkheimians. In the present context, at least two other references are timely. The first is Robert Hertz's unfinished work on *Sin and Expiation* (see Chapter 5 here).

Among the Durkheimians Hertz was, as is well known, the most interested in the 'dark side of humanity', namely in the 'theme of impurity in all its forms' (Parkin 1996b: 17, 1996a; Riley, 2005a). Sin, as is obvious, is a part of Hertz's interest in impurity. If Durkheim and the Durkheimians generally stress the importance of ritual for social solidarity, Hertz stresses the other side of the coin, namely, sin as opposed to ritual action, where transgression of the moral code of society has to be redeemed by means of proper rituals of expiation. The elimination of sin, which in primitive societies equals to the elimination of *evil*, 'is one of the rites that form part of all systems of religious life' (Hertz 1994: 112).

However, the most significant problem Hertz faces in the introduction to his essay is the one related to the definition of sin (and correlatively that of expiation). Sin and expiation, Hertz maintains, are ideas widespread in the spiritual world of Christianity. Therefore, it is not easy to understand whether they are only Christian ideas or if they have a universal value (ibid.: 58–60). But the rejection of the ideas of sin and expiation as 'dark illusions', as Nietzsche argued, on the basis of their Christian definitions, would, according to Hertz, be a terrible mistake. What is required is a 'middle way between these two extremes' (ibid.: 60). As a consequence, most of Hertz's essay is dedicated to the radical criticism of 'rationalist' theologians and the ideas of sin propounded by liberal theologians. For them,[1] sin and pardon form the two extreme moments of an intimate drama which involves only two actors, God and the sinner. The entire action unfolds between these two beings. 'They stand alone, face to face, and are moved by the most generous, deepest feelings of the human heart, without the least constraint, without any suggestion coming from outside to interfere with the free and natural play of their spontaneity' (ibid.: 63). So, 'sincere contrition', 'internal dispositions' of the sinner, and 'individual feelings' are considered the essential elements of sin. According to Hertz, there is nothing irrational in this idea of sin. On the contrary, it is a perfect way to accommodate it 'in the dominant trends of the time' (ibid.: 64). However, the problem is that 'this is to take our contemporary and perhaps temporary desires as a measure of the reality' (ibid.). In fact, 'the *homo religiosus* of the new theology no more exists in reality than the *homo economicus* of classical economics' (ibid.: 69). In this way, liberal Protestant theologians and classical economists are dealt with in one fell swoop! The strict 'specialization and delimitation of religious society [is] in the domain of inner life' (ibid.: 111). It reflects a liberal Protestant bias that considers religious facts, 'past or present which do not fit such a conception ... survivals or pagan distortions of spiritual truth' (ibid.: 65). The point in this case is that contrary to the liberal Protestants' understanding, God and the sinner are not on the stage alone; they are not the only actors in the drama. If they believe in the saving power of expiation, it is because they 'both follow to a large extent the representations and sentiments that society has recommended to them' (ibid.: 66). In other words, even in contemporary spiritualized and individualized conceptions of sin and expiation there is still visible 'a complex tradition informing and determining the conscience [*conscience*] of the believer' (ibid.: 70). Tradition is, as always, according to the Durkheimians' critique of liberal Protestants' understanding of religion, the element neglected by rationalist thinkers. In tradition or, in the end, society: 'it is not the sinner who creates the sin; it is the sin that makes the sinner what he is' (ibid.: 71).

In order to free oneself from the bias of time and culture, Hertz follows an essentially perfect Durkheimian methodology (ibid.: 81–92). It is to 'withdraw ourselves from the religious and moral atmosphere in which we live'.

There is no better way than an ethnological study of 'a particular area of civilization' (ibid.: 91). For Hertz it was the study of the Polynesian totemism.

Based on comparative studies, Hertz maintains that sin and expiation are not just Christian phenomena; neither are they illusory. Basically, sin can be considered a 'transgression which, by the sole fact that it is carried out, tends to bring about death' (ibid.: 99). In the Christian world, this kind of transgression took an internal and spiritual form, so that to 'sin, it is enough that there be a bad intention, a purely subjective rebellion of the creature against the Creator' (ibid.: 107). This is how, among other things, modern societies distinguish sin from crime. Crime resides in 'the carrying out of a forbidden gesture' judged by a social apparatus (judges and penal codes), while sin emerges from a private disposition. But this is 'how the notion of sin presents itself to our conscience [*conscience*] today' (ibid.: 108). Throughout history, as previously emphasized, sin has been understood as something that naturally implies the sinner's subjective recognition, but also the recognition of a socially defined transgression (after all, it is sin that makes the sinner what he is!). At the same time, the expiation of sin presupposes contrition, which is an operation of individual conscience, but, as Parkin notes, 'Hertz still sees the operation of conscience … as a product of social forces, not of individual psychology' (Parkin 1996b: 42). Expiation, on the other hand, is defined by Hertz as follows: 'there is expiation when certain actions, which are in general ritualistic, are capable of re-establishing the state of things prior to the transgression by annulling it and by satisfying justice, without the transgressor and those near to him being crushed thereby' (Hertz 1994: 113). Here, what is more important is that 'elimination of evil' depends on certain kinds of rituals, rituals of expiation, which are a part of 'all systems of religious life' (ibid.: 112). As evil/sin is a social fact that draws its meaning from a tradition, a social moral code that it infringes, so expiation is a social thing too, a way to repair the violation of a shared moral code that takes the form of ritualistic actions.

Worth considering, although perhaps not quite so well known, is Paul Fauconnet's book on *La Responsabilité. Étude de sociologie* (1920).[2] This lengthy volume, dedicated 'à la mémoire de mon maître Emile Durkheim', examines the concept of responsibility from a perfectly Durkheimian perspective. After criticizing the main theories on responsibility, and drawing on ethnographical sources, Fauconnet maintains that 'responsibility of a more profound nature is a product of religious thought, or if one prefers, a product of the same causes that determine the characteristics of religious thought' (ibid: 221). At the beginning, there is no individual or subjective responsibility for sin: 'the cause of pain is not the criminal, but the crime itself' (ibid.: 233). As Hertz maintains that it is sin that makes the sinner what he is, so according to Fauconnet, 'It is not because there are people who are responsible that responsibility exists. Responsibility pre-exists, up in the air as it were, and then fixes itself on various objects'(ibid.: 244). Punishment, in primitive societies, is a true 'un-oriented' vengeance, that, in a not completely arbitrary manner, is transferred onto involved subjects, as a consequence of the well-known phenomenon of taint (Durkheim 1995c: 322–29).

It is only with the development of societies and religion that responsibility develops. Religion and responsibility develop from objectivism to subjectivism. Coherently with Durkheim and Hertz, Fauconnet maintains that the development of the concept of responsibility for evil is characterized by a double process of *individualization*, on the one hand, and *spiritualization*, on the other:

> In one sense, the individualisation of responsibility demands spiritualisation, because individuality is something essentially psychological. If, in the course of social evolution, the relative importance of the individual becomes greater, the conscience [*conscience*] will indeed be developed and enriched. Social life, to the degree that it becomes individualised, becomes more interiorised. The differentiation is one of consciences [*consciences*]. (Fauconnet 1920: 351)

Fauconnet describes in detail this process of individualization and spiritualization that makes responsibility as we know it today. However, once again in a Durkheimian spirit, Fauconnet, who was a graduate student of Durkheim, and not surprisingly against individualistic theories of the time, stresses two important elements. First, that the process of individualization and spiritualization of responsibility is the outcome of a struggle of 'antagonistic social forces': if society needs to punish crimes that offend the collective conscience, other social forces today resist blame. Since during history the individual has acquired importance, unknown up to now, the social interest for individual freedom begins to resist punishment:

> as respect, love and pity increasingly inspire mankind, they come together to limit and modify the notion of responsibility. In the light of this relation, the individualistic cult of the person does not only show itself in the partial interdiction of the treatments that debase or wrong the patient. It also adopts

> a positive form that is the interest that we have in the individual inclines society, which judges him, to understand him and *to put itself in his place*. Sympathy, in the true meaning of the word, opens the heart and mind to our fellow human beings and we carefully give ear to their inner lives. (ibid.: 312)

So, even the individualization and spiritualization of responsibility have to be understood in sociological terms. Secondly, these developments notwithstanding, the very nature of responsibility from primitive societies to modern ones does not change. In fact, a relevant counter-social force pushes responsibility towards new forms of 'reponsabilité communicable', or, in our own terms, towards collective responsibility. Modern penal law recognizes forms of 'responsabilité solidaire' non-distributive (i.e. of associations, foundations) that would seem to be a return to the 'ancient tradition' (ibid.: 340). But if these new cases of collective responsibility are possible it is both because 'individual' responsibility has been widely recognized, and because 'la personnalité des groupes a cessé d'être tenue pour une fiction' (ibid.: 341). So, in Fauconnet's understanding, sin/evil, punishment and responsibility are part and parcel of the same intellectual constellation; that even when this passes through a process of individualization and spiritualization, as in modern societies, it cannot be eradicated from its collective and social roots.

In short, above all after the ethnological shift and the so-called 'revelation' of 1895 (see Pickering 1984: 62ff.), crime, responsibility and punishment are understood within the Durkheimian tradition as deriving from an originally religious context, as secular heir of sin and expiation. However, notwithstanding secularization, individualization and spiritualization, they keep their religious overtones, and consequently continue to be understood as social facts, with the same characteristics of every other social fact. In other words, evil, sin and crime depend on social forces more than on individual agency, they affect society as a whole. Moral taint is a consequence of the social nature of evil. Responsibility is constitutively communicable. Collective expiation, namely collective agency usually *expressed* in ritualistic forms, is the only way to rescue a community from evil. Moral taint, which leaves none completely immune from the evil that affects a society, forces everyone, being part of a moral community, to feel involved in responsibility for evil. They feel involved in the process of expiation, and so render possible a sort of 'politics of compassion' that, as will be evident, is part of the Durkheimian legacy (see Wilkinson 2005: 128–34). All these characteristics of evil, sin, responsibility and expiation made the Durkheimians at odds with modern understanding of the same concepts. This understanding was based on a liberal and individualistic bias that at the time was found particularly in the religious writings studies of Protestant and Catholic modernists.

II. Evil and Responsibility in Contemporary Debate

Today, in the mainstream philosophical discussions on morality in relation to evil and responsibility, many of the individualistic prejudices the Durkheimians criticized are to be found. After Kant, moral philosophy placed a strong emphasis on personal responsibility and accountability for evil deeds (Bernstein 2002). Contemporary discourses on evil, more than on the theological and metaphysical implications of the idea of suffering, focus themselves on individual intentionality, imputability and so on (Cabrera 2001: 17–26; Rosati 2005). Modern and contemporary *Zeitgeist* seems to be incompatible with other views. The category of the subject, the 'who' committed such an evil deed, is usually considered not only the premise of every reflection on responsibility, but also the only one that makes sense. In its most extreme version, responsibility is taken as belonging essentially to the individual, since no one can be considered responsible for others (see Lewis 1991). The notion of 'collective responsibility' is 'barbarous', proper to 'primitive' peoples, to the 'ethic of tribes' or to a traditionalist theological culture, but absolutely incompatible with individualistic moral and epistemological premises (Lewis 1991; see Mellema 1997). In a milder version, still compatible with individualistic assumptions, responsibility can be shared, but never referred to 'superhuman', collective entities (see Sverdlik 1987). From these positions, the refusal of collective responsibility is part and parcel of a defence of Western culture: one of the ways in which contemporary Western culture

> is often contrasted with 'primitive cultures' is in the manner in which moral responsibility is conceived. People in some primitive cultures supposedly think in terms of entire tribes bearing responsibility for the violation of mores or breaching of taboos by one member of the tribe. This collective way of thinking about moral responsibility is based upon the idea of guilt of one individual being transmitted to all members of a clan or tribe and is quite foreign to contemporary Western ways of thinking about moral responsibility. Also, foreign to contemporary Western ways of thinking is the idea that responsibility can be eliminated by destroying a symbolic object such as a voodoo doll. (Mellema 1997: 2)

However, especially after Auschwitz, there are reasons to rethink the very meaning of responsibility (and evil) (Bernstein 2002). As is well-known, Karl Jaspers was the first to reflect on the notions of guilt and responsibility in relation to German identity after the end of the Second World War. He distinguishes between legal, moral, political and metaphysical guilt. According to him, legal and moral guilt are necessarily and always individual. He considers guilt from a legal and/or a moral point of view as that of a whole nation, i.e., it would be, first of all, an 'epistemological mistake', since a *sui generis* identity such as 'the English people', 'the Norwegians', 'the Jews' and so on, just does not exist (Jaspers

2000). On the contrary, political guilt is almost constitutively a collective concept. However, Jaspers also recognizes that sometimes there is something like collective guilt, from a moral point of view, imbued in a collective way of life of which the individual is part. Being part of a community implies sharing – not only from a political, but also from a moral point of view – those habits and feelings that can be related to evil deeds of a political community and its government.

> The Germans – i.e. those who speak the German language – feel affected by everything that springs from the German soul. We are no longer speaking in terms of the responsibility of each citizen of a single nation. On the contrary, it is the state of feeling affected and involved on the part of those who in their status as men are part of German moral and spiritual life together with others of the same language, of the same origin and of the same destiny, a state to which, one cannot simply apply the term guilt but rather something similar to complicity. Moreover, we do not feel simply that we are participating in what is happening in the present, in the sense of complicity only in the agency of our contemporaries, but also in everything that forms part of our own traditions'. (Jaspers 2000)

Here the individual as part of a chain of memory is also influenced by the evil deeds of fellow citizens, even if the individual cannot be considered guilty from a legal point of view.

Hannah Arendt develops her theory of responsibility dialectically with Jaspers and in the same context (see Bernstein 2002: ch. 8; Neiman 2002: ch. 4). Like Jaspers, she refuses to accord any legitimacy to the idea of collective guilt. 'Guilt and innocence', she writes, 'make sense only if applied to individuals' (Arendt 1964: 29). Guilt is related to individual agency, and so is responsibility: 'where all are guilty, no one is'; only in a metaphorical sense can one talk about responsibility for things the individual has not done. Otherwise, the result of a spontaneous admission of collective guilt could be an 'unintended white-wash of those who *had* done something' (ibid.: 28). However, her criticism of collective guilt notwithstanding, Arendt recognizes that Auschwitz is not understandable without extending responsibilities beyond those of Hitler and the Nazi officials. Like Primo Levi, while criticizing the so-called cog theory (Arendt 2003), she indicates the vast area of widespread responsibilities of ordinary people unable 'to think' and 'to judge' (Arendt 1965–66, 1978, 1982) who made Auschwitz possible. So, while defendng a very individualistic and 'Socratic' theory of responsibility and judgment,[3] Arendt maintains, for example, the necessity of a *symbolic act* on the part of the German Federal Republic[4] to expiate collective responsibilities to reconcile – if possible – divided memories, and to strengthen the feeling of a common humanity (Traverso 1997).

The non-tenability of a classical concept of (individual) responsibility to face new challenges has been stressed also by Hans Jonas. With reference above all to ecological global challenges, Jonas formulates a new 'imperative' to substitute the Kantian one. The new one, capable of meeting new social conditions, would sound more or less like this: 'Act in such a way that the consequences of your actions are compatible with the permanence of an authentic life on earth' (Jonas 1985: 35). What is clear from the beginning is the difference between the two: 'the new imperative is directed more towards public policy rather than towards private action, to which it is inapplicable. The Kantian categorical imperative is directed at the individual, and the present is its temporal dimension' (ibid.): a stringent example is the ethics of intentionality. On the contrary, the new 'principle responsibility' has a public dimension, and its temporal dimension is the future. Now, it is clear that global challenges, for example, ecological challenges, the future of human nature with reference to new bio-technologies, questions of global justice etc., cannot be dealt with on the basis of an individualistic ethics of intentionality.

More recently, several moral philosophers have been attempting to think about collective responsibility without regressing into 'primitive' conceptions. Here I would like to mention just a few. D.E. Cooper (1991) criticizes the methodological individualism of Lewis and others, maintaining that in some circumstances the ascribing of collective responsibility cannot be reduced to ascribing responsibility to individuals. Virginia Held (1991) and Stanley Bates (1991) attempt to show that collective responsibility can be ascribed above all to random groups – such as passengers in a subway car – more than to organized groups. Larry May, perhaps one of the most important contemporary writers on the subject, develops a 'social existential' approach to moral responsibility – inspired by Karl Jaspers, Martin Heidegger and Jean Paul Sartre. It is aimed as a corrective to the dominant Western tradition of morality. First of all, he expands the category of agency from individual to collective agency and, secondly, ascribes moral responsibility to people who hold attitudes or traits of their personality, such as insensitivity, with the foreseen potential for causing harm, for example, cases of racism and racial violence. Finally, according to May, collective action, coming together in groups, is an essential element in compensating limits of individual agency (see May 1991a). Joel Feinberg, criticizing the idea that collective responsibility can be only proper of 'primitive' groups and societies, maintains the necessity of finding an 'index' to solidarity, and that 'there is perhaps no better index to solidarity than vicarious pride and shame' (Feinberg 1991: 63). Vicarious pride and shame will be more frequent in what Swinburne calls a 'nurturing community' (Swinburne 1989), namely a community in which the mutual benefit conferred upon all of us within the community creates obligations among the members towards one another, and further, a community in which we feel in debt to the 'fathers' of the community. In such a community, members would have to share the 'burden of guilt', would have to help their fellows to bear their burden of guilt. In other words, as Mellema reminds us, in a nurturing community, we all have moral responsibilities toward others in our community. Among other things, we have responsibilities to deter others from wrongdoing. And, more significantly, we have responsibilities to help others in our communities with their burden. Thus, when a member of a community has a significant burden, then the community has a responsibility to share this burden. (Mellema 1997: 57)

In addition to this general reassessment of collective responsibility and related concepts, there is also another concept, familiar to Durkheimians, that has been recovered in current debates on guilt and responsibility, namely, 'moral taint'. Even if moral taint has been understood in a number of different ways, it seems that it can play a useful role in distinguishing moral guilt from shame for evil deeds – carried out by people with whom we have connections – that we could not prevent (see Appiah 1991; May 1991b; Mellema 1997: ch. 7). We can be tainted by the wrongdoing of others, and shame can be our response to this wrongdoing that faces our moral integrity, without being directly guilty for that wrongdoing. In this sense, taint can be a way of thinking of moral connection among each other in specific circumstances without falling back into regressive conceptions of responsibility.[5]

However, this *philosophical* reassessment of collective responsibility notwithstanding, *collective representations* of responsibility seem in our Western societies far from being less than individualistic. If we do not feel responsible for the acts of others, it depends on the nature of the social groups we belong to. Are there today social groups from which we can exit without losing our own personal identity? As Adam Seligman maintains:

> This possibility of exit brings us to the analytic heart of the matter. For what of those groups from which we cannot exit without losing ourselves, groups from which our withdrawal would in some fundamental sense make us other than we are? What of groups that are constitutive of who we are, rather than simply groups where our membership is voluntary and instrumental toward realizing a certain goal? (Seligman 2000: 75)

In order to feel ashamed for the acts of others, 'one must be tied to others in ways beyond the contractual' (ibid.: 80) and the instrumental, in ways that make a group constitutive of our identity rather than simply instrumental. So, feeling ashamed of or 'tainted' by evil deeds of others is possible only if we feel part of a community. Looking at the relation between responsibility and belonging from another perspective, Arendt wrote that,

> Vicarious responsibility for things we have not done, this taking upon ourselves the consequences for things we are entirely innocent of, is the price we pay for the fact we live our lives not by ourselves but among our fellow men and that the faculty of action, which, after all, is the political faculty par excellence, can be actualized only in one of the many and manifold forms of human community. (Arendt 1968: 50)

If vicarious responsibility is the price, it seems that for modern societies it is too high a price, and that modern individuals choose loneliness in exchange for being left alone.

However, there is no need to adopt an anti-modernist attitude to see the impoverishment implied in the loss of the lexicon of mutual responsibility. A number of cases, taken from different societies, countries, even personal experiences, could be mentioned to show that what is too high is the price paid for rescuing ourselves from the burden of taking upon ourselves vicarious responsibility. The price is the loss of justice, solidarity and consequently inner loneliness.

III. The Durkheimian Legacy

According to Wilkinson, Durkheim's sociology is a 'sociological theory which accounts for why suffering is experienced as a profound sense of inner loneliness and/or as the morbid feeling of being divided against ourselves', and it suggests that 'this may be accompanied at the same time by a greater sensitivity to the suffering of others' (Wilkinson 2005: 77). Above all, in modern societies, the ones in which the cult of individualism seems to be the only possible shared faith, 'feelings of sympathy for the suffering of humanity' (ibid.: 129), or in Durkheim's words 'sympathy for all that is human, a broader pity for all sufferings, for all human miseries, a more ardent desire to combat them and mitigate them, a greater thirst of justice' (Durkheim 1898c, quoted in Wilkinson 2005: 129) could be the premise for a 'politics of compassion that would bring critical attention to bear upon the ways in which the problem of suffering is made to be a part of our social consciousness' (ibid.: 128–29). More violence and precariousness dominate our world, and more mourning would have to inspire solidarity and justice (see Butler 2004).

Mutual responsibility is among the words modernity lost. Restoring this concept to our vocabulary is essential for progressive policies of international and domestic justice and solidarity, for nurturing anamnestic solidarity towards the victims of past evils. However, without feelings of belonging to constitutive groups, there can be no sense of collective responsibility. As long as our representations of evil and responsibility are individualized, there will be no room for vicarious and mutual responsibility, and for the awareness of the importance of symbolic and ritualistic actions of collective expiation in the making and remaking of social solidarity. Herein lies, in my opinion, the importance of the Durkheimian legacy. The Durkheimians fought a harsh battle against the individualization and spiritualization of categories such as evil, sin and responsibility, showing that the categories were basically the outcome of a more general process typical of modern societies that had no universal value. If the Durkheimians could be more than tolerant about Australian totemism and primitive religions, and, on the other hand, critical about

Protestant and Catholic modernism, it was because the former had something to teach to modern societies. With reference to evil and responsibility, Durkheim's (above all later) and his disciples' sociology seem to suggest that modern Western societies must be willing to reassess themselves, not in terms of self-betrayal but with courage and humility, rather than pretentiously displaying their values, bringing them down from the sky in the shape of bombs or other weapons (see Rosati 2008).

Acknowledgements

I am grateful to Maureen Galvin for her generous help in the revision of a first version of this chapter.

Notes

1. For an historical framing see Robert Parkin's and W.S.F. Pickering's Introduction and Preface to Hertz (1994).
2. On Fauconnet, see Besnard (1983).
3. In a number of writings, after the formulation of the controversial notion of the 'banality of evil', Arendt focused on the lack in modern societies of what she called a 'Socratic morality' according to which 'wrong would be whatever I cannot bear to have done, and the wrongdoer would be somebody unfit for intercourse, especially for the thinking intercourse with himself' (Arendt 1965 – 66: 124). From this perspective, evil depends on the inability to think and to judge, and morality is a matter of *personal ethos* much more than a matter of collective norms. This is a very un-Durkheimian point. After the experience of Auschwitz – and also after the new reconversion of Germans to democratic values – Arendt developed a strong distrust towards collective, social morality. Germans proved capable of embracing the Nazis' commandment 'Thou shalt kill' instead of the old one 'Thou shalt not kill', and vice versa, revealing the true meaning of social morality: 'It was as though morality, at the very moment of its total collapse within an old and highly civilized world, stood revealed in the original meaning of the word, as a set of *mores*, of customs and manners, which could be exchanged for another set with no more trouble than it would take to change the table manners of a whole people' (ibid.: 43).
4. The Federal Republic did not proffer any symbolic act until Willy Brandt, in 1970, 'took the burden of the collective guilt of the nation' even though he was innocent as a person, with his now famous action of kneeling while visiting the monument for the victims of the ghetto in Warsaw, and showed the importance of public rituals (rituals of confession in this case), see Giesen (2004: 131).
5. For a fascinating discussion of evil, expiation, responsibility and guilt in the Old Testament, see Von Rad (1962, Vol. 1).

Chapter 8

The Hague Tribunal: Critical Reflections Prompted by Durkheim's Remarks on Suffering

John B. Allcock

I. By Way of Personal Background

This chapter was originally given as a paper for a Study Day in June, 2004, convened by the British Centre for Durkheimian Studies in Oxford. My agreement to undertake the task was shaped by two coincidences. Bill Pickering, the convener, asked me if I would do it the week after the Madrid train bombings. Among my first responses to his invitation was a question. Could Durkheim have had anything interesting to offer in relation to a world which now seems, in many respects, to be so different from his? Two thoughts followed hard on the heels of my own question. The first took the form of images of *la semaine sanglante* (Bloody Week) during which the Paris Commune was savagely suppressed, and the Dreyfus Affair, which shaped the political world in which Durkheim wrote, and perhaps his own political consciousness. The second was the realization that the discipline of sociology has had very little to say on the topic of suffering, preferring to leave this to ethics, or even psychology, and perhaps it is appropriate that we should try to correct that. Given this incentive, what better place to begin than Durkheim, whose aspiration was to found *la science de la morale*?

It is also a fortunate coincidence that for several years now my primary research interest has been the study of the International Criminal Tribunal for the Former Yugoslavia (the ICTY, or for present purposes 'The Hague Tribunal'). My central interests in this institution have fallen within the sociology of politics, and in particular the political consequences of the war crimes process for the states of the former Yugoslav federation. Nevertheless, at the time of Bill Pickering's approach I was working on the events surrounding the creation of the ICTY, and had been struck very forcefully by the fact that without the wave of public outrage which had mounted during 1992 and 1993 over the dreadful events in the Balkans, it is unlikely that the Tribunal would have been founded by UN Security Council Resolution 817, on 25 May 1993. This important innovation in international law can be seen in large measure to have come about because of a widespread popular response to stories of suffering, in the form of 'ethnic cleansing', detention camps, rape and military attacks on civilians.

As a long-term admirer of E.E. Evans-Pritchard, I took these two coincidences as a manifestation of *kwoth* – of 'spirit' – which signalled that it would be auspicious to take up this invitation to reflect upon suffering within a sociological framework.[1] The question arises, however, of the point of articulation between a Durkheimian intellectual context and the specific historical and empirical concerns embodied in my own research. At first the prospects seem limited, because, as Pickering has pointed out, Durkheim's own commitment to liberal humanism inclined him towards a somewhat optimistic view of the world, in which the problem of theodicy occupied a rather peripheral place (1984: 129, 491–94). Nevertheless, several possibilities present themselves.

I start out from the common perception that a significant aspect of the importance of war crimes trials is their value as a response to the suffering of the victims of crime. Summarizing the goals articulated by advocates of the ICTY, including its own officials, an international team of scholars recently placed at the head of their list the following outcomes: 'achieving justice for the victims of violations, and promoting reconciliation among the states and peoples of the region' (Scholars Initiative 2004: 3). As the argument goes, neither of these aims is possible unless the suffering of victims is openly recognized, and the response to it perceived to be just. The Hague Tribunal, through the collection, presentation and testing of evidence, the determination of responsibility and the meting out of punishment, supposedly has a crucial part to play in this process.

The critique which I intend to develop here, however, challenges the expectation that the ICTY (and courts like it) can constitute a fully adequate response to the suffering of the victims of the crimes which they try. My reasons for advancing this view have to do with how we understand suffering; and I find that a very useful point of departure in making that case is provided by Emile Durkheim's observations about suffering and its functions in society.[2]

II. Durkheim on Suffering

Durkheim appears to have addressed suffering in two of its aspects, both of which are most clearly delineated in *The Elementary Forms of the Religious Life* (see Chapter 2 here).[3] The first is his discussion of the 'negative cult', and the second his observations about 'piacular rites'.

In defining the term 'negative cult' Durkheim takes as his point of departure his celebrated distinction between the sacred and the profane, and the importance in ritual life of maintaining the separation between the two realms.

> A whole group of rites has the object of realizing this state of separation which is essential. Since their function is to prevent undue mixings and to keep one of these two domains from encroaching upon the other, they are only able to impose abstentions or negative acts ... They do not prescribe certain acts to the faithful, but confine themselves to forbidding certain ways of acting; so they all take the form of interdictions. (1915d: 299–300)

Subsequently he tells us that: 'owing to the barrier which separates the sacred from the profane, a man cannot enter into intimate relations with sacred things except after ridding himself of all that is profane in him'(ibid.: 309). He then goes on to examine in some detail the 'fasts and vigils or retreats and silence' and other privations which might be deployed to bring about this end.

> But abstinences and privations do not come without suffering. We hold to the profane world by all the fibres of our flesh; our senses attach us to it; our life depends upon it. It is not merely the theatre of our activity; it penetrates us from every side; it is a part of ourselves. So we cannot detach ourselves from it without doing violence to our nature and without painfully wounding our instincts. In other words, the negative cult cannot develop without causing suffering. Pain is one of its necessary conditions. (ibid.: 312)

In the 'negative cult', then, suffering is essential to those ritual experiences by which the boundary is marked between the sacred and the profane, and which by placing them on the side of the sacred constitutes individuals as members of the community.

This 'negative cult' is to be distinguished, according to Durkheim, from 'piacular rites'. These are rites which are performed in expiation of or atonement for something. As Durkheim himself recognizes, it is not always easy to distinguish between these and the 'negative cult'; nevertheless, he endeavours to do so:

> Even though the motions may be the same, the sentiments expressed are different and even opposed. Likewise, the ascetic rites [i.e. the 'negative cult'] certainly imply privations, abstinences and mutilations, but ones which must be borne with an impassive firmness and serenity. Here [i.e. in the case of piacular rites], on the contrary, dejection, cries and tears are the rule. The ascetic [engaged in the negative cult] tortures himself in order to prove, in his own eyes and those of his fellows, that he is above suffering. During mourning [in this case a piacular rite], men injure themselves to prove that they suffer. (ibid.: 396)

My purpose in making reference to Durkheim here is not to indicate that I subscribe without reservation to a Durkheimian account of suffering. This chapter, I emphasize, is not an exegesis of canonical scripture! His ideas, even so, do have value in at least two respects. They remind us, first, that suffering can serve an important function in public and symbolic discourse. It can have meaning both for those who suffer and those who witness their suffering. Second, however, the significance of pain is not that *individuals* suffer, but that their suffering carries meaning and value within *collective* life. We are prompted to enquire more closely, therefore, into the circumstances in which the public rehearsal or celebration of suffering might or might not acquire value in this way.

III. Individual and Collective Suffering

The central point which I wish to develop here relates to the fact that in Durkheim's analysis suffering expressly is not confined in its significance to the *individual*. Suffering is relevant and interesting precisely because, and under circumstances in which, it takes on a *collective* colouring. The interest of this idea can be illustrated and explored in the context of international humanitarian law.

One of the persisting causes of puzzlement and irritation on the part of international lawyers involved in the war crimes process in The Hague is that the character of the Tribunal is 'misunderstood' or 'misrepresented' within the region which is the object of its activity. In international criminal law indictments may only be issued against individuals, and the trial consists of a process by which their personal responsibility (or otherwise) for the actions in question is tested. For this reason, issues relating to whether the conflict in question may be said to be a 'just war' are beyond the competence of the court to determine – and indeed they are irrelevant. It is logically possible for a war which is manifestly 'unjust' to be fought with complete professionalism on the part of the combatants. Equally, it is possible that in the course of a war which is agreed generally to be 'just', individuals might commit acts which all observers would agree to be atrocious, contrary to the 'laws and customs of war' and deserving of punishment. When the Tribunal issues indictments against individuals, therefore, it is expressly without reference to the justice or injustice of the cause which they served. Neither does it take into consideration a wider analysis of the causes that might have brought about that conflict.

Likewise, the opprobrium of having committed these actions is intended to fall entirely upon the individuals in question, and implies no general condemnation of the political or religious group, the ethnic group or culture, to which they belong. The Statute of the Tribunal, in its first five articles, repeats the phrase that 'the International Tribunal shall have the power to prosecute *persons* ...' . Article 7(1) states that:

> A person who planned, instigated, ordered, committed or otherwise aided and abetted in the planning, preparation or execution of a crime referred to in articles 2–5 of the present Statute, shall be *individually* responsible for the crime.[4]

Indictments issued by the Office of the Prosecutor (OTP), therefore, are invariably against named individuals; and, what is more, it is necessary for the prosecution to demonstrate in the course of the trial that the accused was personally responsible for actions listed in the indictment, which invariably list specific places and individual, named, victims.[5] Looked at from the point of view of suffering, therefore, only the suffering of individuals is reckoned to be relevant to the Hague Tribunal – whether this be the suffering of victims, or that which must be visited upon the perpetrators of crimes, by way of punishment.

It is a matter that constantly gives rise to annoyance and puzzlement on the part of the Tribunal, however, that this explicit commitment to the personal character of suffering is frequently ignored in the response to the Tribunal on the part of people from the Yugoslav region. The Office of the Prosecutor is regularly required to rebut allegations to the effect that the ICTY denigrates the Croatian state, or is a part of a deliberate attempt to demonize the Serbs, or fails to take adequate account of the fact that Bosnian Muslims were the victims, as a group, of a genocidal programme. In each case the language in terms of which the Tribunal is criticized adopts phrases which express both guilt and suffering in *collective* terms. This discrepancy in perceptions lies at the heart of the problems which the ICTY has experienced in gaining acceptance in the region.

There can be little doubt that in some measure this kind of misconstruction of the nature of the Tribunal and its work is both deliberate and mischievous, and is undertaken in pursuit of some political intention apart from the achievement of justice. Nevertheless, these views do seem to be so widespread and deeply rooted in popular discourse in the region that I do not believe that they can be explained solely by reference to manipulation. In the central part of the chapter, therefore, I turn to an examination of the factors which have made for the recurrent 'collectivization' of suffering within rhetorics surrounding the ICTY and the war crimes which it tries.[6] In this attempt I look at two aspects of this 'collectivization' process. The first has to do with the way in which the policies of the Tribunal itself can be seen to open the door inadvertently to an emphasis upon communal guilt. The second has to do with the ways in which the actions of the ICTY in prosecuting alleged offenders from the region resonate with local interpretations of the nature and origins of 'The Wars of the Yugoslav Succession', producing rhetorics of collective 'victimhood', and hence communal images of suffering.

IV. ICTY Policy and the 'Collectivization' of Suffering

The scale of suffering occasioned by the wars in the former Yugoslavia was enormous. Early in 1996, shortly after the Dayton Agreements (which ended the conflict in Bosnia) came into force, the UNHCR (United Nations High Commissioner for Refugees) estimated that 686,533 refugees from Bosnia and Hercegovina were located in countries outside the former Yugoslavia and a further 645,300 within other republics of the former Socialist Federation (UNHCR, No. 3–4, 1996: 10–11). At the time, it was estimated that 2,400,000 persons were either 'internally displaced' or 'war affected (vulnerable cases)' (ibid.). I have yet to locate a systematic and comprehensive reckoning of the dead and injured during these conflicts. Nevertheless, it has been estimated reliably that in Bosnia around 100,000 people died.[7] An official Croatian estimate reported that the war in Croatia had left 13,583 people dead or missing, and 37,180 wounded.[8] No authoritative estimate of Serbian casualties appears to be available. Particularly sensitive – and controversial – during the war were the large number of cases of rape that were reported. Although it is highly probable that the numbers of these were subject to propagandistic inflation by various sides, there can be no doubt (even in the absence of accurate statistics) that these ran into many thousands.[9] Relatively early in the war a French source identified no fewer than fifty-six of the notorious detention camps, located throughout Bosnia and Hercegovina (Nouvel Observateur 1993: 477–86).

The scale of suffering adumbrated crudely and incompletely by these figures is enormous. Many of these casualties will have been 'normal' casualties of war, among the combatants. Nevertheless, the prominence and frequency of reports of the bombardment of civilian targets, detention of non-combatants, rape, torture and 'ethnic cleansing' suggest that a high proportion of these casualties will be the results of criminal actions, and the possible number of perpetrators of war crimes will be very large indeed. It became evident from the earliest days of the operation of the Hague Tribunal that it would never be possible to bring to justice all of those responsible. Even though the availability of evidence adequate to support a prosecution would naturally limit these numbers, it would be necessary for the OTP to formulate some policy regarding the priorities which would govern the issuing of indictments. In addition to the need to ensure that evidence could be collected which might make a conviction a realistic possibility, two other important criteria have shaped the pattern of prosecutions. The more serious the crime, the more likely it is that those responsible will be pursued by the OTP. Prosecutions will attempt to 'ascend the ladder of responsibility', ensuring that those in political or military authority, who might be regarded as exercising command responsibility for actions, are more likely to be indicted than individual 'foot-soldiers' who were merely agents of their orders.[10] For these reasons the efforts of the Tribunal have been concentrated on ensuring that individuals such as Slobodan Milošević and Biljana Plavšić, or Radovan Karadžić and Ratko Mladić, are brought to book.

Whereas this policy is entirely understandable in pragmatic terms, it has tended to produce a regrettable, unintended consequence. It is impossible to separate prominent individuals of this kind from their *representative* status. Radovan Karadžić can never be put on trial simply as a private individual who happened to be accused of several serious misdemeanours. He is inevitably perceived as the former leader of Bosnian Serbs in their struggle to ensure that Bosnia was taken into a unified Serb state. Ratko Mladić could never appear at The Hague as no more than the man alleged to be responsible for the massacre at Srebrenica. For Serbs he is primarily the military hero who almost achieved the goal of a unified state, and in pursuit of that aim was willing to defy the might of NATO.

To speak in these terms, however, means that one goes beyond the identification of these individuals (and others like them) as indicted war criminals. At the end of 1993 Bosnian Serb forces controlled perhaps 70 per cent of the territory of the former Yugoslav republic of Bosnia and Hercegovina, and appeared to be on the verge of victory.[11] By the end of 1995, however, things had begun to fall apart to the point at which, aided and abetted by NATO, a joint Bosnian government and Croatian offensive was threatening Banja Luka, and Bosnian Serb forces appeared to be on the verge of a catastrophic defeat, averted by the imposition of the Dayton Agreements which brought the war to a close. Although granted some minimal semblance of statehood, in the form of an ethnic Serb 'entity' within a reunified Bosnia and Hercegovina (*Republika Srpska*), they have been denied, perhaps permanently, the possibility of the unification of all Serbs in one state. In their situation of unexpected defeat and subsequent resentful isolation, therefore, Karadžić and Mladić have taken on a *collective* significance, in which their relentless pursuit by international forces has become a continuing symbol of Bosnian Serb humiliation and 'demonization'.

A story which is similar in some important respects can be told in Croatia. Indictments issued by the Office of the Prosecutor against several former high-ranking Croatian generals have elicited a response of outrage within Croatia, and have resulted in embarrassment for the government, which since the death of the former President Franjo Tudjman has insisted in principle upon the importance of cooperation with the Tribunal. The indictments, in particular, issued against Generals Mirko Norac and Ante Gotovina were construed as undermining the moral basis of the 'Homeland War', which secured independence for Croatia from the former Yugoslavia.[12] For many Croats, it seems, in the hierarchy of moral values the suffering of individuals (the victims of war crimes) ought to occupy a lower level of significance than those actions which resulted in the salvation of the collective dignity of the nation. The prosecution of these men could not be passed off as the visitation of justice upon guilty individuals: it involved a challenge to the very legitimacy of the statehood of Croatia, which had been secured through their actions.

In both of these situations we confront a common problem. The ICTY insists that only individuals stand trial in The Hague, and for crimes of which they are personally accused. In punishing the guilty, therefore, only individuals are required to suffer in expiation of their crimes. This construction of events, however, fails to take account of the manner in which key individuals, who held positions of special political or military responsibility, acquire a public standing such that to place them on trial becomes, in effect, to place the nation on trial. Their punishment comes to be seen as a punishment inflicted upon the whole nation, and their suffering, consequently, takes on the character of collective suffering.

V. Rhetorics of 'Victimhood'

The process of the 'collectivization' of suffering can be illustrated further in relation to the kinds of rhetoric about 'victimhood' which have been developed by different ethnic groups involved in the Yugoslav wars. Once again, these arise in part as an unintended consequence of the nature of the war crimes process. Because, in the nature of the case, the justice or otherwise of the war is expressly beyond the competence of the Tribunal, it is difficult to create the conditions under which a public, independent and objective account of the causes of the conflict, and the character of the struggles which ensued, can be arrived at.[13] In the historiographic limbo which results, therefore, interested, partial and indeed ideologically heavily distorted accounts of events are able to gain currency. Serbs, Croats and Bošnjaci (Bosnians of the Muslim cultural tradition) have all developed rhetorics about the war which place at their centre a view of their people as essentially *victims*. The wars are defined, in other words, in relation to their suffering as communities, and communities are differentiated symbolically by the accounts of their experience as victims to which they subscribe.

An important characteristic of the distribution of ethnic groups in pre-war Yugoslavia was the relatively dispersed settlement of ethnic Serbs. The largest ethnic group in pre-war Yugoslavia was the Serbs, with 35 per cent of the total population. Only 75 per cent of those who declared themselves to be Serbs in the 1991 census, however, actually lived in the Republic of Serbia (as opposed to 98 per cent of Slovenes who lived in Slovenia, or 95 per cent of Macedonians who lived in Macedonia). Large Serb minorities were to be found in particular in Bosnia and Hercegovina (where they constituted 31 per cent of the population of that republic) and in Croatia (11 per cent). The prospect of the break-up of the federation into primarily ethnic states was experienced as especially threatening to Serbs, for whom Yugoslavia represented the only possibility of their living together in a single state.

The contradictory situation of Serbs within Yugoslavia was taken up as a major political issue in the famous *Memorandum* drafted by a group of members of the Serbian Academy, and leaked to the press in 1986. This set out the argument that Serbia had been disadvantaged systematically from an economic point of view throughout the post-1945 period and made the startling claim that Serbs within Yugoslavia had been subjected to 'cultural genocide'. These concerns were used manipulatively by Slobodan Milošević, who became head of the ruling League of Communists in Serbia in 1987, in his subsequent attempt to take control of the federation.

Although the attempt to hold together Yugoslavia by armed force was represented as 'aggression' by Slovenes, Croats and Bosnian Muslims, to Serbs it constituted a natural and justified response to an illegal secession from the federation on the part of other republics, backed by the 'international community'. In this process, Serbs resident in other republics would no longer be citizens on the same footing as all other Yugoslavs, but reduced to minority status, and as such second-class citizens, in states dominated by other ethnic groups.

Consequently, rhetorics about the war in Serbia have used terms such as the 'destruction' or 'breaking up' of Yugoslavia, rather than its 'disintegration', 'dissolution' or 'death' – the former emphasizing a violent action visited upon the country, rather than a process that might be considered natural, however, unfortunate. Serbs have portrayed themselves as victims of a succession of injuries, ranging from the support of the secessionist states by the European Community, guided by the judgments of the Badinter Commission; through economic sanctions; the mounting press criticism of the conduct of the war; the de facto evasion of the UN arms embargo by Bosnian government and Croatian forces; and culminating in the NATO bombing campaign which compelled the Serbian government to abandon its attempt to take control of Kosovo by armed force. Serb accounts of the end of Yugoslavia tend to focus upon the ejection of Serbs from Croatia and Kosovo (as well as, to a much lesser extent, their displacement from parts of Bosnia and Hercegovina). The Tribunal in The Hague has become just one more significant element in this litany of wounds inflicted on the nation.

This may be a highly selective and indeed in some respects wildly distorted account of the history of the past two decades, but it is one which retains a widespread currency among Serbs, and which places at its heart the image of suffering Serbia.[14] One reason for its currency is the manner in which this conceptualization of Serbs as victims resonates with the legendary account of the defeat of the mediaeval Serb kingdom by Ottoman forces at the Battle of Kosovo in 1389, which came to be enshrined in a body of folk literature. In these epic poems, the Serb armies are defeated because their prince, Lazar, chooses in a dream the heavenly over the earthly crown, sanctifying defeat and the consequent suffering of the nation through subjugation by the Turks, and justifying the image of Serbs as a *nebeski narod* – a 'heavenly people'.[15]

Croats, as I have suggested, are likely to interpret 'The Wars of the Yugoslav Succession' in terms of external aggression. This is indicated in the term *Domovinski rat* – the 'Homeland War' – to describe this experience. The theme of aggression is also implied in the use of the term *četnik* to refer to Serb insurgents within Croatia. This was the name adopted by the Serb nationalist guerrilla forces which operated in Yugoslavia during the Second World War. Its rhetorical force is augmented by the fact that it had been delegitimated already in Titoist discourse, and tainted by notions of collaboration with fascism. The role of the Yugoslav Peoples' Army in the war (the JNA) is also undermined by 'serbianizing' it – even during the period when it might have laid legitimate claim to specifically *all-Yugoslav* status.[16] By repeating claims that the armed forces were dominated by ethnic Serbs, which despite their Yugoslav title were in fact close collaborators with Slobodan Milošević in pursuit of the project of creating a 'Greater Serbia' (i.e. not in pursuit of the continuing integrity of Yugoslavia) the *otherness* of the forces against which Croats fought is emphasized.

Croat explanations of the reasons for the war dwell frequently on the supposed existence of a consistently pursued plan of territorial expansion, conceived during the nineteenth century by the Serbian statesman Ilija Garašanin, and shaping Serbian aspirations down to the present day, for the achievement of a 'Great Serbia'. Foiled by the creation of a semi-autonomous Croatian *banovina* (governorship) within the first Yugoslavia in 1938 (and for some, by the Nazi puppet state of 1944–45), but realized in a disguised form in socialist Yugoslavia, this grand design was taken up again by Milošević after 1987. The achievement of an independent Croatia, therefore, is more than a mere consequence of the collapse of Yugoslavia: it signifies the defeat of a historical project of Serbian aggression against Croatia, extending over nearly two centuries.

The imagery of external aggression is sustained in specific events which, for Croats, have come to stand for the war as a whole – the siege of Vukovar, the attack on Dubrovnik, and the bombardment of Zagreb with rockets. Croats too, it seems, were victims – victims once again of external aggression – and it is their suffering that defines not only the war but also the Croat nation.[17]

A third rhetoric of victimhood is encountered among the *Bošnjak* population of Bosnia and Hercegovina, which centres in the main upon the accusation of genocide – the very purpose of the war, they claim, was to eliminate them as a people. To an important extent claims about the genocidal character of the war are lent credence by the rhetorics of the *antemurale* of Christendom against the threat of Islam, adopted by both

Croats and Serbs. Indeed, there has been a strongly anti-Muslim element to Serb propaganda throughout the period in question.[18] The derogatory term *balija* is routinely used by Serbs to describe Muslims – a word which denigrates them as crude and backward. Just as Croats sought to denigrate Serb forces by use of the name *četnik*, in turn Serbs emphasized the alien character of Muslim fighters by labelling them all as *mujahedin*. There was, indeed, a vigorous propaganda campaign to delegitimate the government of Bosnia and Hercegovina, and forces committed to its aim of preserving of a unified, *multi-ethnic* Bosnian state, by reducing them to the level of a specifically *Muslim* faction.[19]

The accusation of genocide is, of course, a particularly powerful one, drawing its force inevitably from that other major European experience of genocide, the Nazi 'final solution' to 'the Jewish question'. Although, in the light of events in Srebrenica and elsewhere, accusations of genocide might seem to be simple statements of fact, it is important to note that a selection is being made here, with respect to the salient characteristics of the war. The Bosnian government position repeatedly emphasized the importance of its *constitutional* aims, in the preservation of a unified, multi-ethnic Bosnian state. To characterize the war in terms of genocide would seem to give special prominence to the significance of the suffering of one ethnic group, allowing the allegiance of many ethnic Croats and Serbs (and others) to that unified state to fall into the background. The choice of genocide as a rhetorical focus, however, highlights the suffering of Bosnians, in a way that constitutional issues could not. Genocide is, by definition, action directed against a *group as a whole*: so that the rhetorical force of the appeal to genocide underscores the *common* suffering of the group which is victimized.

VI. Conclusion: Towards a Sociology of Suffering

It is tempting to try to make the account of war crimes and responses to the war crimes tribunal in the former Yugoslavia fit Durkheim's analysis of suffering, in terms of the 'negative cult' and 'piacular rites'. I believe that, on the whole, this would be to stretch history on the Procrustean bed of theory, and would raise more problems than it provided insights.[20] It may seem at first sight, also, that perhaps the ICTY illustrates well a Durkheimian approach to punishment, in that war crimes can be said to have offended against widespread collective representations, which are reinforced by the punishment of those who have, by their actions, damaged the *conscience collective*. Nevertheless, my primary concerns here are somewhat different.

I believe that Durkheim has provided us with the encouragement to move beyond accounts of suffering which are solely individualistic, whether these are psychological, philosophical or theological in their character. He opens up a space for the examination of suffering as a social phenomenon *sui generis*. Even so, the historical example which I have explored briefly here makes the point that perhaps Durkheim does not go far enough. In noting his remarks about suffering in the *Elementary Forms*, I commended Durkheim for drawing our attention to the collective significance of suffering. What interests him, however, seems to be the suffering of *individuals*, which under certain ritual circumstances take on a symbolic, and hence a collective significance.

What I have illustrated in the material relating to Yugoslav responses to the war crimes Tribunal is that it is also necessary for us to pay attention to the notion that *communities* may also suffer. I have approached this idea in two ways. First of all, I insisted that the representative or symbolic status of individuals who suffer (in this case who are punished for war crimes) can come to be interpreted as a condemnation of the communities which they are seen as representing. In this way, despite the explicit rejection of this point of view by the Tribunal itself, groups experience themselves as being punished, through the medium of exemplary individuals.

In my second illustration I looked at the differing ways in which three ethnic groups in the former Yugoslavia have come to develop 'rhetorics of victimhood', in which an important part of the account of their own history centres upon their claims to have suffered, as a community.

There are several directions in which the study of the sociology of suffering might go from here, based upon the ideas which I have suggested. It is not appropriate to attempt to explore these in detail here, so I confine myself to a few indicative suggestions.

First, it does seem possible that piacular rites, in the form of the public celebration of collective suffering, are relatively common. Communities, and not only in the Balkans, deploy rhetorically 'dejection, cries and tears' precisely in order to 'prove that they suffer'. What is more, the experience of suffering in this way has an important function in the identity formation of the community. Glenn Bowman's discussion of 'constitutive violence' does provide us with a potential tool for analysis here (Bowman 1994). An important corollary of this is that we find ourselves having to deal with suffering, not only as an individual corporeal or psychological fact, but also with what I have called rhetorics of suffering: the forms and manner within which suffering enters public discourse.

Consider further Durkheim's point about suffering demarcating the sacred. Perhaps this is an overstatement of the case, but it seems to be true that a focus upon one's status as a victim, and the character of one's experience as suffering, can function rhetorically to *moralize* the relationship. It is interesting in this respect that the moral standing of the victims is enhanced when it can be claimed that they suffer on behalf of *others*. This heightens the sociological interest of the situation of the sufferer, of course, in that the collective relevance of the suffering is not confined to those who suffer, but it reaches out to embrace the entire community which can be said to have benefited from their suffering. Serbian, but also to a lesser extent Croatian, rhetorics of the significance of suffering in war exemplify this clearly in the image of the *antemurale*. This image of the 'outer defences' of Europe against 'the Turk' is deeply rooted in the history of the region. To some extent it goes beyond mere moralization to the *sacralization* of the position of the sufferer, whose suffering is occasioned by resistance to Islamic 'subjugation' of 'Christian Europe'. I wonder (and this is entirely speculative at this stage) whether the use of suffering in order to sacralize a group in this way renders it particularly difficult for that group then to accommodate to a situation in which it is expected to stand on an equal footing with others in a civic state.[21]

Finally, I return to the ICTY, and the insistence within international law on the sole relevance of individual suffering. The obduracy of the processes of the collectivization of suffering which I have noted raises important questions about the limitations (perhaps necessary limitations) on legal tribunals as mechanisms for dealing with suffering. They exclude as of necessity what will probably turn out to be ubiquitous aspects of the suffering occasioned by war, and especially war crimes. They would seem to allow no place for the rehearsal and public recognition of accounts of collective suffering. Our attention is directed, then, to the real sociological interest of other responses to suffering in these circumstances, such as Truth and Reconciliation Commissions.

I have already mentioned the practical impossibility of bringing to justice all of those who might have been responsible for causing suffering, and the corresponding impossibility that the suffering of all of their individual victims might be heard in court. Non-judicial commissions, such as the South African Truth and Reconciliation Commission, have been cited often as mechanisms which might remedy these deficiencies.[22] The account which I have presented here suggests that in relation to the suffering of communities, these too might have their limitations. The presentation of accounts of the suffering of collectivities typically involves subscribing, not only to different, but also to contradictory explanations of the nature of the events in question. Where the account of suffering is no longer limited to the catharsis provided for individuals, seeking the opportunity to be heard, but becomes an occasion on which to dramatize the suffering of a sacralized community, would the only result of this be a deepening of the differences between communities rather than their reconciliation? It must remain an open question, therefore, as to whether and to what extent they might be suitable vehicles for dealing with collective suffering.

I have suggested that Durkheim is to be commended for the manner in which he opens up for us the possibility that suffering might have relevance beyond the individual, by his analysis of the way in which their suffering takes on significance within ritual contexts. His concern, nevertheless, rests at the level of the somatic or psychological suffering of individuals. What I have attempted to do here is to suggest that it could be useful to pursue further this idea, and that as sociologists we ought to be aware also of the need to encompass within a sociology of suffering the possibility that communities suffer, and that it is important to study the rhetorics through which such suffering is given currency and functions within culture.

Notes

1. The concept of *kwoth* is dealt with in Evans-Pritchard's celebrated study of the Nuer. See Evans-Pritchard (1956, esp. ch. IV).
2. It is important to note that in adopting this critical stance I do not intend to negate the value either of the ICTY in particular, or of international criminal courts more generally. Despite the fact that I acknowledge that there are serious questions to be addressed relating to both the legitimacy in principle of the Tribunal and the manner in which it has gone about its work, I welcome both the ICTY and the more recently created International Criminal Court. It would be entirely inappropriate to attempt to explore these issues in this context.
3. I believe that there are other materials scattered through his work which could be considered here, especially his reflections on anomie, and in particular his writing on suicide. To embark systematically on this enterprise of scholarship would take me well beyond the task I have set myself here, and I will not attempt it. It is relevant to note, however, that his examination of suicide confines itself to a consideration of the personal consequences of social situations, and does not really address the possibility that the suffering of suicides, in turn, might acquire collective significance. In an age in which the suicide bomber has become an item of daily news, however, it would appear that a reappraisal of 'altruistic suicide' is in order.
4. Emphasis supplied by this author in each case.
5. All indictments, and details of the proceedings of each case, together with judgments, appeals and all other related documents, are available on the ICTY website: http://www.un.org/icty/.
6. I prefer to speak of 'rhetoric' rather than the more fashionable 'discourse', as I believe that the latter promises 'discourse analysis', which implies a highly specific technique. I do not pretend to supply this. My usage is not without precedent, however, and I see my work as standing in the tradition of Kenneth Burke. The most accessible introduction to this is probably Gusfield (1989, esp. Part IV, 'Rhetorical Action').
7. According to Mirsad Tokača, Director of the Documentation Centre in Sarajevo, in an interview with the author in 2006, the Centre had confirmed around 93,000 deaths, and estimated the eventual total to be in the region of 100,000.
8. Cited in Allcock, Horton and Milivojević (1998). See the entry on 'casualties', pp. 37–38. I believe that this estimate leaves out Serbian casualties incurred in Croatia.
9. See the article on 'rape' in Allcock, Horton and Milivojević (1998: 233–4), especially for additional bibliography.
10. This was clearly a factor in the two cases at which I served as an expert witness. The events in the Laška Valley focused upon the trials of Dario Kordić, a senior political official, and General Tihomir Blaskić.
11. See the map indicating 'areas of control' in September 1993, in Burg and Shoup (1999: p. 144).
12. Had they not died before indictments could be prepared, it is highly likely that former President Tudjman and his Minister of Defence Gojko Sušak would also have faced

indictments – in which case the sense of Croatian collective outrage would have been all the greater. Although the subject of an indictment, General Janko Bobetko died before the matter of his possible extradition could become the focus of an embarrassing struggle for the Croatian government.
13. To some extent the ICTY is able to play an important role in this respect. The succession of trials which have surrounded the massacre at Srebrenica undoubtedly has played a part in compelling the belated and reluctant acknowledgement of the historical truth of these events among Serbs, who for a long time denied that anything untoward had taken place there.
14. Its currency is suggested by the fact that, at the time of writing, the presidential elections in Serbia might well be won by the candidate for the ultra-nationalist Serbian Radical Party.
15. A useful consideration of this aspect of Serb popular culture is provided in Aznulović (1999).
16. The neologism *srbovojska*, for example, deftly conflates the two ideas.
17. Papers by Mark Biondich and Stevan K. Pavlowitch to the conference *Rethinking the Dissolution of Yugoslavia*, (School of Slavonic and East European Studies, London, June 2004) both suggested that there might be substantial continuities in the way in which Serbs and Croats represented themselves as victims, which were detectable in the 'First Yugoslavia'.
18. In fact Croat attitudes towards Muslims are much more ambivalent, with a strong strain of Croat nationalist thought depicting Bosnian Muslims as specifically ethnic Croats who converted to Islam.
19. The success of this campaign is indicated by the fact that political leaders in the West, who ought to have known better, fell into the habit of referring to the Bosnian government side in the war as 'the Muslims'. The fact that they were led by the Muslim Alija Izetbegović was allowed to obscure the multi-ethnic nature of the Bosnian government and its armed forces, and the primacy of their aim in securing the integrity of a multi-ethnic state.
20. The conspicuous exception to this is perhaps the possibility of studying the Serb use of the Kosovo legends in terms of Durkheim's concept of a 'negative cult'. Here, it seems to me, we do have a case in which a ritualized experience of suffering has come to define the difference between the sacred and the profane, providing the foundation for a process of the sacralization of the nation. This would require, however, another paper. I have made something of a gesture in this direction in Allcock (1993: 157–78).
21. Perhaps this is the key to the paradox of Israeli society, in which despite the experience of the Holocaust – or maybe precisely because of it – Israelis appear to be incapable of imagining, let alone creating a society in which non-Jews could enjoy fully equal citizenship.
22. I believe it is the case that around thirty experiments along these lines have now been tried in different parts of the world. Some comparative investigation of these points might be possible.

Chapter 9

Looking Backwards and to the Future

W.S.F. Pickering

I. Introduction

In various ways the preceding chapters have unearthed hidden or neglected aspects of Durkheim's work with reference to suffering and evil. These studies have also included those of a disciple and others who have followed in his footsteps, but perhaps less enthusiastically. For some readers the findings may be surprising and, indeed, helpful. They have shown that Durkheim did in fact incorporate into his social theory the facts of suffering and evil. Beyond all shadow of doubt he demonstrated that he was not oblivious to the way humans have suffered in one way or another. Other readers, however, may be disappointed to discover that he failed to tackle the larger questions of suffering – the appalling suffering that mankind has inflicted on itself and the terrible pain that has had to be endured as a result of natural disasters.

This book is not only an investigation into the work of Durkheim but also, in the long run, it is meant to be a catalyst in the search for a sociology of suffering. If that is too ambitious a claim, then the editors hope that, at least, the book will encourage sociological studies in the subject of suffering. The latter, as we have mentioned before, have been singularly lacking in the history of the discipline and, in some people's opinion, sociologists are to be criticized for their blindess.

In drawing this volume to a close we would raise several issues that might have a bearing on any future studies in suffering and evil. As such they are in one way or another directly derived from the findings in the previous chapters.

II. What Are We Talking About?

The last contribution focused on suffering of a violent kind that occurred in former Yugoslavia (Chapter 8). It came as a result of the country breaking up after years of communist rule. This form of suffering we labelled at the outset as cataclysmic or calamitous (see Introduction). It usually involves bloodshed, extreme pain or sudden death that affects large numbers of people. It stands in marked contrast to that form of suffering envisaged in most of the other chapters here. On the whole they have given the impression that the suffering alluded to is a universal suffering, common to all people, inevitable in the development of individuals becoming members of a family, a nation, a religion (see especially Chapter 4). For a person to proceed along the path of socialization means, inevitably, walking along a path, the nature of which is painful, but not necessarily excessively so. Here is suffering caused by the eternal conflict between individual desires and ambitions on the one hand, and the demands of an overarching social authority on the other. Such a form of suffering is a *sine qua non* of human and social existence. It is basic to all humanity and every person has to endure it. It might, therefore, be called normal, domestic or institutional suffering, since institutions can be instruments of suffering as well as of healing (see Introduction). One expects to encounter such suffering as one proceeds along the path of daily living. This concords with much that sociology has produced in the past. Parsons described the normal as the basis of sociological discourse. He wrote: 'There is in every system of human action, in every society, a smooth, "normal" pattern of everyday functioning, of ways in which people go "about their business" without particular strain' (Parsons 1952: 292).

But superimposed on that suffering – and the amount of suffering in this respect is open to variation – there is for some people additional suffering in terms of involvement in war or revolution or plague or famine or slavery, to mention only a few of the possibilities. The origins of such suffering are clearly not those arising from socializing processes. Their origin can be within society, but also external to it. In the history of a society one can point to internal suffering such as civil wars, starvation, plagues, persecution, for example; and external to it, the invasion by a hostile force or a tsunami. A sociological study of this kind of suffering appears to have been undertaken by very few academics. One such scholar was P.A. Sorokin, whom we have already mentioned (Introduction).

Any rational discourse depends upon a common agreement about defintions of words, terms, concepts and so forth. When the subject is suffering this demand is crucial, for suffering encompasses a multitude of experiences and extremes of feeling, all connected with physical or mental pain.

Following from this trite but important observation, two issues arise. The first is this. For sociological purposes there is the need for some kind of clarification as to what is meant by suffering; what is implied when one speaks of suffering.

Arising from such a task, but in no way a substitute for it, stands the need for classification – an action well known to sociologists. Leibniz saw such a requirement, even in terms of general discourse. He proposed three types of suffering (see Pickering 1980: 72; ch. 4 here):

1. metaphysical suffering, arising from man's finiteness;
2. moral suffering, arising from man's sinfulness;
3. natural or physical suffering, arising from the laws of nature.

As was noted in the Introduction, von Wiese also pointed to such a need but offered no concrete suggestions. Whether Leibniz's classification, which also incorporates the notion of evil, is of relevance to the sociologist today is probably unikely. To create a modern and adequate classification is a complex task. One must have a criterion for classification, be it the intensity of pain in suffering, the agent of suffering (man or nature), or the numbers of people involved in outbreaks of suffering, and so on. To offer answers to these necessary questions is manifestly beyond the scope of this book. In passing it might be noted that it is extraordinary that no sociologist, to the best of our knowledge, has produced anything approaching an acceptable classification of suffering.

Since the remit of this book does not call for a comprehensive solution of the issues just raised, we would argue that as an initial step towards responding to the need for classification, there is considerable merit in positing two main types of suffering just alluded to: normal or domestic suffering, on the one hand, and calamitous or cataclysmic, on the other. Such a simple division allows us to differentiate 'run of the mill' suffering from excessive or extreme suffering – one might call it unnecessary or senseless suffering. Weber talked about 'senseless suffering': we assume he meant excessive suffering and that can be associated with what we term cataclysmic suffering. Nonetheless Weber did little to develop a classification of suffering.

III. So What of Durkheim?

We would now comment very briefly on what some of the authors of the previous chapters have stated about Durkheim concerning suffering and evil.

First, however, mention might be made of Durkheim's doctoral thesis, *La division du travail social*, published in 1893, of which little has been said until now. It is frequently overlooked that one of the themes of the book is the issue of human happiness but that, *ipso facto*, is related to its generally regarded opposite, suffering (see Book 2, ch. 1). Durkheim rejects the thinking of those who maintain that an unceasing desire for happiness, social and individual, is a valid goal of life. A change in a society's texture, such as that taking place through the division of labour, whether it is seen as gradual or prepared, always brings about a painful (*douloureuse*) crisis (1902b: 220). It does violence to the acquired instincts that oppose it. The changes in the division of labour over the years, however, have not been as satisfactory as they might have been in the light of the need for justice. This state of affairs Durkheim sees as creating inequalities that are *la source du mal* (the source of our ills, surely not evil?). It is none other than a state of anomie that must be overcome by creating an adequate morality so as to eliminate suffering (*souffrance*) (ibid.: 405). Hence anomie is seen as a source of suffering, if not of evil (ch. 3). But anomie is a form of social pathology. Gaston Richard in his book on sociology and theodicy also referred to social pathology as a kind of illness or social malformation that exists in society and threatens social solidarity.[1] For Richard social solidarity forms the subject matter of sociology and pathological states, such as anomie, have to be corrected or ameliorated for the welfare of society (Richard 1943: xiii). This is very much Durkheim's position, too.

Durkheim's specific references to the pathological are also to be seen in his treatment of suicide that was published four years later (1897a; see Chapter 1 here). In Durkheim's eyes, suicide is not only a sociological phenomenon but also a moral one. This is particularly so when suicide is excessive, when it becomes a *mal* – a sickness of society. It is something that undermines the stability of society and, once again, needs to be rectified. It can be argued that those who commit suicide are themselves suffering psychologically (see Chapter 1 here).

A word of warning, however, should be sounded. The term 'social pathology', mentioned in both these early works of Durkheim, is difficult to handle empirically. The normal must logically precede the abnormal or pathological. There is thus initially the crucial problem of defining the normal so as to ensure that the definition is free from subjective or ideological bias. What is held to be normal for one type of society may not be so for another. The ideas of the pathological, therefore, will vary accordingly – what is abnormal in one country is not the case in another. Today sociologists are loath to use the terms normal/abnormal: if that is so, then the notion of pathology disappears. Even within one society particular types of behaviour are unacceptable in one group but not in another. The majority in a democracy will determine what is pathological or what is not. They see that such behaviour may threaten social solidarity, or that solidarity which is of advantage to themselves.

Durkheim held that suffering can be imposed on people by the agency of institutions. Religion is one such institution. It was stated repeatedly in the essay on *The Elementary Forms* (see Chapter 2 here) that suffering and evil are very much part and parcel of society – of life itself. Indeed they exist as a primary condition of society. A society in which there is no suffering cannot be imagined. Most religions call upon their adherents to suffer in some manner: in for example, ascetic rituals, in fasting, in demanding control of personal passions.

However, religions vary enormously in their demands on members. Although many religions give rise to suffering through the administration of rituals and moral demands, such commands are not found in all religions. They are frequently located, for example, in the religions of pre-literate peoples, in early Christianity and in Catholicism, especially in the medieval period. Apart from moral injunctions, acts giving rise to suffering amongst members are virtually absent in most, if not all, Protestant churches and sects. Christian Scientists go so far as to deny the reality of suffering. Further, ascetic rites are totally absent in humanistic forms of religion. And Durkheim saw the cult of the individual as the religion of the future!

Nevertheless, Durkheim emphasized the strong relation between suffering and evil on the one hand, and religion on the other. Could one go further and argue that suffering is to be found as the basis of religion? Although Durkheim in the end rejected the possibility of defining religion in terms of suffering, early in his academic life, he wrote, 'Is it not remarkable that the basic cult of the most civilized religions is that of human suffering (*souffrance*)? (1893b: 243). There have been others, however, who have defined religion in terms of suffering.[2]

Richard pointed out that one of the failures of Durkheim's study of pre-literate societies and their religions was that all too hastily he jumped from the primitive to the modern. The title of his 1912 book shows that Durkheim hoped to bring to light elemental forms of religion that would be of universal application. Without due care, the leap over thousands of years in the history of a religion is, to say the least, questionable. Such enormous jumps are hardly in keeping with the canons of 'science' that Durkheim professed to accept when examining historical and social phenomena.

The last case we point to goes beyond religion and enters a wider sphere of social life. Cladis in Chapter 4 brings home clearly the fact that Durkheim saw the very process of socialization as being necessary for every individual to mature and become a member of society. This, however, means suffering as a result of personal and unhindered desires having to be disciplined. No human being can exist without experiencing this form of suffering. The process is continuous; it does not stop suddenly at some point in time. However, having made this observation, another, but equally important, point is that some societies suffer more than others, just as some individuals endure suffering to a greater extent than others.

Let us now take a wider view of what has just been stated. In the references Durkheim made to *mal* as suffering, social sickness, evil, and by implication anomie, it is evident that he has a basic concern for what might be called suffering within a society in its 'normal' mode (see Introduction). It is the form of suffering one would expect to occur within a society as it exists peacefully over time. It can also be called institutional suffering in so far as there exist institutions which, under normal circumstances, cope with or give meaning to suffering. Durkheim has at the back of his mind this kind of social background when he writes, 'There is then a normal intensity of all our needs, intellectual, moral, as well as physical that cannot be exceeded' (1902b: 219).

Further, Durkheim does not in any way differentiate suffering. For him suffering is suffering *tout court*. He never seems to have accepted the possibility of excessive or useless suffering, frequently present within cataclysmic suffering. Some of the contributors to this book hold, however, that Durkheim did imply what Wilkinson calls existential suffering – a suffering that is experienced by individuals. That is 'real' suffering. It is implied in suffering found in socialization, social pathology, in the administration of certain forms of religion, and in the punishment of criminals. This is also the message of Wilkinson's book of 2005.

But it is possible to look at Durkheim's contribution to the study of suffering in another way. One reason why his approach to suffering has not turned out to be as satisfactory as some would have liked is because he never made suffering his starting point (see Chapter 5). He did not begin with the empirical facts – the social facts – of suffering and evil. Rather, his starting point was with other social phenomena, for example, the division of labour, suicide or religion. He then proceeded, where applicable, to describe how they, in various forms, gave rise to suffering.

Thus, suffering was viewed as a non-operating factor. It was the result of something prior: it was a phenomenon 'out there'. In itself it was not central to sociological research as a subject in its own right.

Such a methodological position may be the reason why Durkheim did not consider any classification of suffering – perhaps he saw it as being too large a general category for sociological analysis.

IV. Evil

Although we have on many occasions coupled suffering with evil, it was noted in the opening chapter that for analytical purposes the two should at some stage be separated. So what of evil? Whereas people may not refer to the suffering that comes to them through the process of socialization as something evil, they are more likely to use the word evil in describing occasions of mass suffering or in referring to political leaders renowned for their cruelty. Hitler has been called evil; so has the Shoah for which he was responsible. Such phenomena are not in themselves evidence of evil. To label something evil is essentially to apply a metaphysical, theological or moral judgement.

What of Durkheim and his use of the word evil? The great problems in dealing with the word evil as used by Durkheim are expounded in detail here by Paoletti (Chapter 3). As was noted in the Introduction, it is difficult to find a French word which unequivocally stands for the English word 'evil'. The French word *mal* is the nearest to it, but that has other meanings as well. In reading Durkheim across the board we see that he never uses the word *mal* in a personalized sense implying Satan or the Devil. Nor does he use it as an evil force that can be located. But, by implication, *mal* contains overtones of moral condemnation. He was outspoken in criticizing what he saw as being damaging to society. He condemned any force or action that would degrade a person. We repeat what we noted earlier: that there is a strong tendency today to translate Durkheim's use of *mal* not by the word evil but by malaise, illness, and so on. This reflects a cultural change in the language of the day, and in this case in the contemporary dislike of language that implies theological and metaphysical overtones. Anyone who ponders issues relating to evil and suffering cannot but come to terms with the intellectual challenges raised by the concept. Those who would disassociate evil from any theological or metaphysical concepts may define evil as moral evil. We may well hold that this is how Durkheim and Richard used the word. Cruel dictators may thus be seen as being evil.

V. Theodicy: A Forgotten Term?

In the past the concept of theodicy was used extensively by theologians and philosophers in connection with suffering and evil. In general it has but a limited usage today. Interestingly enough, in all the previous chapters of this book the word has only been mentioned once, although contributors were free to use it at any time (see Chapter 3). This prompts the question, 'Why?'

At the present time philosophers reject it on account of its theological presuppositions. Theologians find it difficult to support and sociologists in general find their interests lie elsewhere. Nevertheless, the issues it raises are challenging to anyone concerned with the study of suffering and evil, even the sociologist! We would argue that it can be a useful catalyst in giving rise to studies in suffering and evil.

From the time of Leibniz the word 'theodicy' has undergone changes in its meaning.[3] The history of its use and its various meanings is far too long and complicated to be dealt with adequately here. To be brief, four meanings can be observed (Pickering 1980: 64):

1. A narrow meaning where the word theodicy approximates to apologetics in its defence of the traditional Christian doctrine of God.
2. An attempt to tackle philosophically the problem of theodicy formulated by Leibniz as the incongruity between ethical monotheism and human suffering.
3. A later development whereby theodicy becomes equivalent to natural theology or philosophical theology. It focuses on the nature of God in relation to the world. This meaning can also be seen in Leibniz.

4. A wider meaning implies the study of ways in which any religion or ideology attempts to deal with suffering and evil, doctrinally or ritualistically.

Clearly the last meaning is the only one that is, in the main, applicable to sociologists, since the others refer to metaphysical or philosophical discourse. Max Weber was the first sociologist to use it when he examined the major religious systems of the world in order to establish the ways they dealt with suffering and evil.[4] Subsequent sociologists who have employed the word are Talcott Parsons[5] and Peter Berger.

Berger's work calls for a brief consideration. Born in 1929, Peter Berger is a sociologist of a later generation than Parsons. He published a book first called *The Sacred Canopy – Elements of a Sociological Theory of Religion* (1967) and later republished under the title, *The Social Reality of Religion* (1969). It shows clearly how he was influenced by Max Weber. He held, for example, that some theodicies are more rational than others (ibid.: ch. 3). Thus, Hindu theodicy is classified as the most rational of all theodicies on account of the doctrine of karma.

In his general social theory Berger posits an axiom that mankind cannot accept loneliness. Men and women therefore seek the society of others. For society to exist, the self must be surrendered to its demands. This calls for some form of meaning to life in which suffering has a full part. So a theodicy is created by which man finds a way of bridging the gulf between the ideals of society, on the one hand, and what actually happens through experience, on the other. It implies that if one theodicy is rejected, another has to be found. Theodicy for Berger thus becomes a social universal and virtually a *sine qua non* of society. He would equate, or almost equate, the 'meaning of life' with theodicy. Thus, the priority within theodicy becomes meaningfulness in general, not the meaning of suffering per se, unless suffering is defined in the widest terms.

The question arises whether Berger's basic assertion can be supported by empirical evidence. Thus, we might well ask, has there in fact ever been a society without a theodicy? Put in another form, is theodicy as universal as religion is claimed to be? Can a secular society produce a satisfactory theodicy (see below)? Whatever the conclusion, there can be no doubt that Berger made a worthy contribution to sociological theory in attempting to develop the concept of theodicy.

VI. Theodicy and Durkheim

Although Durkheim passed over the concept of theodicy in his sociological writings, he did refer to it in his early lectures on philosophy in the lycée in Sens (Durkheim 2004a: 312–14). He noted that Leibniz came to the optimistic conclusion that the present world was the best of all possible worlds. Bayle, on the contrary, adopted a pessimistic outlook.

Durkheim went on to observe that it was the latter which in his day prevailed in Europe. Apart from this case, Durkheim appears never to have referred to the concept of theodicy again, and never in a sociological context.

It is legitimate to argue that the concept of theodicy often becomes a popular subject in the face of natural disasters or outbursts of evil through the agency of human beings. Two examples immediately come to mind. One is in the more distant past; the other in relatively recent times. The first is the great Lisbon earthquake of 1755 and the other, the Shoah of the last century. In both these cases of terrible suffering, people asked 'why' questions to which theologians and philosophers attempted to produce answers. Voltaire's satire *Candide*, attacking Leibniz's theodicy was written in 1758, three years after the Lisbon earthquake. He ended the book with the cynical remark, 'il faut cultiver notre jardin'. In the more modern example, the Shoah was relatively slow in giving rise to historical and philosophical studies, but now a trickle has turned into a veritable torrent of books. Sociologists, however, have been lamentably slow in making contributions to it and have been severely criticized by the sociologist Zygmunt Bauman for such negligence and indifference (Bauman 1989).

Without referring to theodicy per se, one well might think that Durkheim would at least have taken it into consideration, if not actually used it, prompted by the terrible sufferings arising from the French Revolution or the Paris Commune, or even by the Franco-Prussian war. In fact, in all his writings he never mentions them, with one exception – the Revolution – and then in connection with effervescence (see for example, 1912a: 305–6; 300 n.1). But he says not a word about *suffering* in connection with the Revolution. Surely the events of those turbulent times would have encouraged Durkheim to cast an eye in the direction of theodicy?

Perhaps our judgement is too harsh on Durkheim. We live in a world that has passed through two world wars and a Holocaust and now is in a period of gencocides and wars, albeit small ones. All Durkheim's major works were written before the First World War. We know that the war severely shattered him and during it he had no time to reflect on the appalling suffering it engendered (see 'Reflections on the Death of Emile Durkheim'). And what would he have made of the Holocaust?

The suffering that occurs in normal society is, in Durkheim's eyes, to be accepted as part of nature, of the givenness of the natural and social worlds. It is to be expected and therefore should be seen as inevitable. But there are other cases, as we have seen, such as in the excess of suicides, where Durkheim hoped social forces would arise that would counteract internal 'evils' and produce a 'healthy', 'normal' society. He was an optimist to the extent that he thought it possible to bring about changes in the social fabric by political and moral intervention.

These facts about Durkheim encourage one to speculate as to whether or not he comes close to Leibniz's conservative conclusion. It is that, overall, mankind must accept what happens as there is really no alternative – it has to be accepted that mankind has the best of all possible worlds.

As has just been noted, Durkheim is, in one sense, not a conservative, for he holds that change is possible for the betterment of society; and that means the lessening of suffering. On the other hand, there are aspects of his thinking in which it approaches, but is not identical with, Leibniz's conservative and 'orthodox' conclusion. We can see it in the inevitability of suffering that accompanies the process of socialization – processes that are universal and necessary for individuals to become truly human (Chapter 4). This is unmodifiable, although changes in societal and cultural demands do, in fact, take place over the centuries. The process is changeless, but not the content. Durkheim was very much a realist in so far as he held it was impossible to imagine a world without suffering. Who can see death ever being abolished and illnesses completely conquered? Incidentally, Gaston Richard criticized Durkheim for failing to consider anywhere the issue of death. Durkheim's writings, and not least his letters to Marcel Mauss (1998a), show that he went through periods of optimism and pessimism (see 'Reflections on the Death of Emile Durkheim'). Durkheim is not someone who can be easily pinned down in this matter.

Some people would reject the conservative response to the problems posed by theodicy, that is, they would deny the idea that this suffering world is the best of all possible worlds, with the implication that nothing can be done to change it radically. Rather, they would sound a positive note and point to human progress. One need only recall, they would say, the enormous advances achieved by medicine. They would also cite the ever-growing support through large parts of the world for the dignity of each and every human being, as exemplified by the declaration of human rights. Such developments mean only one thing – the diminution of suffering. This position has been common enough since the nineteenth century. But today can anyone adopt such an optimistic attitude in the face of the enormity of suffering in the world? Can those liberal humanists of a century and more ago find a large following? The answer must be no!

This section has pointed to the concept of theodicy for three reasons. The first is that, as has already been noted, confrontation with the age-old concept brings one face to face with the existence of suffering, especially in the form of cataclysmic suffering. It challenges the complacency of sociologists. The second is a consideration of theodicy as an important first step for those who would seek to develop a new, modern sociological discourse on the question of suffering and evil. Thirdly, the presence of a theodicy, theological or secular, strengthens social solidarity. Grappling with theodicy or trying to establish a meaningful one, at least contributes to the social welfare of a nation or society.

VII. A New Approach?

We may well ask, given what we have just said, whether there are any signs of sociologists developing a theodicy in a non-theological, non-metaphysical, secular form. With the exception of Peter Berger, writers do not appear to have developed the term to any extent, although they sometimes speak of the need to use it. They may argue that, for the strengthening of the solidarity of society, there is indeed the need to have some kind of social understanding of the suffering that individuals or groups must endure. The suffering could be that encountered in 'normal' society or in the form of cataclysmic suffering. As good 'secular' sociologists, some see that more is required than mere description and analysis. Something reassuring and positive is wanted beyond the conservative position of the passive acceptance of suffering.

Not long ago a vigorous attempt was made to highlight such a need. In an article, Morgan and Wilkinson challenged sociologists to address the problem of theodicy formerly treated within the realms of religion and philosophy (Morgan and Wilkinson 2001). They asserted that no sociologists worth their salt can be blind to the miseries and disorder that plague the present world (ibid.: 199). They referred to the sociologists of the 1980s and 1990s who spoke of the need for what amounted to a secular theodicy. Such academics, however, appear to have mentioned that need only *en passant* and have done little to develop the idea (ibid.: 200). In making a positive response to this criticism, Morgan and Wilkinson turned to the word 'sociodicy' which, incidentally, they did not invent. Given so new a concept they expressed the hope that it might give rise to the development of sociological studies in suffering. The advocated change from theodicy to sociodicy is Durkheimian in nature.

The assertion may be expounded as follows. As is so well known, Durkheim postulated, if he did not identify, the religious with the social – with society. When applied to the traditional theodicean problem, there is a simple substitution in one half of the formula. Suffering, sometimes seen as excessive and unnecessary, on the one hand, and the existence of a totally good, loving and all-powerful God, on the other, becomes one where the suffering element remains the same, but God now becomes society. If this is in fact so then, with Gaston Richard, it can be argued that society deified becomes God (Richard 1943: 136ff.). Society, thus viewed, is divine and all-powerful and stands for the good of mankind. The equation God = Society is more complex and subtle than Richard and those who follow him have posited (see Pickering 1984: ch. 13; Strenski 2006: 14–17). One might just add that all the characteristics attached to God or divinity certainly do not match those applicable to society. Suffice it to say that the literalist interretation of Gaston Richard allowed him to argue that Durkheim tried to solve the classical theodicean problem and in so doing gave it, as did Leibniz, the response of acceptance. (Richard 1943: 199).

There is something of a parallel here with Durkheim's use of sociology to solve problems in other disciplines. In *Les formes élémentaires* he attempted to bring light to bear on the philosophical question of categories and pointed to their association with social factors (1912a: 12–28). For this he gained little following among philosophers.

A secular theodicy, now to be called sociodicy, couched in Durkheimian terms or in those of Morgan and Wilkinson, must initially be seen to be a useful contribution to sociological studies in the general area of suffering. It must, however, be carefully defined and developed. Hence a word of caution needs to be sounded.

Quite rightly, Morgan and Wilkinson do not envisage, in the development of the concept of sociodicy, something approaching the more general sociological meaning of theodicy, as seen in Weber and Parsons. They define sociodicy in terms of the 'glaring discrepancy between modernity's ideal expectations of the social world and the lived experience of its history' (2001: 201). This definition reflects Berger's ideas (see above). We repeat what has been said before, that a mere description of suffering offers little or no comfort to those who suffer. Indeed, a simple and straightforward description may trivialize suffering. The task for sociologists is to go beyond description and 'reassess the experience of modernity' in relation to the violence of recent times (ibid.). In brief, it is to attempt to make some sense out of suffering. It is to connect 'the public with the private realm' in order to interpret the meaning of adversity and misfortune (ibid.: 207). The authors conclude their article with these words: 'The task of sociodicy, we have argued, is to explore the ethical and cultural implications of this tension [between expectations and reality], not just to render seemingly "meaningless" suffering and affliction rationally accessible, but in hope that its decivilizing consequences are not perpetuated simply by being ignored' (ibid.: 210).

Any humanist must admire the aspirations of Morgan and Wilkinson to fill a sociological void by their attempt to explore the notion of a secular theodicy. One has to be realistic, however, and say that while they have proceeded further than most in considering the task of providing a meaningful sociodicy, there exists the need to give flesh to the skeleton and to show how sociodicy can be developed. Morgan and Wilkinson are dealing with an age-old problem that is not solved by simply employing a new word. Will sociologists, in developing the concept of sociodicy, be more successful than others in dealing with the issue of suffering and evil? At the very least, any such attempt will demonstrate a concern for suffering.

Can the problem, however, be solved within its own boundaries, as Morgan and Wilkinson propose? Traditional theodicies, based on religious concepts, have been related to and have utilized forces and ideas that are beyond the empirical – sin, salvation, heaven, the suffering of Christ, for example (see note 5). Sociodicy, however, implies that suffering has to be 'explained', 'dealt with' or consolation given to the sufferers, within the closed system of the social. Can remedies be given with 'the tools' that are available within the strictures of society? The difficulty is to break out of the 'here and now'. Or put in another way, can the 'irrational', that is, the utter misery of suffering, be explained by the rational? Berger implied that science cannot answer theodicean questions. And if sociology is a 'science' then can it produce the required answers?

To the majority of people in Europe today, who have no firm or systematic religious faith, or much that is equivalent to it, suffering of all kinds has, by logic, to be accepted as an indelible characteristic of nature. It is a given that is largely unmodifiable and must be held as a fact of life. Medical science can help to alleviate or eliminate certain kinds of suffering and will succeed in giving greater relief as time proceeds. However, as we have emphasized, there are other sufferings and evils in the world that are directly brought about by human beings. So much suffering is excessive and senseless, as the result of wars and genocides. And nature produces earthquakes and plagues for which humans are not responsible. Some suffering may be modifiable, but how much? There have always been those who have seen the problem of classical theodicy as being an intellectually impossible one. Today, many who adopt such a position have usually been moved by the terrible violence of the twentieth century, that is, by its cataclysmic suffering, not least in the Shoah. Writers such as Steiner, Bauman, himself a sociologist, and others, speak of the irrationality, of the unspeakable in suffering, that cannot really be grasped by the human mind (see Morgan and Wilkinson 2001: 207). For them there is no rational or reasonable answer to the question 'why?' And one may well ask: who can find a word to say in the face of the burning of babies and the hanging of young people so that they die slowly, as occurred in the Shoah? So often words about suffering can be platitudinous or banal. Yet perpetual, absolute silence is not the answer. There is the imperative to approach and even enter the evil rather than live in silence or seek an escape. So the sociologist must strive to study and, if possible, to understand the irrationaliy of suffering and evil, at least, in its extreme forms. With the skills and techniques of the discipline, and transcending old-fashioned professional lines of demarcation, the sociologist should *contribute* to some kind of understanding and, indeed, alleviation of the suffering of mankind.

Notes

1. Gaston Richard (1860–1945) followed Durkheim as a lecturer in Bordeaux in 1902 when Durkheim left to take up an appointment in the Sorbonne.. Three years later Richard became professor of social sciences and remained in Bordeaux for the remainder of his life. Early collaboration with Durkheim, in preparing the *Année sociologique,* ended in 1907 where the point of contention was Durkheim's analysis of religion. This was an issue with implications surrounding components of the notion of theodicy. *Sociologie et*

théodicée (1943) contained the last attack Richard made against Durkheim's thought. Richard had an early interest in evil. He first became strongly conscious of the existence of moral evil as a result of studying criminal statistics. Moral evil was, he argued, to be found even in the most civilized countries. He held that a consciousness of evil emerges from an intellectual reflection on the disharmony and disorder that is to be found in the world (Pickering 1975b: 354). For further information on Richard, see Pickering (1975a, 1975b, 1979).

2. In developing his conviction of the existence of moral evil, Richard asserted that, '*toute religion est une solution du problème du mal*' (every religion offers a solution to the problem of evil) (Richard 1905: 468, his italics). And surely *mal* would include suffering? Religion therefore is to be defined in such terms. The anthropologist Bronislaw Malinowski also held that suffering was the basis of religion (Malinowski 1925: 39). Somewhat later, John Beattie adopted a similar position. He based his argument on the hazardous environment in which most pre-literate peoples live. When terrible occurrences cannot be dealt with by proven practical means and techniques people resort to symbolic means, which can be termed religion (Beattie 1964: 227).

3. The word 'theodicy' is directly traceable to the work of Gottfried Leibniz (1646 – 1716). He coined it in his only book, *Essais de théodicée sur la bonté de Dieu, la liberté de l'homme et l'origine du mal*, published in 1710. The word is derived from two Greek words, *theos* and *dikee*, meaning God and justice. The basic argument turns on the nature of God and his relation to mankind. In Christian theology God is held to be both omnipotent and all goodness; yet people suffer, sometimes to a terrible degree. How can God allow this to occur? How can the two sides of the equation be reconciled? Rationalist theologian that he was, Leibniz came to the conclusion that God had created the best of all possible worlds. The practical consequence is that people, made in the image of God, have to accept things as they are. In the end they must live with the paradox: both sides of the equation are to be maintained. Matters are as they are for the good of mankind, and God's work is thus justified! In one sense Leibniz's argument is an apologetic for the existence of God as traditionally conceived in Christianity. His conclusion was a defence of the status quo and of the ambiguity of God's love and omnipotence in the face of human suffering. This position has been vigorously attacked, not least by Voltaire in his book *Candide*, and by many others, including Kant, with his emphasis on morality.

Leibniz, by employing the term theodicy, crystallized problems that go far back in history. They can be seen, for example, in Judaism in the book of Job, where the answer to Job's suffering approximates to that of Leibniz: in accepting things as they are. And in Christianity the issues can be found from its very inception. Richard called it a branch of natural theology (see below). There is scarcely a theologian from St Paul to Karl Barth who has not wrestled with them in one form or another, including Irenaeus and Augustine (see Hick 1966). But further back still, similar problems were also raised by Plato and the Stoics. In trying to solve the theodicean equation theologians have introduced a number of Christian concepts such as the Fall, free will, sin, heaven, hell, purgatory, redemption, atonement, God's will, and so on (ibid.).

4. Max Weber (1860–1920) used the concept extensively, not only with regard to the meanings of life, which seemed for him a priority, but also its application to different world religions. He might well be labelled a student of comparative theodicy.

Religions, especially Christianity, Judaism, Islam and Hinduism, have a doctrine of salvation which is a way of 'solving' the problem of theodicy. Some religious solutions were to be seen to be relatively more rational than others, given the basic principles. For Weber what is rational is meaningful, that is, reasonable.

In developing his comparative theodicy Weber was often criticized, especially by experts in the various religions he examined. We refer to only one example, that of Shmueli's attack on Weber for what he had to say about Judaism. Shmueli held that the great German sociologist based his argument on Jewish theodicy as being related to the pariah class, and then to only one period of Jewish history – that of the eighth-century prophets (Shmueli 1969: 182).

5. Talcott Parsons (1902–79) was considerably influenced by Max Weber. While he referred to theodicy in writing about Weber, he did not shed new light on the concept. However, he pointed to issues that accompany one aspect of theodicy, namely, suffering. He emphasized the fact that life is no paradise, is never smooth: plagues, accidents, famine and so on constantly threaten the well-being of mankind. Death is an inevitability (Parsons 1952: 294ff.). Symbolic techniques and the invention of non-empirical entities such as God, spirit, Satan, heaven, and so forth, are employed to bring some meaning to sufferers for what they are enduring. All religions have a 'transcendental reference' that is related in some way to suffering (ibid.: 297–98).

Some years ago I wrote: 'What is at the heart of Durkheim's [religious] system is really a theodicy and religion thus becomes a means of overcoming suffering in its various forms' (Pickering 1984: 129). They do so by means of collective representations of suffering and by offering rituals of healing and release that may accompany them.

Surely, we are not far removed from Voltaire's closing words in *Candide*: 'il faut cultiver notre jardin', that is, it is imperative that we get on with our everyday affairs and do not worry ourselves about theodicean speculations. This conservative advice is to carry on and accept matters as they are.

Notes on Contributors

John B. Allcock is honorary reader in sociology at the University of Bradford, where he taught sociology between 1966 and 2000, heading the Research Unit in South-East European Studies between 1981 and 2005. His principal research area was the former Yugoslavia and its successors, although he also contributed to Durkheimian studies, editing the English translation of *Pragmatisme et sociologie*.

Mark S. Cladis is professor and chair of religious studies at Brown University, Providence. He is the editor of two books, *Elementary Forms of Religious Life* (2001) and *Education and Punishment: Durkheim and Foucault* (1999). He is also author of *A Communitarian Defense of Liberalism: Emile Durkheim and Contemporary Social Theory* (1992) and *Public Vision, Private Lives: Rousseau, Religion, and Twenty-First Century Democracy* (2006).

Sophie Jankélévitch lives in Paris, and teaches philosophy at the Institut Universitaire de Formation des Maîtres, University of Cergy Pontoise. She is the editor of *Emile Durkheim. L'individualisme et les intellectuels* (2002).

Giovanni Paoletti obtained a doctorate in philosophy from the University of Pisa and then a doctorate in sociology from the Institut d'Etudes Politiques in Paris. He continues to work on Durkheim's philosophical background and, in particular, on his theories of religion and representations. He is now engaged in research on the history of philosophy at the University of Pisa.

Robert Parkin is a departmental lecturer in Social Anthropology in the Institute of Social and Cultural Anthropology, University of Oxford. He is the author of *The Dark Side of Humanity: The Work of Robert Hertz and Its Legacy* (1996) and has translated Hertz and Henri Hubert into English. He contributed chapters on the French school of anthropology to Fredrik Barth et al., *One Discipline, Four Ways: British, German, French, and American Anthropology* (2005). His other interests include kinship, India and Eastern Europe.

W.S.F. Pickering was a founder member in 1991, and then General Secretary, of the British Centre for Durkheimian Studies in the Institute of Social and Cultural Anthropology, Oxford University. Since the 1970s he has written, edited and helped translate various books on Durkheim and his disciples.

William Ramp is an associate professor in the Department of Sociology at the University of Lethbridge, Canada. He has written a number of articles on theoretical linkages between Durkheim and Foucault, and Durkheim and Bataille. His interests are in the cultural and historical development of personal and collective identity, and in the relations between sociology and religion.

Massimo Rosati teaches the history of sociology at the University of Salerno, Italy. His last book in Italian was *Solidarietà e sacro* (2002). He has published articles on Durkheim and Habermas in the *Journal of Classical Sociology* and in *Durkheimian Studies*. He is the editor of the new Italian edition of Durkheim's *The Elementary Forms of Religious Life* (2005).

References

Alexander, J.C., R. Eyerman, B. Giesen, N. Smelser and P. Sztompka. 2004. *Cultural Trauma and Collective Identity*. Berkeley: University of California Press.
Alexander, J.C. 2001. 'Toward a Sociology of Evil. Getting Beyond Modernist Common Sense about the Alternative to "the Good"'. In M.P. Lara (ed.), *Rethinking Evil*. Berkeley: University of California Press.
Alexander, J. and P. Smith (eds). 2005. *The Cambridge Companion to Durkheim*. Cambridge: Cambridge University Press.
Allcock, J.B. 1993. 'Kosovo: the Heavenly and the Earthly Crown'. In Ian Reader and Tony Walter (eds), *Pilgrimage in Popular Culture*. London: Macmillan.
Allcock, J.B., J. Horton and M. Milivojevi. (eds). 1998. *Conflict in the Former Yugoslavia: An Encyclopaedia*. Denver, CO, Santa Barbara, CA and London: ABC-Clio.
Allen, N.J. 2000. *Categories and Classifications. Maussian Reflections on the Social*. Oxford and New York: Berghahn Books.
Allen, N.J., W.S.F. Pickering and W. Watts Miller (eds). 1998. *On Durkheim's Elementary Forms of Religious Life*. London and New York: Routledge.
Appiah, A. 1991. 'Racism and Moral Pollution'. In L. May and S. Hoffman (eds), *Responsibility. Five Decades of Debate in Theoretical and Applied Ethics*. Lanham, MD: Rowman and Littlefield, pp. 219–38.
Arendt, H. 1964. 'Personal Responsibility under Dictatorship'. In H. Arendt, *Responsibility and Judgment'*. New York: Schocken Books.
———. 1965 – 66. 'Some Questions of Moral Philosophy'. In H. Arendt, *Responsibility and Judgment*. New York: Schocken Books.
———. 1978. *The Life of the Mind*. New York and London: Harcourt Brace.
———. 1982. *Lectures on Kant's Political Philosophy*. Chicago: University of Chicago.
———. 2003. 'Collective Responsibility'. In H. Arendt, *Responsibility and Judgment*. New York: Schocken Books, pp. 147–58.
Aznulovi, B. 1999. *Heavenly Serbia: From Myth to Genocide*. London: Hurst.
Bartsch, S. 2006. *The Mirror of the Self. Sexuality, Self-Knowledge, and the Gaze in the Early Roman Empire*. Chicago: University of Chicago Press.
Bataille, G. 1973 [1957]. *Literature and Evil*, translated by A. Hamilton. London: Calder and Boyars.
———. 1985a [1970]. 'The Psychological Structure of Fascism'. In A. Stoekl, C.R. Lovitt and D. Leslie Jr., (eds), *Visions of Excess. Selected Writings, 1927–1939*, translated by A. Stoekl. Minneapolis: University of Minnesota Press.
———. 1985b [1970]. 'The Use-Value of D.A.F. De Sade'. In *Visions of Excess. Selected Writings, 1927–1939*, in Bataille 1985a [1970].
———. 1988a [1979]. 'Sacred Sociology and the Relationships between "Society", "Organism", and "Being"', translated by E. Wing. In *The College of Sociology (1937–1939)*. Minneapolis: University of Minnesota Press.
———. 1988b [1979]. 'Attraction and Repulsion I. Tropisms, Sexuality, Laughter and Tears', in Bataille 1988a [1979].
———. 1988c [1979]. 'Attraction and Repulsion II. Social Structure', in Bataille 1988a [1979].

———. 1989 [1973]. *Theory of Religion*, translated by R. Hurley. New York: Zone Books.
Bates, S. 1991. 'The Responsibility of Random Collections'. In L. May and S. Hoffman (eds), *Responsibility. Five Decades of Debate in Theoretical and Applied Ethics*. Lanham, MD: Rowman and Littlefield, pp. 101–108.
Baudrillard, J. (with C. Bayard and G. Knight). 1995. 'Vivisecting the 1990's; An Interview with Jean Baudrillard'. Ctheory.net, http://www.ctheory.net/articles. aspx?id=66.
———. 1993. *The Transparency of Evil*. London: Verso.
Bauman, Z. 1989. *Modernity and the Holocaust*. Cambridge: Polity Press.
Beattie, J. 1964. *Other Cultures*. London: Cohen and West.
Bellah, R. 1990. 'Morale, religion et société dans l'oeuvre durkheimienne', *Archives des sciences sociales de religion*, 69: 9–21.
Berger, P.L. 1967. *The Sacred Canopy*. New York: Doubleday.
———. 1969. *The Social Reality of Religion*. London: Faber and Faber.
Bergson, H. 1959. *La pensée et le mouvant* in *Oeuvres* (centenary edition). Paris: Presses Universitaires de France.
Bernstein, R. 2001. 'Radical Evil. Kant at War with Himself'. In M.P. Lara (ed.), *Rethinking Evil*. Berkeley: University of California Press.
———. 2002. *Radical Evil. A Philosphical Interrogation*. Cambridge: Polity Press.
Besnard, P. 1987. *L'Anomie, ses usages et ses fonctions dans la discipline sociologique depuis Durkheim*. Paris: Presses Universitaire de France.
———. 1993. 'Anomie and Fatalism in Durkheim's Theory of Regulation'. In S.P. Turner (ed.), *Emile Durkheim: Sociologist and Moralist*. London and New York: Routledge.
———. 2003. *Etudes durkheimiennes*. Genève: Librairie Droz.
———. (ed.) 1983. *The Sociological Domain. The Durkheimians and the Founding of French Sociology*. Cambridge: Cambridge University Press.
Bloch, M. 1992. *Prey into Hunter. The Politics of Religious Experience*. Cambridge and New York: Cambridge University Press.
Boltanski, L. 1999. *Distant Suffering, Morality, Media and Politics*. Cambridge: Cambridge University Press.
Bossu, J. 1982. *Chronique des rues d'Epinal*, Book II. Epinal.
Bouglé, C. 1908. *Essais sur le régime des castes*. Paris: Alcan.
Bourdieu, P. 1987. *Choses dites*. Paris: Minuit.
———. 1997. *Méditations pascaliennes*. Paris: Seuil.
———. et al. 1999. *The Weight of the World. Social Suffering in Contemporary Society*. Cambridge: Polity Press.
Bowker, J. 1970. *Problems of Suffering in Religions of the World*. Cambridge: Cambridge University Press.
Bowman, G. 1994. 'Constitutive Violence and Rhetorics of Identity: a Comparative Study of Nationalist Movements in the Israeli-occupied Territories and Former Yugoslavia'. In B. Kapferer (ed.), *Nationalism and Violence*. Oxford: Oxford University Press.
Burg, S.L. and P.L. Shoup. 1999. *The War in Bosnia-Herzegovina: Ethnic Conflict and International Intervention*. Armonk, NY and London: M.E. Sharpe.
Butler, J. 2004. *Precarious Life. The Powers of Mourning and Violence*. London: Verso.
Cabrera, I. 2001. 'Is God Evil?'. In M.P. Lara (ed.) in *Rethinking Evil. Contemporary Perspectives*. Berkeley: University of California Press, pp. 17–26.
Canguilhem, G. 1975. 'Le normal et le pathologique' and 'La théorie cellulaire', in *La connaissance de la vie*. Paris: Vrin.
Chateaubriand, R. 2003. *René*. Paris: Folio. (First published 1802.)
Cladis, M.S. 1994. *A Communitarian Defense of Liberalism: Emile Durkheim and Contemporary Social Theory*. Stanford: Stanford University Press.
———. 2003. *Public Vision, Private Lives*. Oxford: Oxford University Press.
———. 2006. *Public Vision, Private Lives: Rousseau, Religion, and Twenty-First Century Democracy*. New York: Columbia University Press.

Cooper, D.E. 1991. 'Collective Responsibility (A Defence)'. In L. May and S. Hoffman (eds), *Responsibility. Five Decades of Debate in Theoretical and Applied Ethics*. Lanham, MD: Rowman and Littlefield, pp. 35–46.
Cotterrell, R. 1999. *Emile Durkheim. Law in a Moral Domain*. Edinburgh: Edinburgh University Press.
Cuin, H. 2000. 'Sociologie sans paroles': Durkheim de le discours des acteurs'. In M. Borlandi and M. Cherkaoui (eds), *Le suicide un siècle après Durkheim*. Paris: Presses Universitaires de France.
Davy, G. 1919. 'Emile Durkheim I – L'Homme', *Revue de métaphysique et de morale*, XXVI: 181–98.
———. 1960. 'Allocation' in Divers, *Centenaire de la naissance d'Emile Durkheim*. Paris: Annales de l'Universite de Paris, no. 1, pp. 14–20.
Descartes, R. 1970 [1641]. 'Meditations on First Philosophy'. In *The Philosophical Works of Descartes*, translated by E.S. Haldane and G.R.T. Ross, vol. I. Cambridge: Cambridge University Press.
Douglas, M. 1978. 'The Problem of Evil', in *Natural Symbols*. Harmondsworth: Penguin.
———. 1999. *Leviticus as Literature*. Oxford: Oxford University Press.
Durkheim, E. 1887c. 'La science positive de la morale en Allemagne', *Revue philosophique*, XXIV: 33–58, 113–42, 275–84.
———. 1892a. *Quid Secundantus Politiciae Scientiae Instituendae Contulerit*. Bordeaux: Gounouilhou.
———. 1893b. *De la Division du travail social: Etude sur l'organisation des sociétés supérieures*. Paris: Alcan.
———. 1895a. *Les règles de la méthode sociologique*. Paris: Alcan.
———. 1897a. *Le suicide. Etude sociologique*. Paris: Alcan (tr. 1951a; 2006a).
———. 1898b. 'Représentations individuelles et représentations collectives', *Revue de métaphysique et de morale*, VI: 273–303.
———. 1898c. 'L'indvidualisme et les intellectuels', *Revue bleue*, 4th series, X: 7–13, also in Durkheim 1970a: 261–78.
———. 1899d. Contribution to H. Dagan, *Enquête sur l'antisémitisme*, Paris: Stock, in Durkheim, 1975b, vol. 2: 252–54.
———. 1900b. 'La sociologie en France au XIXe siècle', *Revue bleue*, 4th series, XII: 609 – 13, 647–52.
———. 1901a(i). 'Deux lois de l'évolution pénale', *Année sociologique*, IV: 65–95 (tr. 1992b).
———. 1901c. 2nd edition of 1895a.
———. 1902b. 2nd edition of 1893b. Paris: Alcan (tr. 1984a).
———. 1911b. 'Jugements de valeur et jugements de réalité', *Revue de métaphysique et de morale*, XIX: 437–53 (tr. 1953b).
———. 1911c(2). 'Enfance'. In *Nouveau Dictionaire de pédagogie et d'instruction primaire*. Paris: Hachette.
———. 1911d. 'Préface', in O. Hamelin, *Le système de Descartes*. Paris: Alcan.
———. 1912a. *Les formes élémentaires de la vie religieuse*. Paris: Alcan (tr. 1995c).
———. 1914a. 'Le dualisme de la nature humaine et ses conditions sociales', *Scientia*, XV: 206–21. (tr. 2005a).
———. 1915c. *L'Allegmagne au-dessus de tout: la mentalité allemande et la Guerre*. Paris: Colin.
———. 1915d. *Elementary Forms of the Religious Life*, translation of 1912a by J.W. Swain. London: George Allen & Unwin.
———. 1916a. *Lettres à tous les Francais*. Paris: Comité de publication.
———. 1917a. 'Notice sur André-Armand Durkheim',*Annuaire de l'Association des anciens élèves de l'Ecole Normale Supérieure*, pp. 201–205.
———. 1925a. *L'Education morale*. Paris: Alcan (tr. 1961a).
———. 1928a. *Le Socialisme*. Paris : Presses Universitaires de France (tr. 1958b).
———. 1933b. *The Division of Labor in Society*, translation of 1902b by G. Simpson. New York: Macmillan.

———. 1938a. *L'Evolution pédagogique en France*. Paris: Alcan (tr. 1977a).

———. 1950a. *Leçons de sociologie: physique des moeurs et du droit*. Paris: Presses Universitaires de France.

———. 1951a. *Suicide. A Study in Sociology*, translation of 1897a by J.A. Spaulding and G. Simpson. London: Routledge and Kegan Paul.

———. 1953a. *Montesquieu et Rousseau, précurseurs de la sociologie*. Paris: Marcel Rivière (tr. 1960b).

———. 1953b. 'Value Judgments and Judgments of Reality', translation of 1911b by D.F. Pocock, in *Sociology and Philosophy*. Glencoe, IL: Free Press.

———. 1957a. *Professional Ethics and Civic Morals*, translation of 1950a by C. Brookfield. London: Routledge and Kegan Paul.

———. 1958b. *Socialism and Saint-Simon*, translation of 1928a by C. Sattler. London: Routledge and Kegan Paul.

———. 1960b. *Montesquieu and Rousseau: Forerunners of Sociology*, translation of 1953a, by R. Manheim. Ann Arbor: University of Michigan Press.

———. 1960c. 'The Dualism of Human Nature and Its Social Conditions', translation of 1914a in K. Wolff, (ed.), *Emile Durkheim, 1858–1917. A Collection of Essays*. Columbus: Ohio State University Press.

———. 1961a. *Moral Education: A Study in the Theory and Application of the Sociology of Education*, translation of 1925a by E.K. Wilson and H. Schnurer. New York: Free Press.

———. 1963a. *Primitive Classification*, translation of Durkheim and Mauss of 1903a(1) by R. Needham. Chicago: University of Chicago Press.

———. 1970a. *La Science sociale et l'action*. Paris: Presses Universitaires de France.

———. 1973a. 'The Dualism of Human Nature and Its Social Conditions', translation of Durkheim 1914a by C. Blend, in R.B. Bellah (ed.), *Emile Durkheim: On Morality and Society, Selected Writings*. Chicago: University of Chicago Press.

———. 1975b. *Durkheim, E. Textes*, 3 vols, edited with an introduction by V. Karady. Paris: Les Editions du Minuit.

———. 1977a. *The Evolution of Educational Thought: Lectures on the Formation and Development of Secondary Education in France*, translation of 1938a by P. Collins. London and Boston: Routledge and Kegan Paul.

———. 1982a. *The Rules of Sociological Method and Selected Texts on Sociology and Its Method*, translation of 1901c by W. Halls. New York: The Free Press.

———. 1984a. *The Division of Labour in Society*, translation by W.D. Halls of 1902b. London: Macmillan.

———. 1992b. 'Two Laws of Penal Evolution', translation of 1901a by T.A. Jones and A. Scull, in M. Gane (ed.), *The Radical Sociology of Durkheim and Mauss*. London: Routledge.

———. 1995a. Preface to Octave Hamelin's *Le Système de Descartes*, translation of 1911d by H. L. Sutcliffe, in D. Nemedi and W.S.F. Pickering, 'Durkheim's Friendship with the Philosopher Octave Hamelin, together with translations of two items by Durkheim', *The British Journal of Sociology*, 46, (1): 107–25.

———. 1995c. *The Elementary Forms of Religious Life*, translation of 1912a by K.E. Fields. New York: The Free Press.

———. 1998a. *Durkheim Lettres à Marcel Mauss*. Paris: Presses Universitaires de France.

———. 2001a. *Elementary Forms of Religious Life*, translation of 1912a by C. Cosman of Durkheim 1912a, (ed.) M.S.Cladis. Oxford: Oxford University Press.

———. 2004a. *Durkheim's Philosophy Lectures. Notes from the Lycée de Sens Course, 1883–4*, edited and translated by N. Gross and R.A. Jones. Cambridge: Cambridge University Press.

———. 2005a. 'The Dualism of Human Nature and Its Social Conditions', translation of 1914a by I. Eulriet and W. Watts Miller, *Durkheimian Studies/Etudes Durkheimiennes*, n.s. 11: 33–45.

———. 2006a. *On Suicide,* translation of 1897a by R. Buss. London: Penguin.
———, and M. Mauss. 1903a(i). 'De quelques formes primitives de classification', *L'année sociologique,* VI: 1–72 (tr. 1963b).
———, with E. Denis. 1915b. *Qui a voulu la guerre? Les origines de la guerre d'après les documents diplomatiques.* Paris: Colin.
———, with F. Buisson. 1911c(2). 'Enfance', in *Nouveau Dictionnaire de Pédagogie et de l'Instruction primaire.* Paris: Hachette, pp. 552–53.
Elias, N. 1998. *La Société des individus,* Paris: Agora-Packet.
Evans-Pritchard, E.E. 1956. *Nuer Religion.* Oxford: Clarendon Press.
Fauconnet, P. 1920. *La Responsabilité. Étude de sociologie.* Paris: Alcan.
Fein, H. 1993. *Genocide. A Sociological Perspective.* London: Sage.
Feinberg, J. 1991. 'Collective Responsibility', in L. May and S. Hoffman (eds), *Responsibility. Five Decades of Debate in Theoretical and Applied Ethics.* Lanham, MD: Rowman and Littlefield, pp. 53–76.
Ferrara, A. 2001. 'The Evil That Men do A Meditation on Radical Evil from a Postmetaphysical Point of View'. In M.P. Lara (ed.), *Rethinking Evil.* Berkeley: University of California Press.
Fields, K. 1995. 'Translator's Introduction' to Durkheim 1995c, pp. xvii–lxxii.
Filloux, J.-C. 1977. *Durkheim et le socialisme.* Geneva: Droz.
Fine R. and C. Turner. 2000. *Social Theory after the Holocaust.* Liverpool: Liverpool University Press.
Forsyth, N. 1987. *The Old Enemy: Satan and the Combat Myth,* Princeton: Princeton University Press.
Gane, M. 2003. Review. Michele Richman, *Sacred Revolution, Durkheimian Studies/Etudes Durkheimiennes* n.s. 9: 100–103.
Giesen, B. 2004. 'The Trauma of Perpetrators: The Holocaust and the Traumatic Reference of German National Identity', in J.C. Alexander, R. Eyerman, B. Giesen, N.J. Smelser and P. Szotompka, *Cultural Trauma and Collective Identity.* Berkeley: University of California Press, pp. 112–54.
Girard, R. 2001. *I Saw Satan Fall Like Lightning,* translated by J.G. Williams. Maryknoll, NY: Orbis Books.
Guillo, D. 2006. 'La place de la biologie dans les premiers textes de Durkheim: un paradigme oublié?', *Revue française de sociologie,* 47(3): 507–35.
Gusfield, J.R. (ed.). 1989. *Kenneth Burke on Symbols and Society.* Chicago and London: University of Chicago Press.
Guyau, J.-M. 1885. *Esquisse d' une morale sans obligation ni sanction.* Paris: Alcan.
Halbwachs, M. 1930. *Les causes du suicide.* Paris: Presses Universitaires de France.
Hamelin, O. 1921 [1911]. *Le Système de Descartes.* New York and London: Garland Publishing.
Held, V. 1991. 'Can A Random Collection of Individuals be Morally Responsible?'. In L. May and S. Hoffman (eds), *Responsibility. Five Decades of Debate in Theoretical and Applied Ethics.* Lanham, MD: Rowman and Littlefield, pp. 89–100.
Hertz, R. 1907. 'Contribution à une étude sur la représentation collective de la mort', *Année sociologiqique,* 10: 48–137 (tr. 1960).
———. 1909. 'La prééminence de la main droite, étude sur la polarité religieuse', *Revue philosophique,* 68: 553–80 (tr. 1973).
———. 1913. 'Saint Besse, étude d'un culte alpestre, *Revue d'histoire des religions,* 67(2): 115–80.
———. 1922. 'Le péché et l'expiation dans les sociétés primitives', *Revue de l'histoire des religions,* 86: 5–54.
———. 1960. *Death and the Right Hand,* translation of Hertz 1907 and 1909 by R. and C. Needham. London: Cohen & West.
———. 1973. 'The Pre-eminence of the Right Hand: A Study in Religious Polarity', translation of Hertz 1909 by R. Needham, in R. Needham (ed.), *Right & Left: Essays on Dual Symbolic Classification.* Chicago and London: University of Chicago Press.

―――. 1983. 'St Besse: A Study of an Alpine Cult', translation of Hertz 1913 by S. Wilson in S. Wilson (ed.), *Saints and Their Cults: Studies in Religious Sociology, Folklore and History*. Cambridge: Cambridge University Press.

―――. 1994. *Sin and Expiation*, translation of Hertz 1922 by R. Parkin, Preface by W.S.F. Pickering. Oxford: British Centre for Durkheimian Studies, Occasional Papers no. 2.

Hick, J. 1966. *Evil and the Love of God*. London: Macmillan.

Honneth, A. 1992. *Kampf um Anerkennung*. Frankfurt: Suhrkamp.

Idinopulos, T.I., and B.C. Wilson. 2002. *Reappraising Durkheim for the Study and Teaching of Religion Today*. Leiden: Brill.

James, W. 1985 [1902]. *The Varieties of Religious Experience*. New York: Penguin.

Jaspers, K. 2000. *The Question of German Guilt*. New York: Fordham University Press.

Jonas, H. 1985. *The Imperative of Responsibility*. Chicago: Chicago University Press.

Jones, R.A. 1994. 'Ambivalent Cartesians: Durkheim, Montesquieu and Method', *American Journal of Sociology*, 100(1): 1–39.

―――. 1999. *The Development of Durkheim's Social Realism*. Cambridge: Cambridge University Press.

Jones, S.S. 2003. 'From *Varieties* to *Elementary Forms*: William James and Émile Durkheim on Religious Life', *Journal of Classical Sociology*, 3(2): 99–121.

Kant, I. 1999 [1793]. *Religion Within the Boundaries of Mere Reason and Other Writings*, edited by A.W. Wood et al. Cambridge: Cambridge University Press.

La Rochefoucauld, F. 1974 [1676]. *Réflexions morales*, in *Maximes*. Paris: Garnier.

Lacroix, B. 1981. *Durkheim et le politique*. Montréal: Presses de l'Université de Montréal.

Langer, L.L. 1996. 'The Alarmed Vision: Social Suffering and Holocaust Atrocity', *Daedalus*, 1: 47–66.

Lara, M.P. (ed.). 2001. *Rethinking Evil*. Berkeley: University of California Press.

Léon, X. 1917. 'Nécrologie. Emile Durkheim (1858–1917)', *Revue de métaphysique et de morale*, 24: 749–51.

Lermontov, M.Y. 1854. *A Hero of Our Times*. London: Bogue.

Lewis, H.D. 1991. 'Collective Responsibility'. In L. May and S. Hoffman (eds), *Responsibility. Five Decades of Debate in Theoretical and Applied Ethics*. Lanham, MD: Rowman and Littlefield, pp. 17–33.

Lukes, S. 1973. *Emile Durkheim, His Life and Work: A Historical and Critical Study*. London: Allen Lane.

Maffesoli, M. 2002. 'The Advent of the Tragic', *Space and Culture*, 5(3): 287–89.

Malinowski, B. 1925. 'Magic, Science and Religion'. In J. Needham (ed.), *Science, Religion and Reality*. London: Sheldon Press.

Martin, D., J. Orme Mills and W.S.F. Pickering (eds). 1980. *Sociology and Theology: Alliance and Conflict*. Brighton: Harvester Press. (Reprinted in 2004, Lnden and Boston: Brill.)

Mauss, M. 1925a. 'Essai sur le don', *L'Anneé sociologique*, n.s. 1: 30-186.

―――. 1925b. 'In Memoriam', *L'Année sociologique*, n.s. 1: 7–29.

―――. 1954. *The Gift: Forms and Functions of Exchange in Archaic Societies*, translation of Mauss 1925a by I. Cunnison. London: Cohen & West.

May, L. 1991a. *Sharing Responsibility*. Chicago: University of Chicago Press.

―――. 1991b. 'Metaphysical Guilt and Moral Taint'. In L. May and S. Hoffman (eds), *Responsibility. Five Decades of Debate in Theoretical and Applied Ethics*. Lanham, MD: Rowman and Littlefield, pp. 239–54.

May, L. and S. Hoffman (eds). 1991. *Responsibility. Five Decades of Debate in Theoretical and Applied Ethics*. Lanham, MD: Rowman and Littlefield.

Mellema, G.F. 1997. *Collective Responsibility*. Amsterdam and Atlanta: Rodopi.

Milbank, J. 1995. 'Stories of Sacrifice; From Wellhausen to Girard', *Theory, Culture and Society*, 12: 15–46.

Moore, B. 1972. *Reflections on the Causes of Human Misery and upon Certain Proposals to Eliminate Them*. Boston: Beacon Press.

Morgan, D. and I. Wilkinson. 2001. 'The Problem of Suffering and the Sociological Task of Theodicy', *European Journal of Social Theory*, 42: 199–213.
Mucchielli, L. 1998. 'Autour de la "révélation" d'Emile Durkheim'. In J. Carroy and N. Richard (eds), *La découverte et récits en sciences humaines: Champollion, Freud et les autres*. Paris: L'Harmattan.
Musset, A. 2003 [1836]. *Confession d'un enfant du siècle*. Paris: Folio.
Neiman, S. 2001. 'What's the Problem of Evil?'. In M.P. Lara (ed.), *Rethinking Evil*. Berkeley: University of California Press, pp. 27–45.
———. 2002. *Evil in Modern Thought. An Alternative History of Philosophy*. Princeton: Princeton University Press.
Nemedi, D. and W.S.F. Pickering. 1995. 'Durkheim's Friendship with the Philosopher Octave Hamelin, together with translations of two items by Durkheim', *British Journal of Sociology*, 46(1): 107–25.
Nisbet, R.A. 1993. *The Sociological Tradition*. Somerset, NJ: Transaction Press.
Nouvel Observateur and Reporter sans frontières, 1993. *Le Livre Noir de L'Ex-Yougoslavie*. Paris: Arléa.
Paoletti, G. 2003. *Emile Durkheim et la philosophie*. Paris: Institut d'Étude Politique de Paris.
———. 2005. 'Durkheim historien de la philosophie', *Revue philosophique*, 3: 275–301.
Parkin, R. 1996a. *The Dark Side of Humanity: The Work of Robert Hertz and its Legacy*, Reading and Amsterdam: Harwood Academic Publishers.
———. 1996b. Introduction to *R. Hertz, Sin and Expiation*. Oxford: British Centre for Durkheimian Studies, Occasional Papers no. 2.
———. 1997. 'Durkheimians and the Groupe d'Etudes Socialistes', *Durkheimian Studies/Etudes Durkheimiennes*, n.s. 3: 43–58.
———. 1998. 'From Science to Action: Durkheimians and the Groupe d'Etudes Socialistes', *Journal of the Anthropological Society of Oxford*, 29(1):81–90.
Parsons, T. 1952. 'Sociology and Social Psychology'. In H.N. Fairchild (ed.), *Religious Perspectives in College Training*. New York: Ronald Press.
Pickering, W.S.F. 1975a. *Durkheim on Religion*. London and Boston: Routledge and Kegan Paul.
———. 1975b. 'A Note on the Life of Gaston Richard and Certain Aspects of His Work'. In Pickering 1975a: 343–59.
———. 1979. 'Gaston Richard: Collaborator et Adversaire', *Revue française de sociologie*, XX: 163–82.
———. 1980. 'Theodicy and Social Theory: An Exploration of the Limits of Collaboration between Sociologist and Theologian'. In D. Martin, J. Orme Mills and W.S.F. Pickering (eds), *Sociology and Theology: Alliance and Conflict*. Brighton: Harvester Press.
———. 1984. *Durkheim's Sociology of Religion: Themes and Theories*. London: Routledge.
———. 1993. 'The Origins of Conceptual Thinking in Durkheim, Social or Religious?' In S.P. Turner, (ed.), *Emile Durkheim: Sociologist and Moralist*. New York: Routledge.
———. 1996. Preface to *R. Hertz, Sin and Expiation*. Oxford: British Centre for Durkheimian Studies, Occasional Papers no. 2.
———. 2008. 'Emile Durkheim', in J. Corrigan (ed.), *The Oxford Handbook of Religion and Emotion*. Oxford: Oxford University Press.
Pickering, W.S.F. and H. Martins (eds). 1994. *Debating Durkheim*. London and New York: Routledge.
Poggi, G. 2000. *Durkheim*. Oxford: Oxford University Press.
Portinaro, P.P. 2002. 'Introduzione'. In P.P. Portinaro (ed.), *I concetti del male*. Torino: Einaudi, pp. ix–xxxiii.
Ramp, W. 1998. 'Effervescence, Differentiation and Representation in *The Elementary Forms*.' In N.J. Allen, W.S.F. Pickering and W. Watts Miller (eds), *On Durkheim's* Elementary Forms of Religious Life. London and New York: Routledge.

———. 2000. 'The Moral Discourse of Durkheim's *Suicide*'. In *Durkheim's* Suicide: *a Century of Research and Debate*, eds. W.S.F. Pickering and G. Walford. London: Routledge.

———. 2003. 'Religion and the Dualism of the Social Condition in Durkheim and Bataille', *Economy and Society*, 32(1): 19–140.

Rappaport, R.A. 1999. *Ritual and Religion in the Making of Humanity*. Cambridge: Cambridge University Press.

Richard, G. 1905. 'Sur les lois de la solidarité, *Revue philosophique*, LX: 441–71.

———. 1923. 'L'athéisme dogmatique en sociologie religieuse', *Revue d'histoire et de philosophie religieuse*, pp. 125–37, 229–61. Engish transation in Pickering 1975a: 228–76.

———. 1943. *Sociologie et théodicée: Leur conflict et leur accord*. Paris: Les Presses Continentales.

Richman, M. 2002. *Sacred Revolutions. Durkheim et le Collége de Sociologie*. Minneapolis and London: Minnesota University Press.

Ricoeur, P. 1994. 'Le concept de responsabilité. Essai d'analyse sémantique', *Esprit*, November, now in *Le Just*. Paris: Editions Esprit, 1995, pp. 31–56.

Riley, A.T. 1999. 'Whence Durkheim's Nietzschean grandchildren? A Closer Look at Robert Hertz's Place in the Durkheimian Genealogy', *European Archives of Sociology*, 40(2): 304–30.

———. 2005a. '"Renegade Durkheimians" and the Transgressive Left Sacred'. In J.C. Alexander and P. Smith (eds), *The Cambridge Companion to Durkheim*. Cambridge: Cambridge University Press, pp. 274–301.

———. 2005b. 'The Theory of Play/Games and Sacrality in Popular Culture. The Relevance of Roger Caillois for Contemporary Neo-Durkheimian Cultural Theory', *Durkheimian Studies/Etudes Durkheimiennes*, n.s. 11: 103–14.

Rorty, R. 1989. *Contingency, Irony and Solidarity*. Cambridge: Cambridge University Press.

Rosati, M. 2004a. 'Forms of Radicalism: Radical Thinking and Social Criticism in Durkheim's Thought', *Durkheimian Studies/Etudes Durkheimiennes*, n.s., 10: 10–18.

———. 2004b. 'Review, Michele H. Richman, Sacred Revolutions: Durkheim and the College de Sociologie', *European Journal of Social Theory* 7(4): 552–55.

———. 2005. 'The Evil That Men Suffer. Evil and Suffering from a Durkheimian Perspective', *Durkheimian Studies/Etudes Durkheimiennes*, n.s. 11: 67–85.

———. 2008. 'Inhabiting no Man's Land. Durkheim and Modernity', *Journal of Classical Sociology* vol 8(2): 233–64.

Schmaus, W. 2004. *Rethinking Durkheim and His Tradition*. Cambridge: Cambridge University Press.

Schmueli, E. 1969. 'The Novelties of the Bible and the Problem of Theodicy in Max Weber's Ancient Judaism', *Jewish Quarterly*, 60(2): 172–82.

'Scholars' Initiative', March 2004. Preliminary Report of Group 10, *The International Criminal Tribunal for the Former Yugoslavia*, Department of History, Purdue University.

Seligman, A.B. 2000. *Modernity's Wager. Authority, Self and Transcendence*. Princeton: Princeton University Press.

Smith, P. and J.C. Alexander. 1996. 'Review Essay. Durkheim's Religious Revival', *American Journal of Sociology* 102(2): 585–92.

Sorokin, P.A. 1942. *Man and Society in Calamity*. New York: Dutton.

Stedman Jones, S. 1995. 'Charles Renouvier and Emile Durkheim: Les Règles de la Méthode Sociologique', *Sociological Perspectives*, 38(1): 27–40.

———. 1998. 'Durkheim, Kant, the Immortal Soul and God'. In N.J. Allen, W.S.F. Pickering and W. Watts Miller (eds), *On Durkheim's* Elementary Forms of Religious Life. London: Routledge.

———. 2001. *Durkheim Reconsidered*. Cambridge: Polity Press.

Steiner, P. 2000. 'Crise, effervescence sociale et socialisation'. In M. Borlandi and M. Cherkaoui (eds), *'Le Suicide', un siècle après Durkheim*. Paris: Presses Universitaires de France, pp. 63–85.

———. 2005. *L'école Durkheimienne et l'économie*. Genève and Paris: Librairie Droz.

Stone, D. 2004. 'Genocide as Transgression', *European Journal of Social Theory*, 7(1): 45–65.
Strenski, I. 2006. *The New Durkheim*. New Brunswick, NJ: Rutgers University Press.
Sverdlik, S. 1987. 'Collective Responsibility', *Philosophical Studies*, 51: 61–76.
Swinburne, R. 1989. *Responsibility and Atonement*. Oxford and New York: Clarendon Press.
Taylor, C. 1989. *Sources of the Self*. Cambridge: Cambridge University Press.
Tekiner, D. 2002. 'German Idealist Foundations of Durkheim's Sociology and Teleology of Knowledge', *Theory and Science* http://theoryandscience.icaap.org/content/vol 003.001/tekiner.html
Timasheff, N.S. 1963. *Sociological Theory: Its Nature and Growth*. New York: Random House.
Traverso, E. 1997. *Histoire déchirée. Essai sur Auschwitz et les intellectuels*. Paris: Editions du Cerf.
Trilling, L. 1972. *Sincerity and Authenticity*, Cambridge, MA: Harvard University Press.
UNHCR March/April 1996 *Information Notes*, No. 3–4.
Van Gennep, A. 1909. *Les rites de passage*. Paris: Emile Nourry.
Von Rad, G. 1962. *Theologie des Alten Testaments*, Vol. 1, *Die Theologie der geschichtlichen Überlieferungen Israels*. München: Chr. Kaiser Verlag.
von Wiese, L. 1934. 'Sociology and Suffering', *International Journal of Ethics*, 44(2): 227–35.
Watts Miller, W. 1996. *Durkhheim, Morals and Modernity*. Montreal and Kingston, London: McGill-Queen's University Press.
———. 2005. 'Total Aesthetics. Art and the *Elemental Forms*', *Durkheimian Studies/Etudes Durkheimiennes*, n.s. 10: 88–118.
Wilkinson, I. 2005. *Suffering. A Sociological Introduction*. Cambridge: Polity Press.
Wolff, K.H. 1969. 'For a Sociology of Evil', *Journal of Social Issues*, 25(1): 111–25.
Wright, N.T. 2006. *Evil and the Justice of God*. Downers Grove, Illinois: Inter-Varsity Press.

Index

A

Alexander, J.C., 6–7, 61, 130, 131, 134n1
Allcock, J.B., 148–62, 161nn8–9, 162n20, 179
Allen, N., 62n7, 134n4
anomie, 32–35, 37, 39–40, 45, 167; *and see* social malaise
Appiah, A., 145
Arasse, D., 48n3
Arendt, H., 58, 143, 145, 147n3
Aristotle, 39, 48n3
Ascetic, asceticism, 50–51, 58, 126, 150
St Augustine, 84, 97, 176n3
Auschwitz, 143, 147n3
Aznulovic, B., 162n15

B

Balkans, war crimes, 148–62; wars in 1960s, 153–55
Barth, K., 176n3
Bartsch, S., 134
Bataille, G., 8, 54, 118–19, 127–34, 135n13
Bates, S., 144
Baudrillard, J., 132–33
Bauman, Z., 6, 171
Bayle, P., 64, 170
Beattie, J., 176n
Bellah, R., 60, 62nn10–11
Berger, P., 170, 173–75
Bergson, H., 35, 89
Bernstein, R., 122, 142–43
Besnard, P., 47n1, 59, 62n9, 70, 79n1, 80n9, 117nn2–3, 147n
St Besse, 117n4, 117n8
Biondich, M., 162n

Blaskic, T., 161n
Bloch, M., 130
Bobetko, J., 162n
Boltanski, L., 6
Bossu, J., 25, 26n3
Bouglé, C., 17, 21, 116
Bourdieu, P., 6, 32, 34, 35
Bowman, G., 159
Brandt, W., 147n4
Brunetière, F., 73, 89
Burchell, G., 47
Burg, S.L., 161n11
Burke, K., 161n6
Buss, R., 9
Butler, J., 146

C

Cabrera, I., 119, 142
Callois, R., 118, 133
Canguhilhem, G., 35, 41, 48n7
Chateaubriand, F-R., 39, 41
Cicero, 48n3
Cladis, M.S., 52, 81–100, 100n8, 167, 179
Collège de Sociologie, 118–35
Comte, A., 45, 48n11, 113
Cooper, D.E., 144
Cotterrell, R., 137
crime (and punishment) 69, 137, 140
Cuin, C.-H., 47n2
cult of the individual, 146
'dark side of humanity' 104, 138

D

David (King), 14
Davy, G., 12–15, 17, 26n4

death, 107–9, 115; representations of, 125–26, 146
Degouy, A., 27n9
Denis, E., 17
Descartes, R., 75, 118–24, 126, 128, 133, 134
Division of Labour in Society, 37, 44, 66–67, 75, 136–37, 165–66
Dodd, L., 113
Douglas, M., 125, 134n3
Dreyfus Affair, 72–73, 148
Durkheim, A. (son), 13, 14, 15, 17, 26n6, 58
Durkheim, E., 5, 9, 10–28, 31–48, 49–62, 63–80, 81–100, 103–17, 118–35, 136–40, 146–47, 148–51, 158–60, 162n20, 163, 165–74, 175n1, 176–77n1
  His illness and death, and André's death, 13–15, 58; burden of work, 16–18; cancer, 23–25; and conflict, 90–94, 116; death, likely causes, 11–28; depression, 19, 21–23; domestic life, 18–19; pessimism, 97–98; recalcitrant nature, 45–47; work load, 13
Durkheim, L. (wife), 14, 19, 25, 26n7
Durkheim, M. (father), 18
Durkheim, M. (mother), 22, 25
Durkheim, R. (sister), 18

E

Eastern Orthodox tradition, 98
effervescence, 53, 77–79, 127
Elementary Forms of the Religious Life, 47, 49, 62, 72, 76–79, 81–82, 94–96, 120, 149–51, 166, 174
Elias, N., 48n9
Eliot, G., 39
euphoria/dysphoria, 52–53, *and see* effervescence
Evans-Pritchard, E.E., 149, 161n1
evil (*mal*), 54, 110, 142, 168–69; concepts of, 63–80; and expiation, 56; function of as in Jewish and Christian traditions, 65, 121; problems of, 49–50, 54, 63–6; radical, 122; and responsibility today,

142–44; and truth, 127; types of, 54, 60, 64–66
Evolution Pédagogique en France, 75–76

F

Fauconnet, P., 16, 27n8, 139–41, 147n2
Fein, H., 6
Feinberg, J., 144
Ferrara, A., 123
Fields, K., 61, 62n6
Fine, R. 6
Fish, J., 134n1
Flaubert, G., 39
Forsyth, N., 121
Foucault, M., 99
Freud, S., 23, 47, 60, 62n11, 84, 90, 94, 128

G

Galen, 38
Galvin, M., 147
Gane, M., 188, 134n1
Giesen., B., 147n4
Gillen, F.J., 59
Girard, R., 130–31
God, 121–22, 138, 169, 173
Goethe, W., 39
Gotovina, A., 154
Guillo, D., 75
guilt, 143; *and see* sin and expiation
Gusfield, J.R., 161n6
Guyau, J.-M., 33

H

Habermas, J., 129
Hague Tribunal, 148–62
Halbwachs, M., 33–35, 39–41
Halphen, E., 14, 26nn 3–4
Hamelin, O., 20–22, 118–20, 122–23, 125, 132–33
Hartmann, H., 69
Heidegger, M., 144
Held, V., 144
Hertz, A., 113
Hertz, R., 5, 54, 103–18, 138–40, 147n1
Hick, J., 176n3
Hippocrates, 38

Hobbes, T., 89, 116
homo duplex, 'Dualism of Human Nature', 90–96
Honneth, A., 61
Horton, J., 161n9
Howitt, A.W., 59
human nature, 78, 81, 95; becoming human, 81–100; and necessary suffering 83–85; *and see* suffering

I

Idinopulos, T.I., 62n7
individual/social (society) 82, 85, 89–90, 92
individualization 140–41
Islam, 158
Izetbegovic, A., 162n19

J

Jacobs, A., 79
James, W., 91–92
Jankélévitch, S., 31–48, 179
Jaspers, K., 142–44
Jonas, H., 143–44
Jones, R.A., 56, 62n7, 62n11, 134n2

K

Kant, I., 34, 57–58, 84, 94, 96–97, 99, 121–24, 129, 133, 134nn4–5, 142, 176n3
Karadzic, R., 154
Kennedy, C., 13, 26n4
Klibansky, R., 48n3
Kordic, D., 161n10

L

Lacroix, B., 23, 62n11
Lamartine, A., 39
Langer, L.L. 6
La Rochefoucauld, F., 41
Leibniz, G.W., 64, 165, 169, 171–73, 176n3
Léon, X., 12, 14–15, 20, 26n6
Lermontov, M., 39
Levi, P., 143
Lévi, S., 62 n7
Levi–Strauss, C., 106, 115

Lévy–Bruhl, L. 16
Lewis, H.D., 142
liberalism, Catholic and Protestant, 136–37, 141, 146–47; *and see* modernism/anti-modernism
Life and death 112–15, 125
Lukes, S., 12, 18, 20, 22, 26n1, 62n11, 117n1

M

MacLaine, G., 26n2
Maffesoli, M., 134n1, 134n9, 134n9
mal de l'infini, 38; *and see* social malaise
Malinowski, B., 176n2
Marcel, J.-C., 134n1
Martins, H., 17
Marx, K., 35, 104, 114, 117, 128
Mauss, M., 11, 12–19, 24–25, 58, 62n, 103–4, 106, 107, 116, 118, 120, 127–28, 172
May, L., 144–45
Mellema, G.F., 142, 144–45
Mellor, Ph., 134n1
Mestrovic, S., 134n1
Milbank, J., 130
Milivojevic, M., 161n9
Milošević, S., 154, 156–57
Milton, J., 122
Mladic, R., 154
modernism/anti-modernism, 57–59; *and see* liberalism
Montesquieu, C-L., 100n4
Moore, B., 6
Morgan, D., 6, 173–75
Morrison, K., 134n1
Mucchielli, L., 23
Müller, M., 54
Müller-Lyer, F.C., 4
Musset, A., 39, 40–41

N

Neiman, S., 57–58, 119, 143
Nemedi, D., 21, 121
Nietzsche, F., 54, 96, 113, 115, 118, 138
Nisbet, R., 40
Norac, M., 154
normal/abnormal, 31–35, 67–69, 166–68; *and see* anomie

P

Panofsky, E., 48n3
Paoletti, G., 56, 59, 62n9, 63–80, 75, 169, 179
Parkin, R., 103–17, 113–14, 116, 117n4, 138–39, 147n1, 179
Parsons, T., 164, 170, 174, 177n5
St Paul, 176n3
Pavlovitch, S.K., 162n17
Pearce, F., 134n1
Physique des moeurs, 73–74
Pickering, C., 79, 134n1
Pickering, W.S.F., 3–10, 5, 11–28, 20–21, 49, 51, 53, 54, 62n3, 62n7, 65, 79, 121, 141, 147n1, 148–49, 163–77, 165, 169, 173, 175n1, 177n5, 180
Pigeaud, J., 48n3
Plato, 31, 84, 96, 97, 176n3
Plavšic, B., 154
Plutarch, 48n3
Poggi, G., 54, 58–59, 62n3
Poincaré, R., 17
Pope, T., 134
Portinaro, P.P., 65
profane, 50–52, 27; *and see* sacred

R

Ramp, W., 56, 118–35, 126, 132, 180
Rappaport, R., 58
Rawls, A.W., 62n7, 134n1
religion, 49–59, 82, 120, 140, 167; and Durkheim 19–20
Renouvier, C., 134n4
Richard, G., 5, 166, 169, 172–73, 175–76n1, 176n2
Richman, M., 54, 118, 134n1
right hand and left, 109–10
Riley, A.T, 54, 113–14, 134n1, 138
ritual, rite, cult, 50, 52, 57, 61, 78, 94, 106, 125–29, 138, 149–50; *and see* cult of individual
Robertson Smith, W., 51, 55, 62n7
Robespierre, M., 113
Rorty, R., 60
Rosati, M. 3–10, 49–62, 56, 62n4, 77–78, 118, 123, 124, 134n1, 136–47, 142, 147, 180

Rousseau, J.J., 34, 64, 84–90, 97, 98, 100n4, 100nn 7–8, 105, 106, 116
Rules of Sociological Method, 31–32, 66–69

S

Sabine, 100n2
sacred, 50–54, 106, 128; *and see* profane
sacrifice, 55, 58, 81, 94, 114
Sade, D.A.F., 118, 135n14
Saint-Simon, C.-H., 113
Salinger, I., 62n5
Sartre, J.P., 144
Saxl, F., 48n3
Schmaus, W., 134n4
Schopenhauer, A., 68, 97
Segal, R.S., 62n7
Seligman, A.B., 58, 145
Semblat, M., 17
Seneca, 48n3
Sheldon, J., 26n1
Shilling, C., 134n1
Shmueli, E., 176–77n4
Shoup, P.L., 161n11
St Silouan, 81, 98
Simpson, G., 9
sin (and expiation), 66, 111–12, 116, 136–41
Smith, A., 65
Smith, P., 134n1, 181
social life, society, 51, 55; fragility, 59; health of, 31, 71; nature of, 71; representation of, 75
social malaise, social pathology, 21, 31, 34, 46, 59–60, 70, 166
social solidarity, 138
sociodicy, 173–75
sociology, sociologists, of evil, 130–34; lack of studies of suffering, 5–6, 148; reasons for lack of study of suffering, 7–0, role of, 31, 36, 64, 196; starting point of 8–9, 36; of suffering 158–61
Sorokin, P.A., 4, 5, 164
Spaulding, J.A., 9
Spencer, Sir B., 59
Spencer, H., 42, 45, 48n11
Spinoza, B., 74, 75

Stanner, W.E.H., 51
Stedman Jones, S., 57, 62n7, 134n4
Steiner, P., 62n5, 77
Stone, D., 133
Strehlow, C., 59
Strenski, I., 62n7, 173
suffering, 82, 123–25; collectivization of, 153–55; concept of, 84; defining, 85; in *Elementary Forms*, 47–62; individual and collective, 151–52, 155; normal 164; presence in the world, 3–4, 104; psychological, 31–48; studies of 4–5; theory of, 115, 146; types of, 165; *and see* evil, theodicy, sociodicy
suicide, *Le suicide*, 31–48, 69, 71; definition of, 32, 36, 70; diagnosis of, 31–36; egoistic, 37–39, 45–46; and Halbwachs, 33–35, 40–41; and melancholy, 36; and solitude, 40; types of, 72; *and see* anomie
Sušak, G., 162n
Swanton, J.R., 59
Swerdlik, S., 142
Swinburne, R., 144
Sztompka, P., 181

T

Tekiner, D., 134n4
theodicy, 54, 65–66, 72, 76, 169–70, 175; and Durkheim 170–72
Timasheff, N.S., 5
tissu (holes in the fabric), 41–44
Tokača, M., 161n7
Tolstoy, L., 39
Traverso, E., 143
Trilling, L., 61
Tudjman, F., 154, 162n12
Turner, C., 6

V

Vigny, A.V., 39
violence, 120, 146
Volante, P., 79
Voltaire, 122, 171, 177n5
van Gennep, A., 106
von Wiese, L., 4
von Rad, G., 147n5

W

Watts Miller, W., 49, 59, 62n7, 134n1
Weber, M., 4, 13, 50, 91, 116–17, 165, 170, 174, 176–7nn4–5